*White Love

and Other

Events in

Filipino

History*

American Encounters/Global Interactions
A series edited by Gilbert M. Joseph and Emily S. Rosenberg

This series aims to stimulate critical perspectives and fresh interpretive frameworks for scholarship on the history of the imposing global presence of the United States. Its primary concerns include the deployment and contestation of power, the construction and deconstruction of cultural and political borders, the fluid meanings of intercultural encounters, and the complex interplay between the global and the local. American Encounters seeks to strengthen dialogue and collaboration between historians of U.S. international relations and area studies specialists.

The series encourages scholarship based on multiarchival historical research. At the same time, it supports a recognition of the representational character of all stories about the past and promotes critical inquiry into issues of subjectivity and narrative. In the process, American Encounters strives to understand the context in which meanings related to nations, cultures, and political economy are continually produced, challenged, and reshaped.

AMERICAN ENCOUNTERS / GLOBAL INTERACTIONS

A series edited by Gilbert M. Joseph and Emily S. Rosenberg

white love

and Other Events in Filipino History

Vicente L. Rafael

Duke University Press

Durham & London 2000

© 2000 Duke University Press
All rights reserved
Designed by Rebecca M. Giménez
Typeset in Minion with Bodega
display by Keystone Typesetting, Inc.
Library of Congress Cataloging-in-
Publication Data appear on the last
printed page of this book.

Acknowledgements for the use of
copyrighted material appear on page
287, which constitutes an extension
of the copyright page.

To the memory of Bayani S. Rafael

Contents

List of Illustrations xi

Acknowledgments xiii

Introduction
Episodic Histories 1

1. White Love
   Census and Melodrama in the U.S. Colonization of the Philippines 19

2. Colonial Domesticity
   Engendering Race at the Edge of Empire, 1899–1912 52

3. The Undead
   Notes on Photography in the Philippines, 1898–1920s 76

4. Anticipating Nationhood
   Identification, Collaboration, and Rumor in Filipino Responses to Japan 103

5. Patronage, Pornography, and Youth
   Ideology and Spectatorship during the Early Marcos Years 122

6. Taglish, or the Phantom Power of the Lingua Franca 162

7. Writing History after EDSA 190

8. "Your Grief Is Our Gossip"
   Overseas Filipinos and Other Spectral Presences 204

   Notes 229

   Bibliography 265

   Index 277

Illustrations

1. Schedule sheet 30
2. Keyboard punch card 31
3. Negritos (Aetas) 38
4–5. Wild non-Christian peoples 39
6. Civilized Christian people 40
7. Portraits of census supervisors 41
8. "Negritos in the island of Luzon" 78
9. "An elaborate tattoo" 79
10. "Bagobos, island of Mindanao" 80
11. "Native chiefs of Mindanao, Philippines" 80
12. "A pure Tagalog type of the lower class girl of Manila" 82
13. "Filipino Boy—Upper Class" 82
14. "Type of high-class woman of Manila" 82
15. "Evolution of a Bontoc Igorot constabulary soldier—1901" 84
16. "Evolution of a Bontoc Igorot constabulary soldier—1902" 84
17. "Evolution of a Bontoc Igorot constabulary soldier—1903" 84
18. "The prison band 'sounding off' at retreat, Bilibid Prison" 85
19. "Typical scene in a trade school" 85
20. "Filipino elites in the colonial legislature, 1918" 86
21. "Dead insurgent officer and soldier on the road to San Pedro Macati" 87
22. "Burying the Filipino dead" 88
23. "At the battle of Caloocan" 89

24. "The American Artillery did wonderful execution in the battles with the insurgents" 88
25. "Tating dear, Let this picture of your friend remind you of our companionship. With love, Apolinar" 94
26. "Heartily dedicated to my dearest Enchang as a sign of everlasting friendship. Lovingly yours, Cleofe" 94
27. "A Mi Amada Cristeta, Dedico este retrato en prueba de nuestro cariño, Teang" 95
28. "To Chimang, To prove once more the sincerity of my true love. Otelio" 95
29. "Kay Genoveva—Ala-ala ko ito sa iyo tanda ng di ko pagkalimot. Ang iyong kaibigan, Luming" 96
30. "A mi distinguida y buena prima Agueda, Mi mas humilde recuerdo. La Original" 97
31. "To my dear Estrella" 98
32. Don Mariano Ponce and Dr. Sun Yat Sen in Yokohama, Japan 104
33. Ferdinand Marcos as Malakas 123
34. Imelda Marcos by Claudio Bravo 144
35. Imelda by Federico Aguilar Alcuaz 146
36. Imelda by Antonio Garcia Llamas 148
37. "Merry Crises-mas!" 175
38. "Let's make baka, don't be takot!!!" 178

Acknowledgments

The writing of this book was aided by grants from the Social Science Research Council, the Humanities Research Institute at the University of California, Irvine, the East-West Center at Honolulu, Hawai'i, the Rockefeller Foundation in Bellagio, Italy, and several grants from the Committee on Research at the University of California, San Diego.

The imaginative depth and intellectual rigor of the work of Reynaldo Ileto continues to place my writing in his debt. The generosity of Doreen Fernandez, Ambeth Ocampo, Karina Bolasco, Eduardo Jose Calasanz, Tina Cuyugan, Jessica Zafra and Ray Vi Sunico have enriched me over the years, especially during my frequent trips to the Philippines. Their contributions to this book are far more than I can ever acknowledge. I have profited perhaps more than I'm entitled to from the friendship of John Pemberton and Marilyn Ivy, both of whom have made many useful comments on a number of the chapters in this book. John Sidel also carefully read through the manuscript and offered many valuable suggestions.

Over the years, it has been my great fortune to have had the advice and support of Benedict Anderson and James T. Siegel. Their writings, so distinct from one another, inform and inflect many of the terms with which I have approached recurring questions about language and history. Many others provided me with occasions to discuss and publish parts of the chapters that appear here, pointing me in directions I would otherwise have missed had I not come into contact with their work. A very partial list of these people includes: Itty Abraham, Warwick Anderson, Belinda Aquino, Enrique Bonus, Carol Breckenridge, Suzanne Brenner, Oscar Campomanes, Fenella Cannell, Yvette Christianse, Michael Cullinane, Cathy Davidson, Vicente Diaz, Jean-Paul Dumont, Steve Fagin, Nancy Florida, Susan Harding, Val Hartouni, Robert Horwitz, Florence Howe, Susan Jeffords, Amy Kaplan, Webb Keane, George Lipsitz, Henk Maier, Michael Meeker, Rosalind Morris, Rudolf Mrazek, Chandra Mukerji, Brian Mussumi, Donald Pease, Mary Pratt, Danton Remoto, Lulu Reyes, Renato Rosaldo, Michael Salman, Doris Sommer, Ann Stoler, Neferti X. Tadiar, Ricardo Trimillios, Anna Tsing, C.J. Wee Wan-ling, and Geoff White. I am also grateful to Ken Wissoker for his many years of encouragement and editorial advice.

    I cannot imagine how a single sentence could have been written here without the material and emotional labor of my families spread out across the Pacific Ocean: Jose and Rosemarie; David and Rina; Enrique and Menchie; Yoshiko, Craig and Cristi; and most important, the two C.'s who parenthesize my life: Catalina and Carol.

When we name a thing, we furnish it with a name. But what about this furnishing? . . . [T]o name is to call something into its word. What is so called is then at the call of the word. What is called appears as what is present, and in its presence it is secured, commanded, called into the calling word. So called by name, called into a presence, it in turn calls. It is named, has the name. By naming, we call on what is present to arrive. Arrive where? That remains to be thought about. In any case, all naming and all being named is the familiar "to call" only because naming itself consists by nature in the real calling, in the call to come, in a commending and a command.—*Martin Heidegger, "What Calls for Thinking?"*

But if the [Spanish] corporal was a bad philologist, he was, on the contrary, a good husband; he would teach his [native] wife what he had just learned and so continued her education.

"Consola, what is the name of your d— country?"

"What else should I call it? As you have taught me, Felifenas!"

"I'll knock you with this chair, you b—! Yesterday, you were pronouncing it much better, the modern way. But now, you have to say it the ancient way: Feli, or rather Filipinas! . . . Say it you b— or I'll hit you with this chair!"

Consolacion saw the movement, thought for a while, and stammered, breathing heavily, "Feli . . . Fele . . . File . . ." Pum! Crracc! The chair completed the word.

The lesson ended in fisticuffs, scratches, blows. The corporal grabbed her hair, and she, his goatee and other parts of his body . . . ; blood flowed, one eye grew redder than the other, a shirt was torn to shreds, body parts came out from their hiding places, but Filipinas did not emerge.

Adventures like these happened every time the matter of language came up.—*Jose Rizal,* NOLI ME TANGERE

Introduction
Episodic Histories

Few countries give the observer a deeper feeling of historical vertigo than the Philippines. Seen from Asia, the armed uprising against Spanish rule of 1896, which triumphed temporarily with the establishment of an independent republic in 1898, makes it the visionary forerunner of all other anticolonial movements in the region. Seen from Latin America, it is, with Cuba, the last of the Spanish imperial possessions to have thrown off the yoke, seventy-five years after the rest. Profoundly marked, after three and a half centuries of Spanish rule, by Counter-Reformation Catholicism, it was the only colony in the Empire where the Spanish language never became widely understood. But it was also the only colony in Asia to have had a university in the nineteenth century. In the 1890s barely 3 per cent of the population knew "Castilian," but it was Spanish-readers and -writers who managed to turn movements of resistance to colonial rule from hopeless peasant uprisings into a revolution. Today, thanks to American imperialism, and the Philippines' new self-identification as "Asian," almost no one other than a few scholars understands the language in which the revolutionary heroes communicated among themselves and with the outside world—to say nothing of the written archive of pre-twentieth century Philippine history. A virtual lobotomy has been performed.—*Benedict Anderson, "The First Filipino"*

The chapters that form this book were composed during the last decade of the twentieth century. They are as much the products of the "virtual lobotomy" that Anderson writes about as they are belated attempts to come to terms with its operations. Written from the place of forgetting, the United States of America, these essays relate events in the cultural and political history of the Philippines and Filipinos from roughly 1898 till the middle of the 1990s. They do not tell a complete and unified story about the nation and its fragments but instead offer versions of what could be told based on archival remains and the wealth of official, scholarly, and popular interpretations of certain events. And although they deal with historical topics, they are indebted to the critical vocabularies of anthropology and literary studies as well. At bottom, what holds them together is an interest in understanding the languages of rule, resistance, and collaboration as these are conjugated by the technologies of imagery in the production of colonial and national histories. In engaging the related legacies of colonial interventions and nationalist responses, however, I have also pursued the emergence of other historical possibilities that either exceeded or fell short of these narratives. Precisely those moments, in other words, that somehow cannot be neatly mapped onto either discourse, that seem incidental or peripheral to the grand moral (and moralizing) narratives of both. These concerns, inescapably overdetermined, are enmeshed in a number of contexts, two of which are worth citing.

To begin with, this book explores the fractious history of a nation-state at a time when both the nation form itself and the scholarly genre for addressing it—area studies—are undergoing intense scrutiny and face uncertain futures in the United States.[1] The end of the cold war; the intensification of capitalist penetration across national borders; the emergence of new nationalisms within older ones coinciding with the rise of ethnic conflicts, of postcolonial neoliberal regimes alongside religious fundamentalisms and growing economic disparities in the so-called third world: such a history, as is well known, has characterized the fin de siècle. One of the developments arising from this history has been particularly important to the writing of this book: the mass migration beginning in the mid-1960s to the present of Filipinos in search of alternatives—economic, political, cultural—to the pressures of uneven developments and unrealized desires that they face in the Philippines. Such movements have, in turn, given rise to a new generation of hyphenated and racialized Filipinos, especially in North America, increasingly curious about their origins. Uneasily affiliated with while doubly alienated from the land of their birth and places of their work, residence, and/or citizenship, these migrant, immigrant, and second-generation Filipino-Americans have become crucial sources of financial aid by virtue of the remittances they send to the Philippines.[2] By the same token, they have also become significant interlocutors in the political debates and formation of knowledge about Filipinos in the Philippines and elsewhere. This all takes place as area studies, the dominant post–World War II social science genre for coming to terms with the "alien" and modes of alienation among peoples outside the United States, has come under considerable pressure to justify its institutional existence to funding agencies, private and public alike. While area studies has historically been used to extend and refine U.S. hegemony in the world as part of the cold war, it has also provided channels of communication and exchange between scholars, resulting in an extensive body of work critical of the very agencies and figures that have sought to instrumentalize knowledge of the other. These two facts—the emergence of what, for want of a better term, might be referred to as a diasporic Filipino culture on the one hand, and the crisis in the culture of area studies in the United States on the other—have in part shaped the shifting textures and tonalities of this book. The chapters that follow can thus be read as tokens in an ongoing engagement with these recent, far from clearly demarcated developments.

The second context for these essays has to do with the history of nationalism in the Philippines. They appear against the backdrop of various Filipino centennial celebrations of the anticolonial revolution of 1896 and anti-imperialist war against the United States of 1899–1902. Both of these momentous events were punctuated and eventually overcome by counterrevolution, beginning with the Tejeros Convention of 1897, and followed by the Malolos republic of 1898–1899 and the colonial Philippine Assembly of 1907. Centennial festivities in the Philippines as well as among most Filipino overseas and immigrant communities have tended to portray all these events as part of a smooth continuum—the story of the struggle against colonial bondage leading to national sovereignty—rather than events that exist in dialectical tension with one another.[3] Such a view grows out of and serves to consolidate the triumphalist official nationalism that has emerged in the wake of the 1986 People Power Revolt (another stunted revolution) under the Aquino, Ramos, and Estrada regimes of the late 1980s and 1990s. It has coincided with the stultification of revolutionary nationalism within the Communist Party of the Philippines, whose leaders as of this writing remain in obdurate exile in the Netherlands, at odds with their increasingly factionalized cadres back home. This book is partially a response to these fluid and disparate conditions in a country where a certain conservative nationalism has become ascendant, and populist expressions of nationhood seem so readily taken up and contained by varieties of Christianity, the forces of the state, and the lures of the marketplace.[4]

The form that this response has taken is something not unfamiliar to the tradition of Filipino critical and historical writing: the essay. I follow in the wake of those writers who have sought to render an episodic rather than epic account of the Philippines.[5] Where a major tendency of nationalist historiography has been the epic recollection of the "passion"—the suffering, death, and resurrection—of the Filipino nation, there has existed as well a "minor" style of episodic narrative, which treats in a more condensed and concise manner clusters of historical details and reflections that do not easily fit into a larger whole. The usefulness of such a form of writing lies in its ability to attend to the play of contradictions and moments of nonheroic hesitation, thereby dwelling on the tenuous, or we might say ironic, constitution of Philippine history. Where the epic, with its concern for the heroic, seeks to form the very consciousness of the people whom it speaks to and about, the episodic digresses, circling around recurring motifs and recalcitrant obsessions. For this reason, the latter necessarily assumes an ironic relation to the former. Irony forestalls and interrupts the establishment of a single, overarching narrative about the nation.[6] Rather than relay *the* event of nationhood, episodic histories linger on the thresholds of meanings. Dwelling in the shadow of details, they convey the eventhood of events, that is, the conditions of possibility and impossibility for the historical emergence of the nation and its various states.[7]

Names and Naming We can begin with the ironies encysted in the names *Philippines* and *Filipinos*. The archipelago was named after the heir to the Hapsburg throne, Felipe II, by the Spanish explorer Ruy Lopez de Villalobos most likely in 1543. In search of the spice islands, his crew inadvertently landed on the shores of Samar and Leyte, the easternmost region of what is now called the Visayan Islands in the central

Philippines. Like Columbus confronting the islands of the New World, Villalobos took conceptual possession of these, naming them *las islas Filipinas*. The boundaries of this Spanish invention, however, were far from settled. Originally, it referred to those two islands where Villalobos's men were able to secure provisions. By 1565, with the arrival of Miguel Lopez de Legazpi and the establishment of the first permanent colonial settlement on the island of Cebu, the term encompassed those parts of the archipelago that had come under Spanish control, including most of the lowlands of Luzon.[8]

Through the two centuries of Spanish rule, the limits of Filipinas kept shifting. At one point, it would have included parts of Borneo and the Moluccas in the south and Formosa and Macao in the north, both of which had served as Spanish outposts only to eventually be abandoned in the seventeenth century. Spanish expeditions during this period were also sent to conquer Malacca, parts of present-day Cambodia along with what in the nineteenth century would be known as Indochina, and the Marianas and Caroline Islands. Only the Marianas expeditions were a success, resulting in the incorporation into the Spanish realm of the island of Guam, which in the nineteenth and early twentieth centuries would be used as a site to incarcerate Filipino nationalists. By the same token, had the Dutch defeated the Spaniards in the protracted wars of the seventeenth century, the archipelago would have been part of the East Indies and present-day Indonesia. For a brief period in the mid-eighteenth century, 1762–1764, Manila was part of the British Empire as a consequence of the Spanish defeat in the Seven Years' War. The colony was eventually returned to Spain in the peace settlement that followed. However, British, and to a lesser extent German and North American, merchant capital came to dominate the economic realities of the colony by the late eighteenth through the nineteenth centuries. Thus was Filipinas doubly colonized, belonging to Spain (and until 1821, administered as a Mexican province through the trade connection between Manila and Acapulco) but also to the expansive geography of a world capitalist system that stretched across the Pacific and Atlantic Oceans. From sugar mills to railroads, British, German, and North American merchant houses financed what amounted to an agricultural revolution that linked the colony to overseas markets and created a mestizo middle class from which the leaders of the nationalist movement would emerge.[9]

Nonetheless, until the end of the Spanish era in 1898, parts of the colony's territories—the upland regions of the Cordilleras and the mountainous terrains of the southern Tagalog and eastern and western Visayas, as well as the Muslim-populated areas of Mindanao and the Sulu archipelago—clearly stood on the periphery of colonial control, offering refuge to those seeking to escape and undo its hold. These were areas interior to Filipinas yet exterior to its hegemony. As the great writer Nick Joaquin observed, "The might-have-beens of Philippine geography are staggering. . . . It could have been less or even non-existent as a separate entity. There could have been no 'Philippines' at all. The labor of the Spanish period was not only to create a geography but to *preserve* what had been created."[10] Even American colonial officials in 1898 chose to maintain this Spanish geography after some short-lived discussions of partitioning the colony. The outlines of the cartographic image of Filipinas that is familiar to every Filipino schoolchild today was, in fact, first sketched in 1734 by the Jesuit Pedro Murillo Velarde and engraved by Francisco Suarez and Nicolas de la Cruz, both of whom referred to themselves as *indio tagalo en Manila*. It was this colonial geography, instigated by the hallucinations and contingencies of voyages and conquest, that came to be taken as naturally fated and organically whole by the leaders of the Philippine Revolution and all other nationalists who have come in their wake. But unlike the eighteenth-century engravers Suarez and de la Cruz, late-nineteenth-century nationalists referred to themselves as Filipinos rather than indios. How did this shift come about?

The Spaniards, like Columbus, tendentiously misnamed the native inhabitants of las islas Filipinas indios, placing them in the same racial pot as the inhabitants of the New World. The term *Filipino* likewise had curious beginnings. As late as the end of the nineteenth century, it referred to the sons and daughters of Spanish parents born in Filipinas. Like the Americano, the Filipino was thought to be racially distinct and consequently inferior to the Spaniard who hailed from the peninsula regardless of his or her educational attainment or class background. At the same time, he or she enjoyed a more privileged social position in a plural society compared to the lowly indio, the untrusted but economically essential *Sangley*, or Chinese, and the equally educated and Hispanicized mestizos, both Spanish and Chinese. Indeed, the very term

Filipino emerges in the first place as a way of accounting for the existence of those who, looking like Spaniards, were in actuality born outside of Spain, in the colonies where the climate and civilization were seen to be so radically different from that of the motherland.[11] We could thus think of Filipino as that which initially referred to a liminal group, to individuals who were native neither to the place of their parents nor that of their birth. Indeed, it was not until the spread of nationalist consciousness in the last two decades of the nineteenth century that the term began to take on another meaning: those who would claim a fatal attachment to the *patria* regardless of their juridically defined identity. Such a condition has led Benedict Anderson to remark that by the end of the Spanish colonial regime in 1898, there existed a territorially demarcated country—las islas Filipinas—with a centralized state apparatus and an economy tied to global capitalist markets, but whose population was only beginning to refer to itself self-consciously as Filipinos, thanks to more than two decades of nationalist stirrings climaxed by a revolution that was then quickly followed by counterrevolutionary actions sealed by American imperialist intervention.[12]

Las islas Filipinas, in short, existed for more than three centuries before there were any Filipinos who would lay claim to its reality and proclaim loyalty to its existence. It is this ambivalent fit between the name of a place and the name of a people that has long haunted nationalisms, both official and popular. And given the prevailing ethnolinguistic and religious diversity of the archipelagic nation, an ongoing civil war between the republic and the Communist Party of the Philippines that dates back to the 1960s, separatist wars with Muslim groups in the south from the 1970s, the steady migration since the mid-1960s of its middle-class population to work or live in virtually every part of the world, and the recent resurgence of fundamentalist Christian sects across a wide array of social classes since the 1980s, attempts at establishing a clear and undisputed fit between the Philippines and Filipinos is far from complete, and in fact, may never be realized. Hence, when nationalist scholars, area studies specialists, or second-generation Filipino-Americans refer to Filipinos as the "native" inhabitants of the Philippines whose existence begins with the prehistoric Tabon Caves and remains essentially unchanged through the centuries and comes to include such disparate practices as Igorot crafts and tattoos, locally produced rock music, and late-nineteenth-century Tagalog peasant movements—they simultaneously acknowledge and erase the historicity of the term. These and other anachronistic usages of Filipino indicate the term's ironic origins, even as that irony is set aside.

Colonial Tracings The imperfect alignment between the name of the nation and the name of the people, who since the last nineteenth century have laid claim to this nation as their homeland, is precisely the trace of the colonial conditions within which both came about. It is well worth reiterating the extent to which Spanish colonialism introduced profound disjunctions into the native societies that it conquered. We can see this, for example, on the level of language. As I have argued elsewhere, the very possibility of writing the names of the nation and the different vernaculars of its inhabitants depends on a technological complex introduced by the Spanish missionaries: that of the Latin alphabet and phonetic script that replaced the Sanskrit-derived syllabic scripts so widespread on the islands at the point of contact. The ease with which these local scripts were replaced had, in part, to do with the fact that they were connected neither to royal literary traditions nor to elaborate cosmologies such as Hinduism and Islam, both of which had only the most superficial influences on precolonial societies. The exigencies of Christian conversion so essential to the consolidation of Spanish rule required that the Spanish missionaries learn native languages and thereby encode their grammar and publish dictionaries, religious sermons, and devotional literature in these various languages rather than in Spanish or Latin. What emerged at the end of Spanish rule was a Catholicized lowland majority speaking a variety of mutually unintelligible languages and made dependent on the linguistic and political mediation of the Spanish clergy to make their desires known to those at the top of the socioreligious hierarchy.[13] The cultural reality of las islas Filipinas cohered, then, in a linguistic hierarchy—of local languages conceived as derivatives of the language of the colonizer, and both considered to be derivatives of the language of God; and of local signifying conventions (from modes of writing to animist forms of spirit beliefs and rituals) as inferior, and thus, subject to those of the colonizer.

Harnessed primarily to the needs of evangelization (which in turn was the legitimating basis of colonial conquest), the technologies of

Spanish signification—Latin characters, grammar books, dictionaries, religious literature, laws, and decrees, all of which were reproduced and disseminated mechanically via print and backed by the machineries of the colonial military and state bureaucracy—effected the consolidation and regularization of the colony's linguistic diversity. To this day, such a diversity flourishes at the expense of a national language. Unlike other Southeast Asian and Latin American countries, the Philippines does not have a national language. Instead, it has a history of state and elite *attempts* to institute a national language based on Tagalog in the face of the persistence of a linguistic hierarchy, where the last colonial language, English, continues to be hegemonic.[14] As I will argue in chapters 4, 6, and 7, the persistence of this linguistic hierarchy has been coterminous with, if not constitutive of, the persistence of socioeconomic divisions in the country.

The Philippines and Filipinos are thus permeated with foreign origins, their historical realities haunted by the ghosts of colonialism. Nationalist revolution and counterrevolution have sought to lay these ghosts to rest with uneven success and unsettling effects. From its beginnings, nationalism in the Philippines has been divided and conflictual. Loving the nation has never been a simple matter. Historically, it has taken on various tendencies that defy synthesis. In its inception in the 1880s and 1890s, nationalist sentiments veered between assimilationist aspirations and separatist ambitions vis-à-vis the mother country, Spain. It was not, in fact, uncommon for the two sentiments to coexist in the writings of individual nationalist figures.[15] A brief review of the history of the revolution reveals as much.

Cross-class coalitions and ethnolinguistic alliances in the face of an increasingly reactionary Spanish regime (which, it is important to note, counted on the collaboration of many "natives" in its military and bureaucratic apparatus) made possible the geographically limited successes of an anticolonial revolution in the latter half of 1896. But these successes were brought about by a leadership made up of low-level bureaucrats and provincial elites led by Emilio Aguinaldo that quickly sought to contain the more radical social aspirations of the revolution. To this end, Aguinaldo and his followers installed a revolutionary government through what were likely fraudulent elections, then carried out the execution of the so-called father of the revolution, Andres Bonifacio, when he protested the results and conspired to launch a coup. Shortly thereafter, confronted with Spanish reinforcements, Aguinaldo and his generals retreated from their provincial base, eventually striking a deal with Spanish authorities brokered by the wealthier and more Hispanicized members of the Manila elite. By the end of 1897, they agreed to lay down their arms and go into exile to Hong Kong in exchange for large sums of money.[16] Aguinaldo, on the eve of their departure, readily professed to a Spanish journalist in his halting and heavily accented Castilian his continuing loyalty to the colonial government and desire for assimilation despite the fight that he had led against Spain.[17] But once in Hong Kong, Aguinaldo and his junta lost no time in seeking ways to purchase guns and solicit foreign aid to revive the struggle even as revolutionary fighters in the Philippines continued to engage in local battles against colonial troops.[18]

By May 1898, war broke out between Spain and the United States. Returned to the Philippines by U.S. naval forces, Aguinaldo was enlisted by George Dewey to aid in the fight against Spanish troops until the arrival of ground reinforcements. As U.S. ships aimed their guns at the colonial capital, Aguinaldo resumed the revolutionary struggle, quickly routing the demoralized Spaniards and declaring independence in June. In August, the Spaniards in Manila consented to what amounted to a mock battle with American troops in order to save face and keep Filipino forces from entering the capital city. The Filipino revolutionaries, prevented from claiming victory, had to establish their capital to the north, in Malolos, where they formed a republican-style, elite-dominated government. Unable to gain recognition of their sovereignty from the United States, however, the republic was driven to war with the new colonizers in February 1899.

Although the war came to an official end in 1902, sporadic resistance from peasant armies in other parts of the archipelago continued until 1912. Nevertheless, within the first five years of U.S. rule, the overwhelming majority of revolutionary leaders had surrendered to the occasionally genocidal ferocity of the conquering force.[19] Elites, in time, saw their own survival as entirely dependent on their collaboration with the new colonial state. Through U.S. colonialism, nationalist elites consolidated their prominence, finding in the new regime the economic, military, and political means with which to ward off the demands for radical change from below and secure their privileged positions to speak for and of the nation through the patronage of those above.

How can we understand these events? Revolution had stirred the populace—first in the Tagalog regions and then in places that had come under Spanish rule. Ironically, word of the revolution traveled along the same communicative routes established by the colonizers—initially in the Castilian language and eventually in the vernaculars that had been conserved by the missionary orders. It spread among students at colonial universities, was incubated in secret societies styled after Masonic lodges, was inveigled from church pulpits, and appeared in newspapers published in Spain and the Philippines. Social hierarchies threatened to collapse as indios, mestizos, and Filipinos demanded recognition from Spaniards as equals. And when their appeal was construed as either ingratitude or intimations of criminal intentions by the colonial state and church—both already paranoid about their losses in Latin America and the revolution in Cuba—these groups found themselves linked under a common name as "filibusteros," or subversives: enemies of the state, subject to surveillance, deportation, torture, and execution.[20]

The expectations of freedom that swept through many parts of the archipelago in the wake of the revolution were not uniform; indeed, the meaning of *freedom* was never clear-cut. As the historian Reynaldo Ileto has shown, it ranged from the Enlightenment notion of political independence and representative government familiar to the nationalist bourgeoisie, whereby they would figure as the natural rulers of the land, to the more vernacularized, Catholic-inflected notions that saw the revolution in millenarian terms as the redemptive leveling of all social distinctions.[21] What was so revolutionary about the revolution was precisely that it placed different social groups and classes into unprecedented contact and communication. Revolutionary nationalism came to be infused with the agency of an irresistible newness, suggesting the emergence of possibilities yet unthought and a history that could not be foreclosed. In the language of some of its more radical participants, the revolution promised not only freedom from colonial domination but also release from unequal relations of all sorts.[22]

As we have seen, however, the possibility of a social revolution was quickly overtaken by the forces of counterrevolution by 1897 and increasingly after 1899. Elite attempts to contain revolutionary impulses by organizing a revolutionary state, then formalizing it into a republican form of government wholly dominated by Spanish-speaking elites, amounted to the resuscitation of the social hierarchy. While war against the United States revived revolutionary hopes, military defeat and political collaboration consolidated social differences. Throughout the years of U.S. rule, there emerged a remarkably resilient oligarchy. With a rural base in a plantation economy; it enjoyed tariff-free access to markets in the United States and dominated national politics under U.S. sponsorship. Many (though not all) of these elites collaborated with the Japanese regime during World War II, and then repudiated it with the return of the Allies in 1945; survived not only the Hukbalahap peasant rebellion that followed in the late 1940s and 1950s but also the Marcos dictatorship of the 1970s through early 1980s; and have continued to dominate Philippine political and cultural life in the aftermath of the People Power uprising in 1986.[23]

The tragic—and therefore ironic—relationship between revolution and counterrevolution forms one of the most enduring motifs in Philippine history. Conservative impulses have conflicted with but also complemented more radical views. The desire for social leveling has alternated with the desire for hierarchy, often within the same nationalist figures and the same class formations. Even peasant-instigated movements critical of colonial and elite domination were waged in a language of devotion and submission, taken from the colonial idiom of Catholicism and fused with the residues of animistic, precolonial beliefs. Utopic longings for freedom also betrayed a generalized wish for an order of perfect reciprocity ruled over by a benevolent patron.

We can see this irony, for example, in Ileto's highly suggestive excavation of the meanings of the Tagalog word for freedom, *kalayaan*. It is derived from the root word *layaw*, the carefree state associated with childhood when all of one's needs are taken care of by one's parents. As such, kalayaan could be used as a vernacular token in the moral critique of oppressive conditions caused by the neglect of those below by those on top of the social hierarchy. Yet it also indicates a state of sublime dependency that assumes unending access to an inexhaustibly generous patron/parent prepared to grant every desire. Freedom here simultaneously undermines and idealizes hierarchy, positing not an end to dependency but the possibility of its perfection. In this sense, the notion of kalayaan echoes the Christian one of salvation, which puts forth a transcendent realm that would relieve one from daily sufferings by granting him or her a place of perfect subordination to God.[24] Freedom as sublime dependency is reflected not only in lower-class discourses but in a wide range of nationalist imaginings as well. These include the middle-class projects of campaigning for assimilation into Spain, exploring protectorate status from Japan on the eve of the revolution, invoking the patronage of the "great North American nation" right in the declaration of independence of 1898, or submitting to devotional practices and prophetic figures acting in the name of a higher power, whether they be peasant leaders in the mountains of the Visayas or *ilustrado* (enlightened) leaders in Manila.

The double connotations of freedom are, of course, directly related to the complexities of nationalism's history. As the chief means for undoing colonialism's effects, nationalism is inextricably linked to that which it seeks to repudiate. Attempting to exorcise the ghosts of colonialism, nationalism also marks the point where colonialism returns, particularly in the forms of the modern state apparatus and socioeconomic inequalities registered in the persistence of a linguistic hierarchy. The coherence and appeal of Filipino nationalism comes, in part, from its continuing relationship to colonialism's power—whether Spanish, North American, or to a lesser extent, Japanese. This is not to say, however, that it is a derivative discourse, to use a current term. That would clearly be a mistake. Rather, the history of Filipino nationalism shows it to be inhabited and strangely enabled by the very forces it has sought to distinguish and expel from itself. Seeking to repossess and expropriate colonialism's legacies, nationalism also finds itself possessed by its spectral returns. Thus the fundamental irony of Filipino nationalism. It has engendered militant resistance and remarkable acts of sacrifice and courage, just as it has provided an alibi for self-serving collaboration with new regimes and the systematic repression of those opposed to them. In an era marked by diaspora, nationalism has provided a language for organizing and mobilizing overseas and immigrant communities in response to racial and sexual discrimination and often in alliance with other similarly marginalized groups, both in the host country and the Philippines. Still (as we shall see in chapter 8), it has also functioned to reify identities, freeze the past, and encourage the commodification of ethnicity that situates Filipinos abroad in a touristic—that is to say, neocolonial—relationship with the Filipinos at home.

Interruptions The chapters that follow delineate some of the ways in which the tracings of colonialism continue to embroider, and thus ironize, Filipino nationalism; but they also reveal how the ironies of nationalism have acted on and problematized colonial attempts at institutionalizing social order. Although arranged in rough chronological fashion, each chapter proceeds by way of juxtaposing and dispersing certain figures and motifs. In chapter 1, I examine the colonial census of 1903–1905—already a hybrid text made up of statistics, ethnological reports, and photographs—in relation to the "seditious" Tagalog nationalist melodramas whose performances evoked a revolutionary nationalism at odds with the racialized imperial order imposed by the United States. At stake in both was the casting of a certain Philippines as an object of supervision and attachment at a time of uncertainty and violence. Chapter 2 considers the writings of women from the United States during the first decade of U.S. rule, probing into the contradictory construction of Anglo-American notions of domesticity in an irreducibly foreign setting. By focusing on the crisis of embodiment experienced by white women within a vastly different racial order in the colony, this chapter calls attention to the mimetic relationship between these women and the native and Chinese servants working in their homes. Such a relationship will resonate, as we shall see with the predicaments of mestizo and mestiza nationalism in the period during and after the Second World War.

In both chapters, a consideration of the racial and gender aspects of U.S. colonialism in the Philippines reveals it to be far from an exception to, and in some ways continuous with, the European colonialisms of the early twentieth century. We can also sense how the nature and place of the colonized could never be definitively circumscribed. Collaborations and resistances characterized Filipino responses to the technologies of the U.S. rule. We see this not only in the form of the nationalist theater but also in the use of photographic portraiture, the subject of chapter 3, to elicit alternative identities and modes of identification among the living and, even more significantly, those who come after the dead. It is precisely this play of identifications, the contrasting and contradictory vectors of "Filipino-ness," that is the subject of chapter 4. Here, it is the juxtaposition of the rhetoric of collaboration with the circulation of rumor during the Japanese occupation of Manila that indicates how recurring moments of misidentification, already at work among the first generation of nationalists in the late nineteenth century, make up the pleasurable, but also anxious, basis of national identity held in an anticipatory mode as that which is always yet to come.

The pleasures and anxieties of nationalist identification in the postwar decades are taken up in chapter 5 in the context of the Marcoses' rise to power. This chapter looks at the ways in which the First Couple mythologized their romance and capitalized on the contradiction between the moral economy of patronage, on the one hand, and the amoral economy of commodity exchange, on the other, in order to project (but also frustrate) the desire for nationalist modernity and intimate the beginnings of an authoritarian aesthetic. It closes with a brief examination of the rise of youth politics and the ways it challenged the language of patronage espoused by the Marcoses. The linguistic dimension of nationalist modernity and its link to popular culture is the subject of chapter 6. Where chapter 5 deals with the political culture of nationalism during the formative Marcos years, this chapter explores the cultural politics of the era leading up to and past the martial law period. It focuses on the emergence of Taglish, itself the product of the juxtaposition of languages, and shows how it takes on varying historical significance, capable either of going against the grain of the prevailing hierarchy of languages (and the social hierarchy it implies) or reconfiguring and reinforcing both. Chapter 7, written as an introduction to the work of Ambeth Ocampo, one of the most widely read historians in the Philippines today, further reflects on the hazards of popular culture and the phantomlike existence of the lingua franca in the period after the EDSA uprising of 1986.[25] Finally, in chapter 8, I seek to bring together what otherwise might seem like a set of categorically distinct entities: overseas Filipinos, gossip, and ghosts. Their conjunction, made possible by the twinned legacies of colonialism and capitalist development, allows us to see the ways in which the emergence of overseas Filipino communities places new strains, but also new possibilities, on the articulation of official and popular nationalism in recent times.

True to their episodic quality, these essays were conceived with different audiences in mind and for different occasions, primarily in the United States and the Philippines. They could not have been written without close readings of and sustained contacts with vernacular languages and local sources of knowledge, which of course are the very practices associated with area studies. Yet they are also addressed to anonymous and accidental audiences who might be drawn to see the Philippines as a case that forms part of their larger wholes, or as an allegory about the specific materializations of modernity. In this sense, these pieces exist at a remove from any single public or place. It is tempting to say that this book is written from a place of exile, as if the possibility of return and resettlement had been taken away from the author. Yet exile seems so full of pathos, so poignant a condition, that it would leave little room for considering the many pleasures and productive shocks of estrangement. Even more important, exile brings to mind the epic possibilities of heroism and the longing for redemption for oneself and one's people. It dreams of a path to progress and liberation even if the exile him- or herself cannot, like the prophet, share in its realization. We might think of exile, then, as an ironic condition that sees itself as such yet also dreams of abolishing such irony.

But this book is so full of interruptions, so taken with and by the fragments and leftovers of texts, and so drawn to what escapes power rather than what fulfills or definitively overturns it, that it cannot even pretend to be heroic in scope or in its aspirations. While it shares in the sense of the exilic as that which hopes for the return of justice (often seen to be coterminous with the return to the homeland), it remains skeptical about the possibilities of that return under the current conditions. It thus tacks its way back and forth between the place of its writing and the nation that it is writing about, moving between the debates on nationalism and contemporary studies of colonialism in the West, and the dense historical deposits of nationalism in the Philippines. Each chapter is the product of the aleatory conditions under which it was written as much as it is a signpost for future projects, the beginnings of which have only been sketched. As such, the chapters are full of gaps and hesitations, imperfect arguments that already anticipate their revisions. Such revisions, in fact, are already under way as another work is now in progress to address, in a more sustained fashion, the origins of nationalism and relationship between revolution and counterrevolution that I have hastily sketched above.

Nonetheless, it is my hope that this book as a whole might provoke other connections and conjectures on the part of the reader and that its shortcomings might furnish the provisional points from which counterarguments, novel comparisons, and alternative interpretations may arise. Here, I am reminded once again of Nick Joaquin. In a gesture reminiscent of Jorge Luis Borges, Joaquin responds to the nativizing tendencies in some nationalist writings by producing a list of what he considers to be the most important events in Philippine history. Beginning with the introduction of the wheel, he cites such milestones as the introduction of paper and printing, the Roman alphabet, the calendar and clock, and the *guisado*, characteristic of a wide variety of Filipino cooking. He ends with the example of the guava tree, which, like the items above, has a Spanish colonial provenance (by way of the New World) all-too-readily forgotten in the nationalist accounts of the Philippines. As Joaquin writes, "The Filipino boy washing the fresh wound of his circumcision in guava-leaf ointment seems so immemorially a part of our aboriginal culture that we are startled to discover that the guava tree came to us only with Spain."[26]

Joaquin's argument is that Filipinos qua Filipinos are descended not from precolonial natives but from a mixture of cultures and blood that began as recently as 1521. Hence the appropriateness of their name. They owe it to their great ancestor, whom they have now almost wholly forgotten, Don Felipe II. They live in the modern nation-state that not only bears his name but whose historical reality was initiated by that act of naming, however violent and bloody its consequences were at times. To which we might add, recalling the racial politics of the term itself, that if the Filipinos are related to Spaniards, they are so by virtue of a family romance gone awry. Looked on as bastards by the Spanish fathers, and accused of being parricides for having overthrown by force of arms *los padres* and *La Madre España*, Filipinos had rebelled against what they deemed to be the latter's criminal neglect of *los hijos y las hijas filipinas*. Joaquin's revisionary history thus recalls what has often been forgotten. And that recollection frequently comes as a surprise: for example, the recollection of the alien origins of the guava tree used for supposedly traditional rites of circumcision, or of a revolution not only unfinished but unresolved, steeped in acts both courageous and criminal. They draw one to think of impure origins and foreign genealogies, of national selves ineluctably inhabited by foreign others.

Although I did not intend it, this book shares an affinity with at least this aspect of Joaquin's project. Part of my father's generation who came of age during and immediately after the Japanese occupation, Joaquin writes and lives in Manila, whereas I write across the very Pacific once traversed by the Spanish galleons. Yet we find ourselves sharing a familiar predicament. For him, it entails thinking of Filipino as "an identity in progress"; for me, it is the name of a history that, coming from the outside, continues to arrive from the future. The difference may not be so great. In either case, the task is one of historicizing the uncertainty of such names and namings, thereby momentarily interrupting the workings of colonial and national lobotomies. It should be clear, though, that the effects of such interruptions can never be fully determined. Standing on the threshold of a revolutionary epoch, the national hero Jose Rizal had sought to contemplate a cure for his diseased country by tearing away the veil that hid the "social cancer" of *la patria* in his novel *Noli me Tangere*. Our situation is of course different. For in these postcentennial (and arguably counterrevolutionary)times, we can hope at the very least to approach the sense of vertigo—epistemological and comparative—that comes with apprehending las islas Filipinas and Filipinos as they slip in and out of various attempts to master and comprehend them.

1

White Love
Census and Melodrama in the U.S. Colonization of the Philippines

Arriving in Manila in March 1899, Dean C. Worcester, professor of zoology at the University of Michigan and member of the Schurman Commission appointed by President McKinley to investigate conditions in the Philippines, tells of witnessing the signs of war between the United States and the Filipino forces led by Emilio Aguinaldo. Worcester describes how he walked toward the Filipino trenches after one such battle, "counting the dead and wounded, as I had heard wild stories of tremendous slaughter and wanted to see just how much damage the fire of our troops had really done."[1] Wishing to discredit the claims made by anti-imperialists in the United States regarding the severity of the Filipino-American War,[2] Worcester conceives of the dead bodies of "insurgents" as objects to be counted and data for official sources of information. To do so, he erases the particularity of those bodies, as the task of counting replaces the ritual of mourning. The extent of the erasure of the Filipino dead becomes even more stunning at the conclusion of Worcester's story when he talks not about the dead at all but the wounded: "At the time we visited the Insurgent trenches, not all our own killed and wounded had been removed, yet every wounded Insurgent whom we found had a United States canteen of water at his side, obviously left by some kindly American soldiers. Not a few of the injured had been furnished hard tack as well. All were ultimately taken to Manila and there given the best care by surgeons" (ibid.).[3]

Benevolent Bondage   For Worcester, colonial warfare was not meant to conquer and exterminate the native populace. It was instead a kind of police action that would quell the disorder on the islands caused by the stirrings of deluded peasants and workers led by a gang of ambitious, mixed-blood Filipinos. These Filipino leaders, beginning with the Chinese-mestizo Aguinaldo, were illegitimate representatives of the Filipino people. Indeed, there were no Filipino people as such, only a heterogeneous collection of imperfectly civilized tribes and "wild men" speaking a bewildering variety of languages, bereft of a common culture and subject to impulsive and irrational behavior (Worcester, 2: 921–22, 938).

Given this putative absence of a Filipino nation, the U.S. presence in the archipelago could not be construed as usurping another people's sovereignty. Intervention was understood, in official accounts, as an altruistic act motivated by America concern for the natives' welfare on the part of the United States. U.S. troops did not shoot Filipinos to kill them but to save them from killing one another. Hence, in the Senate hearings of 1901, David Prescott Barrows, head of the Bureau of Non-Christian Tribes who would go on to run the colonial public school system before becoming professor of anthropology at the University of California, Berkeley, could state that the U.S. practice of administering the water cure—forcing water down prisoners' bodies to compel them to talk—could not possibly have harmed Filipinos; and that they willingly abandoned their homes and sought U.S. protection in concentration camps at the height of the war in order to lead easier, more secure lives. William Howard Taft similarly claimed that there were Filipinos "who . . . said they would not say anything unless they were tortured" and that "there never was a war conducted, whether against inferior races or not, in which there was more compassion and more restraint and more generosity [than this war against the Filipinos]."[4] Secretary of War Elihu Root could only concur a year later, praising the "splendid virile energy . . . accompanied by self-control, patience, [and] magnanimity" on the part of the U.S. troops. In spite of thousands of Filipino deaths resulting from artillery fire, disease, and famine, as well as considerable ecological havoc, the war was "characterized by humanity and kindness to the prisoner and non-combatant."[5] For in the end, the war had been a valuable learning experience for the Filipinos, a real "blessing," as Barrows would write in 1901 in his diary, "for without it the Filipinos would never have recognized their own weaknesses; without it we would never have done our work thoroughly."[6]

Indeed, U.S. colonialism in the Philippines was rhetorically driven by what President McKinley had referred to as "benevolent assimilation," whereby the "earnest and paramount aim" of the colonizer was that of "win[ning] the confidence, respect and affection" of the colonized.[7] Colonization as assimilation was deemed a moral imperative, as wayward native children cut off from their Spanish fathers and desired by other European powers would now be adopted and protected by the compassionate embrace of the United States. As a father is bound to guide his son, the United States was charged with the development of native others. Neither exploitative nor enslaving, colonization entailed the cultivation of "the felicity and perfection of the Philippine people" through the "uninterrupted devotion" to those "noble ideals which constitute the higher civilization of mankind."[8] Because colonization is about civilizing love and the love of civilization, it must be absolutely distinct from the disruptive criminality of conquest. The allegory of benevolent assimilation effaces the violence of conquest by construing colonial rule as the most precious gift that "the most civilized people" can render to those still caught in a state of barbarous disorder.

But instead of returning their love, Filipino "insurgents" seemed intent on making war. "Why these hostilities?" the Schurman Commission asked. "What do the best Filipinos want?" By demanding recognition of the independence that they had just wrested from Spain, Filipinos appeared to have "misinterpreted" the "pure aims and purposes of the American government and people," and thus, were attacking U.S. forces.[9] In resisting, the Filipinos were being unreasonable. As with errant children, they needed to be disciplined, according to McKinley, "with firmness if need be, but without severity so far as may be possible." A crucial part of the "high mission" of colonization, then, was the need to "maintain the strong arm of authority to repress disturbances and to overcome all obstacles to the bestowal of the blessing of a good and stable government upon the people of the Philippine Islands under the free flag of the United States."[10]

A certain kind of violence underwrote the allegory of benevolent assimilation. The measured use of force was deemed consistent with the tutelary aim of colonization: making native inhabitants desire what colonial authority desired for them. The mandate to institute "democratic aspirations, sentiments, and ideals" brought with it the need to enforce discipline and constant surveillance among the Filipinos. Filipinos were called on to accept the "supremacy of the United States . . . and those who resist it can accomplish no end other than [their] own ruin."[11]

What may seem like a fundamental contradiction at the heart of the colonial enterprise was due to assumptions regarding the aptitude of Filipinos. They lacked "the experience possessed by us"—namely, that of "self-government"—and by implication, the self-consciousness that marks a people's readiness for independence (Worcester, 2:981–88). Filipinos, as Taft observed, were "in a hopeless condition of ignorance . . . subject, like the waves of the sea, to the influence of the moment. . . ." As with children, they were highly impressionable, unable to reflect on their own conditions, and capable only of mimicking the actions of those they perceived to be above them. In their present state, Taft asserted, they cannot possess themselves; they can only be possessed by others. This situation made it all the more imperative for the United States to intervene. For only after the natives "have been elevated and taught the dignity of labor . . . and self-restraint" can they be allowed to decide their own future.[12]

The allegory of benevolent assimilation thus foresaw the possibility, if not the inevitability, of colonialism's end. But equally important, it also insisted on defining and delimiting the means to that end. While colonial rule may be a transitional stage of self-rule, the self that rules itself can only emerge by way of an intimate relationship with a colonial master who sets the standards and practices of discipline to mold the conduct of the colonial subject. In other words, the culmination of colonial rule, self-government, can be achieved only when the subject has learned to colonize itself. As Woodrow Wilson wrote with reference to the Philippines,

Self-government is a form of character. It follows upon the long discipline which gives a people self-possession, self-mastery, and the habit of order and peace . . . the steadiness of self-control and political mastery. And these things cannot be had without long discipline. . . . No people can be "given" the self-control of maturity. Only a long apprenticeship of obedience can secure them the precious possession.¹³

Made up of disparate characteristics, Filipinos lacked the "character" with which to control themselves, thereby requiring "a long apprenticeship." In this way can benevolent assimilation indefinitely defer its own completion, in that the condition for self-rule, self-mastery, can be made identical to the workings of colonial rule, the mastery of the other that resides within the boundaries of the self. White love holds out the promise of fathering, as it were, a "civilized people" capable in time of asserting its own character. But it also demands the indefinite submission to a program of discipline and reformation requiring the constant supervision of a sovereign master.¹⁴

Conjoining love and discipline, benevolent assimilation was meant to ennoble the colonizer as it liberated the colonized. What secured this link between an ideology of benevolence and the repressive-productive institutions of discipline? How was it possible to sustain the fiction, fostered by U.S. official discourse and eventually accepted with varying degrees of alacrity by Filipino collaborators, that colonial rule amounted to democratic tutelage? How did white love and native subjugation become mutually reinforcing?

I want to suggest that the link between benevolence and discipline was made possible through representational practices that recast Filipino appearances. The re-formation of natives as colonial subjects required that they become visible and therefore accessible to those charged with their supervision. Through continuous and discrete observations, the targets of benevolent assimilation could be identified, apprehended, and delivered for democratic tutelage. Whether it was in the areas of public order or public health, education or elections, incarceration or commerce, such supervision sustained the articulation of colonial rule at both the ideological and practical level. By rendering visible the subjects of colonization in particular ways, colonial supervision amounted to a powerful form of surveillance, setting the limits of colonial identities within the borders of the state.

This is not to imply that the circuits linking supervision, representation, and control were perfectly insulated, making the colonial state all powerful and unchallenged. Indeed, recent scholarship has shown the extent to which U.S. colonial rule, like its Spanish predecessor, was constantly compromised by forces and events it could not control, much less comprehend. The very agents of the state were often divided in their personal loyalties and ideological inclinations. U.S. military and civilian officials, for example, were clearly at odds over the appropriate techniques of conquest and colonization owing to their varying appraisals of Filipino capacities, just as the colonial government was subject to the vagaries of policy shifts among elected officials in the metropole. Similarly, differences existed among Filipino collaborators in terms of their earlier involvement with the revolution as well as their personal and political ties with colonial patrons. Collaboration was fraught with disagreements over legislation, taxation, budgets, and racially tinged debates regarding Filipino fitness for self-rule. Equally significant, class conflicts pitted colonial authorities, U.S. and Filipino elites alike, against peasant and workers' groups, at times erupting into local revolts that were brutally suppressed.[15] Nonetheless, an examination of the rhetoric of colonial rule suggests the existence of a dominant desire informing the state: that of creating a continuum between an ideology of benevolence, disciplinary practices, and networks of supervision—in short, a desire to consolidate the relay between knowledge and power. My interest here lies in inquiring about the formation of this colonial desire and the limits to its institutionalization.

In the early period of U.S. rule, one of the most instructive documents of the colonial wish to establish total and continuous supervision for the sake of tutelage was the four-volume *Census of the Philippine Islands*, begun in 1903 and published in 1905.[16] In what follows, I want to consider the various ways in which the census functioned as an apparatus for producing a colonial order coextensive with the representation of its subjects. It is important to stress, however, that the census's salience as a discursive practice can best be understood within the larger context of the Filipino-American War. As such, I attempt in the latter part of this chapter to link the census with one of the most popular forms of nationalist expressions among Filipinos during this period: vernacular plays whose performances were deemed seditious and ultimately banned by the colonial regime.

Historically coincident with the taking of the colonial census, performances of the nationalist dramas between 1899–1905 sought to contest the means with which to delineate and authorize the difference between Filipino and North American—and as I shall suggest, between men and women—at a time of catastrophic changes when a U.S. colonial state was yet to be stabilized amid the ruins of Spanish imperial hegemony and the collective memory of Filipino revolutionary victory over Spain. Seen in their historical conjuncture, both the census and plays were struggles over the representation of the Philippines growing out of the violence of nationalist revolution and imperialist intervention.

Surveying Subjects Census reports are curious texts. They contain no single author, for standing behind them is not a person but a state apparatus made up of a veritable army of enumerators, clerks, and statisticians managed by a hierarchy of supervisors and directors. It is not, therefore, the case that a census has no author but that the bureaucratic nature of its writing renders its authorship and authority dispersed and anonymous. Consequently, while the workings and results of census reports are never completely visible to an individual, censuses can claim to see everything that can be individuated, that is, counted, tabulated, and classified. No single reader can exhaust the entirety of a census report, just as no single reading can comprehend its meaning insofar as its myriad tables and graphs of statistical data escape total recall. Compiled in a mechanical fashion, census reports exceed narrative synopsis. The power—that is to say, the persuasiveness—of a census to convey what appears to be an objective representation of the world derives, in part, from its remarkable capacity to picture in quantitative terms the totality of the world's multiplicity. Thus the value of census reports to the colonial (and to any modern) state: they represent the state's ability to represent, and so govern itself. In enumerating and classifying the resources and population of the state, censuses render visible the entire field of colonial intervention.[17]

As the first Philippine census under U.S. rule, the 1905 report was conceived as both a confirmation of and means for consolidating the "pacification of the archipelago." The Congressional Act of 1902 made the cessation of the "insurrection" a precondition for conducting the census. The creation of a Census bureau under the direction of General Joseph P. Sanger (who had supervised earlier census reports for Puerto Rico and Cuba) was a way of officially asserting that the war was over. It was left to the victor to make an inventory of its new possessions. One reason for doing so was to set the conditions for holding elections within two years of the census's publication for Filipino representatives to the colonial legislature, to be known as the Philippine Assembly. Such a legislature was designed to consolidate the practice of Filipino collaboration, thereby rendering more efficient and cost effective the running of the colonial state while containing all remaining nationalist challenges to U.S. hegemony. Collaboration was seen as an index of the success of tutelage, the measure of the Filipino's recognition of their subordination to and desire for white authority. "The taking of the census," Governor-General Taft wrote, "will therefore form a test of the capacity of the Filipinos to discharge a most important function of government.... The census is to be taken solely for the benefit of the Filipino people, ... [and] they should lend their unanimous support to the successful taking of the census" (*Census*, 1:20).

Calling for Filipino collaboration both as local supervisors and enumerators, the census would serve as a kind of test of Filipinos' ability to perform a task. Discipline was called for by the census: that was why it could serve both the practical and ideological route to self-government in the future. As an instrument of white love, it was meant to give Filipinos an opportunity to perform before the solicitous gaze of U.S. tutors. The census would be an exercise, as it were, in character building, where the capacity to count was coterminous with the ability to be accountable to a colonial hierarchy. Not only would the census provide the empirical grounds for shaping the direction of colonial legislation and facilitating the influx of U.S. capital investments in the archipelago; as with the colonial legislature, it would also function as a stage on which Filipinos were to be represented as well as represent themselves as subjects of a colonial order: disciplined agents actively assuming their role in their own subjugation and maturation.

The U.S. project of a centrally organized and nationally coordinated census superseded that of the Spanish state's. For its census data, the Spanish colonial regime had relied mainly on the irregular and far-from-comprehensive records kept by parish priests on their local flocks. In addition, Spanish efforts at more systematic census gathering met with enormous resistance from the people inasmuch as they were geared primarily for the levying of taxes and conscription of labor

(*Census*, 1:13).¹⁸ The U.S. census of the Philippines, by contrast, was supposed to elevate rather than exploit the populace. The groundwork had been prepared by a number of U.S. surveys between June 1898 and 1903. In the face of ignorance about the archipelago in the United States, such surveys were charged with collecting facts on the Philippines as well as encouraging collaboration from native informants. The most important of these were the Philippine Commissions of 1899 and 1900 presided over by academic experts and the Ethnological Surveys carried out by such anthropologists as David Barrows, Dean C. Worcester, and Albert Jenks between 1900 and 1905. These surveys produced voluminous reports on the conditions of the country, generously illustrated with photographs of native scenes and types. As Paul Kramer has shown, the American project of amassing what was considered scientific knowledge was dependent not only on progressivist notions of expertise but also on an already existing body of Spanish colonial writings on the Philippines. Even more significant, these surveys would not have been possible without the active collaboration of natives, especially local elites, as indispensable sources of support and information. Published and republished, cited widely in newspapers, congressional testimonies, schoolbooks, and scholarly studies, such surveys established the basis for a kind of colonial common sense in the interest of countering revolutionary expectations.¹⁹

The Census Bureau followed existing practice, laying great stress on seeking Filipino cooperation in order to neutralize whatever local resistances still existed in the country. Conducting the census, then, was of a piece with U.S. attempts at co-opting Filipinos of all classes, thereby consolidating a counterrevolutionary nationalism that had emerged as early as 1898.²⁰ With appointments to the colonial judiciary beginning in 1899, the establishment of the Philippine Scouts (1901), and the election by limited suffrage of municipal officials (1905) and, later, representatives to the Philippine Assembly (1907), Filipinos were drawn into a pattern of collaboration with the colonial state.²¹ There were practical and pedagogical reasons for Filipinos, particularly members of the provincial and municipal elites, to be used as census personnel. To do so was, as Census Chief General Sanger put it, "to identify them with the census and to test their capacity to perform duties never undertaken before, and which in this country are supposed to require at least average intelligence" (*Census*, 1:13). Altogether, 7,502 Filipinos were employed, 40 of whom were women. Like the surrendering insurgents, local supervisors and enumerators were required to take an oath of allegiance to the government of the United States; they also received instructions on how to manage the canvassing of their districts. To supplement the ranks of U.S. and Filipino supervisors, the Census Bureau pressed into service all provincial and municipal officials as well as U.S. army officers and the Philippine Constabulary (*Census*, 1:16, 18–19, 36).

The gathering of census data was an enormous undertaking involving the mobilization of a vast army of clerks in the colonial capital and the deployment of enumerators across as much of the archipelago as possible. Although President Theodore Roosevelt had declared the Filipino-American War officially at an end by July 1902, guerrilla resistance continued in many parts of the country. In provinces such as Albay, Sorsogon, Bulacan, and Rizal, census takers were challenged by the guerrillas, now referred to under the criminal sign of *ladrones*, or bandits, by the colonial government. The enumeration of the population necessitated their pacification. Constabulary forces often intervened to suppress the guerrillas and secure the areas to be canvassed. In parts of Mindanao, a "show of force" by the colonial army was usually required to gain access to sources of local information, while in other parts of the country, local elites were pressed into providing information on and arranging for the surrender of local ladrones (*Census*, 1:22–23).

The census thus illustrates the indispensable link between the policing of colonial borders and annexation of local populations into the space of colonial knowledge. Census workers, white and native alike, labored under the watchful eyes of a hierarchy of supervisors even as they kept their eyes out for alleged insurgents. They surveyed the populace and were themselves surveyed by the state. In this sense, the census functioned as a machine for totalizing observation. Through the collection and classification of statistical data, it kept watch over the population, mapping their social location and transcribing them as discrete objects of information and re-formation. And through the bureaucratization of supervision underwritten by the organized deployment of violence, the census differentially disciplined those who managed as well as those who were targeted by its operations.

In order to better understand the manner in which supervision promotes assimilation—that is, how it lays the circuits that run between benevolence and discipline—I want to look in more detail at the mechanisms for gathering census data. Two forms were utilized: a schedule for enumerating and classifying people in a given area, and a keyboarded punch card for identifying each individual in relation to a set of categories indicated in the schedule. One served as an index for the other. Where the schedule sheets were designed to divide and distribute a person's identity into a series of delimited categories, the punch cards were meant to reconstitute him or her as the referent of a specific set of signs (*Census*, 2:9–14).

The schedule sheet was written in Spanish for the sake of Filipino enumerators unfamiliar with English. A facsimile of the schedule in English translation appears in the census report (fig. 1). The schedule consists of a series of vertically arranged categories such as "Location," "Name," "Relationship," "Personal Description," "Race," "Age," "Sex," "Marital Status," "Occupation," and so forth for the supposedly civilized (that is, Christian) population and a simpler, more abbreviated series for those deemed wild (that is, non-Christian). Enumerated on the sheet, one can imagine one's existence flattened and neatly spread out as a set of numbers across a table. It is as if becoming a subject of the colonial state entailed taking on a different kind of particularity. Plotted on a grid, one's identity becomes sheer surface and extension, abstracted from any historical specificity. Put differently, the census schedule projects a skewed profile of colonial society by divorcing identity from biography. Where biography entails the articulation of the subject as an agent of its own history, the schedule positions its subjects as a series of aggregates locatable on a table of isolated and equivalent values.

Through the schedule, the census sought to transcribe the person into a series of numbers grafted onto a closed set of categories. In tabulating the results of the schedule, however, the census also attempted to reconstitute the subject as an individuated, and therefore retrievable, item within the vast repositories of the colonial archive. This was done through what amounted to a massive filing system in the form of keyboarded punch cards designed to tabulate population tables—similar to the cards used in 1900 for the twelfth U.S. census. Each card contained an array of numbers and letters that corresponded to the data on the

Census of the Philippine Islands taken under the direction of the United States Philippine Commission.

SCHEDULE No. 1.—POPULATION.

Supervisor's district, No. ——.
Enumeration district, No. ——.
Municipality, ——; barrio, ——; institution, ——.
Enumerated by me on the —— day of ——, 19—. —— ——, Enumerator.

Province, ——.
Judicial district, ——.
Sheet No. —. Page 1.

	LOCATION.					RELATIONSHIP.	PERSONAL DESCRIPTION.					NATIONALITY.	CITIZENSHIP.	OCCUPATION.	EDUCATION.				OWNERSHIP OF HOMES.			
	In cities or pueblos. Street.	In cities or pueblos. Number of the house.	Number of the house in the order of visitation.	Number of the family in the order of visitation.	Name of each person who resides with this family or in this house.	Relationship of each person to the head of the family.	Color.	Sex.	Age at the last birthday.	Whether married or single, widowed or divorced.	Insane, deaf, dumb, blind.	Country of birth of this person.	Filipino, American, Spaniard, Chinese, Japanese, etc.	Occupation, trade, or profession of each person of 10 or more years of age.	Months of school attendance during the past school year.	Primary. Can read.	Primary. Can write.	Superior.	Is the occupant of the house the proprietor of the house, or land, or of both, or of neither?	Which is rented, the land or the house?	What is the monthly rent?	Is the house of nipa or of more durable materials?
	a	b	1	2	3	4	5	6	7	8	9	10	11	12	13	14	15	16	17	18	19	20
1																						
2																						
3																						
4																						
5																						
6																						
7																						
8																						
9																						
10																						
11																						
12																						
13																						
14																						
15																						
16																						
17																						
18																						
19																						
20																						
21																						
22																						
23																						
24																						
25																						

Census of the Philippine Islands taken under the direction of the United States Philippine Commission, 1903.

[Special statistics for non-Christian tribes of the Philippines.]

SCHEDULE No. 7.—POPULATION, SCHOOLS, AGRICULTURE.

Supervisor's district, No. ——.
Municipality of ——.
Enumerated by me this —— day of ——, 1903. —— ——, Enumerator.

Province of ——.
Judicial district ——.

	PUEBLO OR RANCHERÍA.	Tribe.	INHABITANTS.								SCHOOLS.						AGRICULTURE.											OTHER INDUSTRIAL PRODUCTS.				
			Of more than 15 years of age.		Under 15 years of age.		Total.					Teachers.		Pupils.		What is the approximate average of the inhabitants who can read and write?	Total area cultivated.	Products cultivated.					Number of domestic animals.									
			Males.	Females.	Males.	Females.	Males.	Females.	Births in 1902.	Deaths in 1902.	Total number.	Males.	Females.	Males.	Females.																	
	1	2	3	4	5	6	7	8	9	10	11	12	13	14	15	16	17	18	19	20	21	22	23	24	25	26	27	28	29	30	31	32
1																																
2																																
3																																
4																																
5																																
6																																
7																																
8																																
9																																
10																																

NOTICE.—When it is not possible to answer a question even approximately, write "Ign." instead of "Ignorado." The box headings of columns 18 to 32 have been left blank and should be filled out in accordance with the information collected. There should only be written down the products cultivated or harvested, such as hemp, tobacco, copra, vegetables, gutta-percha, etc. The names of these should be written in the box headings, and the quantities cultivated and harvested during the year 1902 should be written down in the columns underneath the numbers indicating the columns. If there are more products than the number of columns of the box headings, paste on an extra piece of paper and write down on this the quantities of the latter. The same method should be observed in connection with domestic animals, such as carabao, horses, sheep, cattle, fowls, etc. In columns 28 to 32 write down any other industries of the pueblo, such as pottery, textiles, cutlery, mats, hats, etc., and take notice of the instructions regarding agriculture and domestic animals given above.

Fig. 1. Schedule sheet (*Census of the Philippine Islands*, 1903)

schedule sheets. In addition, a numbering system tied the cards to the name of a specific person and the area where she or he was counted (fig. 2). By punching the appropriate holes—say, "B" for *blanco* (white), "M" for *moreno* (brown), "A" for *amarillo* (yellow), "V" for *varon* (male), "H" for *hembra* (female), etc.—the cards functioned to index a range of information regarding an individual's race, sex, age, occupa-

DIAGRAM OF KEYBOARD PUNCH CARD.

Gang punch.		Dwelling.	Families to dwelling head.	Persons to a dwelling.		Persons to a family.		Color.	Sex.	Age.					Conjugal condition.			
1	2 3 4	X	X					M	V	M0	M1	M3	M6	M9	S	O		Not defective.
5	6 7 8	Dw	J	0	50	0	5	0	50	0	5	A	H	1	2	3	4	5	C	C	X	Blind.
1	2 3 4	B	1	10	60	1	6	10	60	1	6	Mx	10	15	18	20	21	25	CM	L	X	Insane.
5	6 7 8	X	2	20	70	2	7	20	70	2	7	B	30	35	40	45	50	55	V	M	X	Dumb.
a	b c d		3	30	80	3	8	30		3	8	N	60	65	70	75	80	85	D	'S	X	Deaf.
1	2 3 4	5+	4	40	90	4	9	40		4	9		90	95	100				F	N	Native or foreign.
5	6 7 8	Nl	50	0	CR	Am	81	88	V	0	5	0	5	~0	0	Jp	Yo	Jp	As	Fm	Bi
1	2 3 4	Fu	100	1	TR	Ca	No	NN	VI	I	6	1	6	1	1	In	Al	UK	Al	Ta	Ca
5	6 7 8	Em	Tr	2	Un	Te		SN	VII	II	7	2	7	2	2	Fr	Ch	Fr	Ch	Vi	Ig
1	2 3 4	Un	Pd	5		OO			VIII	III	8	3	8	3	3		Xa	OA	Xa	Zs	Il
1	2 3 4		Un	10		TO			IX	IV	9	4	9	4	4		Am	OX	EU	Ot	Mo
5	6 7 8		X	25		Da			Un	X		5		6	5	Ot	Ot	IO	X	Pr
Gang punch.		Material of house.	Amount of monthly rental.	Owned or rented.	Higher education.	Literacy.	Months at school.		Occupation.						Citizenship.	Country of birth.		Name of tribe.

Fig. 2. Keyboard punch card (*Census of the Philippine Islands, 1903*)

tion, and so on. "By means of the gang punched holes and numbers," declared the census, "any one of the approximately 7,000,000 cards corresponding to the population of the Philippines could be identified and the correctness of the punching verified" (*Census*, 2:13).

The cards moved in the opposite but complementary direction to the schedules, citing an individual as a possessor of a range of qualities rather than a collection of numbers attached to a set of categories. The schedule itemized an individual's characteristics, whereas the card individualized the items on the schedule. In this sense, the census worked like an archive, cross-referencing characters with characteristics. On the one hand, it attempted to constitute a population by enumerating the totality of heterogeneous peoples and recording them onto a grid of reified categories. On the other hand, the census sought to affix to each member of the population an essentialized, regulated, and therefore retrievable identity. As Benedict Anderson has remarked, "The fiction of the census is that everyone is in it, and that everyone has one and only one extremely clear place."[22]

The census could serve as an infinitely expandable repository for accumulating all that could be quantified and empirically known in the colony to the extent that it provided the grammar for classifying its objects of knowledge as subjects of a colonial order. As with the practice

31 *White Love*

of enumeration, this grammar of classification was far from disinterested. Rather, it was crucial in imaging the terms of colonial society as, above all, a racial hierarchy.

Recoding Race   White love for "little brown brothers," as Taft referred to Filipinos, was predicated on white supremacy enforced through practices of discipline and maintained by a network of supervision. General Sanger in his introduction to the census of 1903 remarked how Filipinos would, in the course of time, become good citizens in that some of them had already proved themselves to be "excellent soldiers" capable of following the orders of their white officers. Similarly, census workers under white supervision had shown the natives' potential for performing complex state functions. With appropriate training, there was no reason why the rest of the population could not become a disciplined people. As Sanger contends,

Under the guidance of a free, just and generous government, the establishment of more rapid and frequent means of communication, whereby they could be brought into more frequent contact with each other, and with the general spread of education, the tribal distinctions which now exist will gradually disappear and the Filipino will become a numerous and homogeneous English-speaking race, exceeding in intelligence and capacity all other peoples of the tropics. (*Census*, 1:40)

Encapsulating the benevolent-disciplinary trajectory of colonial policy in general and the census in particular, Sanger reiterates the possibility, indeed the desirability, of molding colonial subjects into a single people, here conceived of as a "homogeneous English-speaking race." Predictably, homogenization can only come after a process of tutelage, one aimed at superseding if not suppressing existing "tribal distinctions." To do so, however, the general outlines of those distinctions need to be surveyed and accounted for. In order to transform the native races into *a* people, their differences had to be produced and reassembled.

The population tables of the census divide the inhabitants of the Philippines into roughly twenty-five linguistic groups, distinguishing at least five skin colors ranging from "white" to "black," and where relevant, types of "citizenship" and locations of birth. These seemingly incommensurable groupings were then reduced into two broad categories: "civilized" and "wild." Their differences initially had less to do with their material culture than their religious characteristics. Those labeled civilized were seen to adhere to a common Christian culture, while those marked wild were either Muslims or subscribed to animism, both clearly outside the Christian order. The former, comprising the majority of the archipelago's inhabitants, owed their civilized state, the census assumed, to the effects of Spanish rule. The latter—whether "pagan" headhunters in the mountains, nomadic forest dwellers, or Muslim peoples in the south—had steadfastly resisted Spanish conquest and were thought to live in "stages between almost complete savagery and dawning civilization" (*Census.* 1:22–23).

It is important to note, though, that the distinction between civilized and wild peoples is regarded in the census as relative and transitional. Wild peoples owed their "barbarous" state to the historical failure of Spain to conquer them, a condition that a more vigorous U.S. regime would remedy. Indeed, colonial accounts, especially those of Worcester's, are filled with glowing reports regarding the "wild men" as ideal colonial subjects. Because they were free from the so-called corrupting influence of Catholic Spain and lowland mestizo elites, wild men were seen to be far more receptive to the firm, straight-talking, tough love of white men. Hence could wild men be more easily disciplined through such tasks as massive road constructions that would link the lowlands with the mountains, mining explorations for U.S.-owned companies, North American–style athletic competitions staged for visiting colonial dignitaries, and the policing of the wild country from warring tribes to secure the safety of colonial hill stations and outposts. Wild men were ripe candidates for tutelage to the extent that they seemed most susceptible to subjugation.[23]

Conversely, so-called civilized Filipinos were more recalcitrant, even resistant, to the call of benevolent assimilation. As "insurgents" fighting to assert their sovereignty after having defeated the Spanish army, declared a republic, framed a constitution, organized a cabinet, and convened a congress by 1899, they were deemed dangerously ambitious and inherently deceptive. By their conduct in the war, these Filipinos had showed themselves to be wild and barbarous. And when they chose to collaborate with the new colonial power, they remained shifty, opportunistic, and often lazy. Spanish colonization and the Catholic religion had done no more than imprint the natives with the outward signs of civilization. Inwardly, they remained inadequate to the task of civilizing themselves.

One of the most commonly cited character traits in colonial sources that suggested the semicivilized state of Filipinos was their supposed penchant for mimicry. Incapable of original thought, they could excel only in copying their colonial and class superiors. Sanger's remarks on the ability of Filipino soldiers to follow orders under competent white officers seemed to ratify this belief. The census repeatedly quotes passages from various colonial sources and travel accounts from the late sixteenth century to the early twentieth that retail this notion of native mimicry. Typical were the comments of Major Frank S. Bourns, army surgeon and, later, chief of the Bureau of Health:

The race is quick to learn and has a fairly good natural ability, but such a class will have to be educated before great responsibility can be placed in its hands. . . . My idea [is that] if [Filipinos were] associated with . . . a sufficient number of Americans who are honorable and upright in their dealings, there would be a very strong tendency on their part to do as their colleagues do. They are natural imitators; it is a racial characteristic. (*Census,* 1:505; see also 1:494, 497, 499, 500–502, 507–8).

As "natural imitators," Filipinos perforce depend on external stimuli to shape their internal disposition. Merely reactive rather than reflective, they existed in immediate and sensuous relationship to their surroundings rather than as self-conscious agents of their own transformation. If they had committed "atrocious crimes" during the war, according to Governor-General Taft, it was only because they were imitating the actions of their mestizo leaders (who, in turn, were imitating the actions of their Spanish masters). Taft, like Bourns, attributes this tendency of the Filipinos to blindly follow their racial superiors to the fact that "they are an Oriental race. . . . Like all Orientals, they are a suspicious people, but when their confidence is won, they follow with a trust that is complete" (*Census,* 1:530).

Mimicry on the part of the natives is construed as a sign of inferiority borne out of racial difference. But precisely for this reason, as Taft states, it is also an invitation to white supervision: "[The Filipinos] are merely in a state of Christian pupilage. They are imitative. They are glad to be educated, glad to study some languages other than their own, glad to follow European and American ideals" (*Census* 1:530). Just as the untainted state of the wild peoples provided white men the opportunity to display their manly love, the civilized but imitative and corrupted peoples of a hybrid Oriental-Christian culture called for the studious and diligent care of white tutors and commanders.

Wildness and civility were thus contingent and interchangeable terms. In mapping population differences, the census also projected their future reconfiguration. Such was possible because the religious difference between wild and civilized peoples was subsumed by larger considerations of color and race. Whether they were Christian or non-Christian, marked or unmarked by European influences prior to U.S. rule, both types were seen to display "great homogeneity" with regard to their "brown" color, live in "tribes" with regard to their sociolinguistic organization, and be "Malays," a species of Orientals with regard to their race (*Census*, 1:411–12, 2:42–65). Hence is the census able to imagine civilized and wild peoples existing side by side on the same map of the Philippines (*Census*, 2:50–51). While their separate locations are indicated by the various colors of the map, one gets an acute sense of how their borders were encompassed and flattened out on the same homogeneous surface by the surveying eye of the state. Their identity as wild or civilized peoples was relative to their place on the colonial geobody, just as their distinct characteristics came into focus with reference to the assimilative gaze of white benevolence. The census not only mapped the structure of racial difference; it also established the privilege of a particular race to determine the borders of those differences.

This racial privilege was endowed with a genealogy. In the census section titled "History of the Population," then Chief of the Bureau of Non-Christian Tribes David Barrows writes about the peopling of the archipelago in terms of waves of migrations of different "races" from the outside. In doing so, he reiterates the speculations of other colonial accounts regarding the prehistory of the Philippines—speculations that, since the archeological advances of the 1960s, have been definitively discredited. My interest in pointing out the census's use of the wave migration theory has less to do with disproving its accuracy than with showing how its currency in official accounts grew out of the colonial concern with racializing Philippine history.

The original inhabitants of the islands were supposedly the Negritos (a Spanish term that literally means "little Negroes"), or Aetas, "aboriginal black dwarfs" whose origins, according to Barrows, remain shrouded in mystery. With their shorter stature, dark skin, "woolly hair," nomadic forest existence, and austere material culture, they seemed to Barrows and other writers from the United States to be so racially distinct as to be historically removed from the rest of the population. "They probably approach as nearly to the conception of primitive man as any people thus far discovered," Barrows notes. The aboriginal Negritos were then said to have succumbed to a succession of more culturally sophisticated and physically better endowed Malays from the south. Arriving in large boats, they conquered the islands, pushing the aboriginal populations into the forests while occasionally intermarrying with them. Later migratory waves brought even stronger Malays, some in possession of an Islamic faith acquired from Arabs, driving the older Malays into the mountains. The spread of Muslim Malays, however, was checked by the arrival of the Catholic Spaniards in the sixteenth century, marking the break between the prehistoric and properly historic epochs in the Philippines. The Spanish conquest also led to an influx of a "Chinese element" into the population, as traders settled and intermarried with the Malays, giving rise to a small but economically and socially significant mestizo population (*Census*, 1:411–17, 454, 532).[24]

This narrative of the peopling of the archipelago imagines the Philippines to have been a tabula rasa settled by successive waves of colonizers. As such, the racial and tribal diversity of the population can be explained in temporal terms as the inevitable retreat of darker-skinned, more savage inhabitants in the face of advancing groups of lighter-skinned, more civilized, and physically superior conquerors. Indeed, the epochal break between the prehistoric to the properly historical era occurs only with the arrival of the Spaniards. Racial differences result then from a long history of colonization culminating, presumably, in the arrival of the strongest, most progressive, and lightest-skinned colonizer to date: whites from the United States. The effect of racializing both the social structure and cultural history of the Philippines is to position the population in a derivative relationship to the outside. It is as if the country was naturally destined for conquest just as the United States was manifestly destined to colonize it. The historical recounting of the population, like its statistical accounting, renders colonial subjects visible from a transcendent, posthistoric vantage point, one occupied by what we might designate as the white gaze. Spatially, it is a gaze that dreams of surveying and cataloging other races while remaining unmarked and unseen itself; temporally, it is that which sees the receding past of nonwhite others from the perspective of its own irresistible future.[25]

The privileged poise of seeing a regulated and well-policed future already prefigured in the heterogeneous and disorderly past comes across with special clarity in the photographs of Filipinos that appear in the census report. Set off from the textual and statistical sections of the census, the photographs are arranged to form an album of colonial subjectivities. "Typical" examples of wild and civilized peoples are featured in the photographs in the first volume, along with pictures of native enumerators and their local supervisors. Dressed in their tribal attire for the camera's lens, images of colonial bodies are wrenched from their historical and social contexts. In their frozen state, they suggest the appearance of specimens undergoing different stages of tutelage. At the lowest extreme, the scantily clad Negritos hunched over the ground, with tangled hair and minstrel-like grins, are made to appear farthest removed from the civilizing touch of colonial rule (fig. 3). Head-hunting Igorots, those putative descendants of the first wave of Malay conquerors, along with Muslim Malays appear more erect, even regal, decked out in their tribal ornaments signifying their more advanced state (figs. 4 and 5). Closest to civilization are the Western-clad census workers. Set against a background of American flags, their appearance suggests well-disciplined bodies, while the portraits of local supervisors identified by name and area of responsibility produce images of bourgeois respectability assimilated into the state machinery (figs. 6 and 7).

Within the context of the census's racializing frame, such photographs constitute a visual complement to the statistical tables, a distinct but related way of seeing native subjects as objects of knowledge and reform. Where statistical tabulations abstract native identities into faceless numbers, the photographs give a kind of composite face to the statistics. Shadowed by the notion of typicality—which I take to be the reduction of cultural differences into an ordered range of variations and

Fig. 3. Negritos (Aetas) (*Census of the Philippine Islands, 1903*)

a set of representative figures—these photographs form part of the same enumerative and classificatory optic of colonial knowledge.

Photographs of wild and civilized Filipinos are reproduced not only in the census report but in various official documents of the colonial archive. Many were taken by government officials themselves, most prominently Dean C. Worcester, as part of their regular trips to survey the peoples and conditions of the country. Within a colonial context, these photographs make a claim analogous to that of the census: while a diverse collection of tribes may exist in the archipelago, they can be encoded within the same racial hierarchy and enclosed within a single visual field. Constructed as examples and exemplars of native types, photographic images of colonial subjects map cultural differences within the same representational grid. That is to say, they bear the marks of a colonizing gaze that is able to arrogate for itself, in remaining discrete and dispersed, the privilege to rank and assess the comparative value of the native inhabitants and their world. They image the subjects of colonialism as objects of transitional significance whose present is bound to fade into the past as they are wholly annexed to the civilizing embrace of the future. Mementos of conquest, such photographs serve as dioramas of benevolent assimilation. Like the census tables and graphs, they work to erase the traces of violence at the origin of U.S. rule

Figs. 4–5. Wild non-Christian peoples (*Census of the Philippine Islands, 1903*)

and instead pay tribute to the technologies of supervision and classification that maintain the disciplinary devotions of white love.[26]

Short-circuiting Surveillance Were there other ways of reading benevolent assimilation that went against the grain of the census? Did alternative styles of envisioning the Philippines exist that called into question the racializing narratives of the Philippine past along with the disciplinary prescriptions for its present and future?

At about the same time that the census—with its dream images of a benevolent empire—was being conducted and published between 1903–1905, a series of nationalist plays in the Tagalog vernacular were being performed in and around Manila. Written and performed largely by urban, working-class artists, some of whom had been active in both the revolution against Spain and war against the United States, these plays were extraordinarily popular among working-class audiences as well as

39 *White Love*

Fig. 6. Civilized Christian people (*Census of the Philippine Islands, 1903*)

members of the nationalist elite critical of U.S. rule. Occupying the same historical terrain as the colonial census, nationalist melodramas mark the limits of the census's reach. While the census serves as an important foundation in the construction of a larger colonial archive—one that would eventually come to include transcribed and translated examples of Tagalog "seditious" plays as part of the colonial court records—nationalist dramas performed a history whose meanings eluded the imperial logic of benevolent assimilation and surveying gaze of the archive.

Under the Sedition Law, the colonial Supreme Court banned these nationalist dramas, claiming that they tended to "incite the people of the Philippine Islands to open and armed resistance to the constituted authorities" and "inculcate a spirit of hatred and enmity against the American people and the Government of the United States in the Philippines."[27] Forced to go underground in order to evade the constant scrutiny of colonial authorities, playwrights and casts were frequently arrested, fined, and imprisoned. Through such coercion, the colonial government managed to curtail and finally extinguish the production of nationalist plays after 1905.

Official anxiety over these nationalist dramas had to do with the extent of their popularity among Filipinos. Playing to crowded houses

Fig. 7. Portraits of census supervisors (*Census of the Philippine Islands*, 1903)

in Manila, such dramas also attracted "every man, woman and child" in the outlying barrios. It was not uncommon for an audience to "cheer on its feet, rabid with fury and frenzy for three hours" after a performance, as one U.S. observer nervously wrote. "When the seditious plays appeared, the people rose to it as one man, recognized that it told their story and patronized them liberally" (Riggs, xi, 45, 57). In order to evade colonial surveillance, theatrical groups relied on such tactics as publicizing plays under different titles, staging impromptu songs and speeches advocating Philippine sovereignty, and dressing the cast in costumes that, when brought into formation on stage, momentarily created an image of the outlawed Philippine flag. They used visual props such as the rising red sun symbolic of the revolutionary organization Katipunan, which had led the revolution against Spain, and structured their stories as allegories of romance and kinship to invoke recollections of recent events and provoke sympathy (*damay*) for the sufferings of the motherland (*Inangbayan*). Through the characters, the playwrights staged debates about the present and future of the nation, crafting lengthy soliloquies and pointed exchanges that questioned U.S. pronouncements of benevolent assimilation and critiqued the practice of Filipino collaboration. Indeed, colonialism and collaboration were seen in the plays as mutually reinforcing, working to enslave (*alipinin*) the population and disrupt the affective ties that constituted the borders of the national community.

Nationalist plays drew their formal coherence from the melodramatic conventions of nineteenth-century vernacular genres, especially the *komedya*. By the nineteenth century, the increasing commercialization of agriculture and opening of the Philippines to world trade laid the conditions for the emergence of secular art forms tied to the marketplace rather than the Catholic Church. Theatrical genres such as the komedya were part of these cultural developments. They were local versions of medieval Spanish romances featuring forbidden love, melodramatic conflicts, and predictable resolutions between Christian and Muslim princes and princesses and their respective families. Performed in the vernacular language, komedyas rearticulated Spanish forms. They highlighted spectacular stage effects, densely choreographed movements such as sword fights and marches, brightly colored costumes, and elaborate rhetorical modes of address. Focusing on the social conflicts generated by the proscribed love of Christian for Muslim, komedyas took up the themes of transgressive desire, filial betrayal, the crisis of parental authority, and by extension, the unmaking and remaking of the bonds of reciprocity on which such authority was based. Set amid the fantastic surroundings of imagined but distant medieval European kingdoms, nineteenth-century popular theater translated and so conventionalized the persistent presence of the foreign in one's midst in ways that escaped clerical and colonial representations. It thus opened up an alternative space for conceptualizing and addressing colonial conditions in terms other than those authorized by the church and state.

Komedyas, furthermore, were linked to the marketplace as much as to the communities where they performed. Out of this genre, a notion of the author as owner and origin of his or her work began to form (such as in the case of the best-known playwright, Francisco Baltazar), and certain performers became widely recognizable to different audiences across geographic divides, allowing them to charge more for their appearances. Theatrical troupes were portable and mobile, making money by traveling from one town fiesta to the next rather than enjoying the patronage of the state or church.[28] With the outbreak of revolution, theatrical forms were politicized and performative conventions rearticulated toward more radical ends. Reynaldo Ileto, for instance, has demonstrated such transformations in the case of the *Pasyon*, the epic story of Christ's passion performed in the vernacular during Holy Week and mobilized to frame the tumultuous events of the revolution in millenarian terms.[29] It comes as no surprise, then, that the melodramatic conventions of the komedya should also lend themselves to being retooled to respond to the force of events relating to the war and onset of U.S. colonial rule.

The plots of nationalist dramas served as screens for projecting profoundly felt and widely shared social experiences of revolution, colonial occupation, war, and the intense longing for freedom (kalayaan).[30] They usually revolved around the relationship between a female beloved and her male lover-protector or between a mother and her children. One personified the nation and freedom; the other stood for the patriot and the people. In either case, their relationship is invariably threatened by a male foreign intruder harboring designs on the woman-nation. He is aided by a local collaborator, who in betraying his siblings and parents, substitutes the love of nation for the lust after money. Together, they abduct the woman-nation, thereby precipitating a crisis of filiation. Encouraged by their mother-land, the male-patriot and his supporters battle both foreigner and collaborator to regain the freedom of the beloved-nation. Extended calls to mourn (damay) those who had perished in the fighting are issued by the motherland (Inang-bayan). She appeals to her sons and daughters to recall the sacrifices of the dead, thereby turning death into an occasion to celebrate the bonds that unite them. Although the endings of the plays may vary in their details, they all envision the spectacular reunification of the beloved nation, whether in the present or future, with her lover-patriot returning from imprisonment or death itself to lead the people to victory against foreigners and collaborators alike.

Whereas the allegory of benevolent assimilation regarded imperialism as the melodrama of white love for brown brothers, seditious plays used the language of melodrama to express the love of nation. We can see how language is politicized in the plays by looking at the conventions for naming different characters. Playwrights generally used common nouns and adjectives to denote each character and have each character signify a particular concept or social entity as gleaned from the play's dramatis personae. For example, in Juan Abad's *Tanikalang Guinto* (*The Golden Chain*), Liwanag (literally "light," signifying "freedom") is betrothed to K'ulayaw ("defender," standing for the patriot), the son of Dalita ("suffering," connoting the captive condition of the motherland). Liwanag, however, is desired by Maimbot ("avarice," that is, the U.S. colonial government), who enlists the aid of the collaborator Nag-tapon ("one who is thrown away"). Nag-tapon accepts money from Maimbot and thus betrays his brother, K'ulayaw, and mother, Dalita (Riggs, 497–542).

Similarly, in Juan Matapang Cruz's *Hindi Pa Aco Patay* (*I Am Not Yet Dead*), Macamcam ("avaricious"; again, the colonial state), the son of Maimbot seeks by force and deception to wed Karangalan ("dignity" or "respect," connoting the natural resources of the country), the daughter of Pinagsakitan ("she who suffers," or the motherland). Macamcam and Maimbot employ the services of the son of Pinagsakitan, Ualanghinayang ("shameless one," the Filipino collaborator), who in exchange for money, helps to engineer the abduction of Karangalan. However, Karangalan's lover, Tangulan ("protector," the Filipino patriot), the nephew of Katuiran ("reason" or "justice," signifying Filipino rights), attempts to rescue her by challenging Macamcam to a duel. Macamcam seems momentarily victorious, and everyone believes that Tangulan is dead. But as the wedding between Macamcam and Karangalan is about to take place, Tangulan suddenly appears on the stage, declaring to the wild applause of the audience, "I am not yet dead!" (Riggs, 543–606).

In one of the most famous seditious dramas, *Kahapon, Ngayon, at Bukas* (*Yesterday, Today, and Tomorrow*), by the prolific writer Aurelio Tolentino, Philippine history is depicted not as the successive waves of conquests described in the census report but as the progression of anticolonial struggles against foreign invaders and local collaborators. In act 1, "Yesterday," Inangbayan ("motherland") rallies her people, led by

Tagailog (literally, "from the water," a reference to the Tagalogs), to defend their land, Balintawak (a reference to the site where the revolution of 1896 against Spain began), against the incursions of the "Chinese" despot Batang Hari ("child-king," perhaps a reference to the seventeenth-century "Chinese" pirate, Limahong, who had threatened to invade the Spanish colony). Batang Hari is aided by the machinations of the collaborator Asalhayop ("behaves like an animal"). In act 2, "Today," Tagailog escapes from prison by killing the collaborator Dahumpalay ("venomous snake"), concealing his identify, and rousing his fellow Tagalogs to rescue Inangbayan—then in the process of being buried alive by Matanglawin ("hawkeye," the Spanish colonial government), his wife, Dilatnabulag ("sighted but unable to see," Spain herself), and Halimaw ("monster," the Spanish friar). Finally, in act 3, "Tomorrow," Tagailog presses a condescending Malaynatin ("one whom we don't know," the U.S. government) to live up to his promise of granting independence to the people. Inangbayan also pleads with Malaynatin's wife, Bagongsibol ("fresh spring," the U.S. nation), to convince her husband to accede to Tagailog's demands. The latter prepares an army to attack Malaynatin should he renege on his promise. But such a plan proves unnecessary, as Bagongsibol finally succumbs to the entreaties of the children of Inangbayan and gives the country its independence. "Tomorrow" ends on a hopeful note with everyone celebrating the new freedom of Inangbayan (Riggs, 607–51).

Arthur Stanley Riggs, who compiled an extensive dossier on these plays for the colonial government, remarks on the practice of using common words to denote the names of characters:

Such names . . . are to the native mind filled with the keenest suggestion, and the artful connotation of the playwright in thus making the very names of his mimes tell more than their set speeches has had a tremendous effect. Every time the common nouns were employed in the body of the text, the audience saw not only the characteristic properties suggested by them, but also swiftly imagined the particular characters to which the names belonged. . . . The result was a quick, lively, and entire confidence established between author, players, and audience impossible to obtain in any other way. (Riggs, 122)

In nationalist melodramas, mimicry acquires a value different from that assigned to it by colonial sources in relation to native characteristics. Characters on stage mime the qualities suggested by their names with the active and complicitous understanding of the playwrights and audiences. In this case, mimicry becomes a sign of acute, even ironic, self-consciousness geared toward acting out historical narratives that ran counter to official versions. Common names are invested with new meanings and remade by characters into emblems of collective experiences. They become hieroglyphs, as it were, for recalling the nation's history and redrawing its moral boundaries. In this sense, the commonality of words becomes proper not only to the individual character on stage but to the particular vernacular community from and to which that character addresses her- or himself.

The practice of naming in nationalist melodramas bears comparison to the representational conventions of the census report. As we have seen, the latter designated the population as the aggregate of quantitatively visible entities within a closed set of categories. Reifying identities into schedules, cards, and photographic specimens of the typical, the census consigned both their naming and interpretation to a bureaucratic apparatus. Translatable into numbers and locatable on a grid, names were regarded as part of an ensemble of objectifying devices with which to regulate and supervise the relationship between knower and known, state and subjects, white and nonwhite peoples.

By contrast, nationalist plays turned common names into new sites for public life, rendering their referents easily accessible to actors, audiences, and authors who shared the same vernacular. The practice of naming was a way of establishing an imagined continuity between communication and community. Thus could names speak more than their characters inasmuch as they provided not merely a way of marking one from the other on stage; they also opened up a space from which to address all those who considered themselves affiliated with the nation. Where colonial archives characterize and classify in order to render their subjects available for discipline, nationalist melodramas resignify the vernacular so as to reclaim the capacity of people to nominate themselves as agents in and interpreters of their experiences.

The narrative of those collective experiences was shaped by a thematic of kinship ties. As with many Southeast Asian island societies, Filipino relations are bilaterally reckoned. Individuals trace their links equally on both the mother's and father's sides. Bilateral kinship descent allows for the cultivation of extended families through both ritual and extraritual means. Historically, such ties tended to be idealized along the lines of an economy of reciprocal obligations: that is, through conventions of deference, respect, and expectations of mutual caring between parents and children, older and younger siblings, husbands and wives, lovers and beloveds, landlords and tenants, masters and servants, and any other configuration of superordinate and subordinate relations. Reciprocal obligations are, in a way, the "grammar" of kinship ties, determining the lines of filiation and affiliation between self and other as simultaneously personal (face-to-face) and political (hierarchic and subject to conflict and change). Put differently, kinship is a way of conceiving the self as fated, and thereby obligated to the other and to a social order predicated on the circulation of mutual indebtedness. In a sense then, to acknowledge one's kin is to imagine the limits of one's social experience.[31]

By mapping the national community onto the extended family—and conversely, by imaging colonization and collaboration as the disruption of that family and the subversion of an economy of reciprocal indebtedness—nationalist dramas reenact the relationship between the personal and political. As melodramas, they regard kinship as the terrain of conflicts and alliances that bear simultaneously on the private and public spheres—indeed, that call attention to their mutual constitution. To better understand how these plays dramatize the link between the personal and political, it is instructive to look at the ways in which they engender the image of a nation by placing gender itself in motion.

As we saw earlier, the discourse of benevolent assimilation was predicated on a racial hierarchy that surveyed as it sought to discipline colonial subjects. Yet the census also differentiated the population as males and females, coordinating gender distinctions with race, age, occupation, cause of death, disability, and the like. Worth noting is the fact that while racial difference was conceived of in spatial and temporal terms as organized by and subordinate to whiteness, gender distinctions were posed without commentary, as if they were wholly natural. Indeed, the category of gender was not used at all, but rather that of sex, so that the distinction between men and women appears to be "natural" and beyond any sort of social convention.

The extent to which gender seems unproblematic in the census is, I think, a function of the overwhelmingly masculine construction of colonial order. There is never any doubt in official sources that white love is paternal and the task of colonial administration, though it employed women as teachers in public schools and nurses in public health programs, is by and large men's work. Colonial politics was conceived of as a homosocial affair involving the tutelary bonding between white fathers and their male native-mestizo apprentices. To be coded female of whatever race was, in effect, to be consigned to a marginal position in the public sphere of colonial society. Gender was thus conflated with sex as the representation of sexual difference was naturalized in relation to the paternalism of the colonial state. Just as racial difference was organized from the vantage point of whiteness, sexual difference was structured from the state's masculine perspective. To be classified as male or female meant becoming visible as such to the gaze of white fathers.

Nationalist melodramas, by contrast, do not contain a discourse on race. Whatever hostile references these plays may have to supposed foreigners, such characters are never distinguished by color or race but in terms of behavior and language. Hence, characters standing for the U.S. colonial government are depicted as loud and disrespectful, given to excessive drinking and crude behavior (as Filipinos often witnessed U.S. soldiers do during the war), and untrustworthy by virtue of having reneged on past obligations. In Tolentino's play, the foreigners representing the United States are even more complex, depicted in a sympathetic light as potentially responsive to the rights of Filipinos, and by implication, assimilable into the family. The occasional reference to Chinese invaders may reflect a sense of anti-Sinitism cultivated by Spanish colonial policies in the past, but these Chinese remain so vaguely drawn and unracialized as to be tokens in a larger discourse about nationalist resistance to colonial rule.[32]

Indeed, race as a trope for difference and power is remarkably absent in these plays. What seems crucial in drawing social distinctions, however, is gender. The importance of gender is apparent in the names and plots of the dramas. Figures for the beloved nation (such as Inangbayan, Pinagsakitan, Karangalan, and Dalita) and desired freedom (Liwanag, Bituin, Malaya) are invariably cast as women. Those who desire her, whether patriot-protectors or colonialists and collaborators, are always cast as men. It is as if these dramas triangulate social desire, casting nationhood in terms of the masculine struggle over a feminized object. The relationship between the nation and nationalists and colonizers alike is thereby mediated by what appear to be gender stereotypes. While men act—they threaten or protect, abduct or rescue, wage war or make peace—women react and watch the spectacle of men seeking them out.

Yet in the text of the plays, these gender stereotypes are provisional and shifting. In attributing a gender to the characters, the plays also problematize the meaning of those roles, particularly under the severe conditions of revolutionary upheaval and colonial dislocation. In *Hindi Pa Aco Patay,* for example, Karangalan calls out to Tangulan to rescue her from Macamcam. Nonetheless, it is she who ends up rescuing him in the forest by shooting a predatory bird symbolizing the colonial Philippine Constabulary. It is from her, too, that we hear the most incisive critique of collaboration as mere enslavement to money and the most resonant refutation of U.S. assessments regarding the unfitness of Filipinos for self-government. *Luhang Tagalog (Tagalog Tears),* an earlier play by Tolentino, features a wife, Bituin ("star," signifying independence), who protects her husband from the murderous designs of his collaborationist father. She also counsels the mothers and wives of those going off to war, offers a trenchant critique of war as an arena of masculine privilege, and eloquently exposes the link between benevolent assimilation and colonial subjugation (Riggs, 352–422). As the suffering motherland (Busilak in Tomas Remigio's *Malaya* [*Freedom*], Pinagsakitan in *Hindi Pa Aco Patay,* and Inangbayan in *Kahapon, Ngayon, at Bukas*), women do not serve as passive spectators to their own rescue. Rather, they initiate the call to struggle by putting forth the need to remember the dead. They invoke the importance of mourning (damay), which because it rekindles ties between the living and dead, the past and future, constitutes the historical and affective boundaries of the national community.[33]

Women personify the beloved nation waiting to be rescued; yet they also generate the conditions that make their rescue both possible and desirable. As nurturing mothers and vulnerable lovers, woman-nation figures take up arms, plan battles, and demand accountability from characters and audiences alike. They are objects of masculine contention, but they are also active interlocutors in the debate over the future disposition of their body politic.

Part of what renders women's position so complex is the remarkable fact that fathers are either marginal or absent in these plays. The foreigners who covet the woman-nation are constructed as illegitimate or unacceptable fathers. Collaborators are often depicted as less than human, almost animal, because of their association with money. Patriot-protectors, as lovers, are not yet husbands and tend to occupy shifting positions as characters in need of defense as much as they seek to defend the nation. When taken together, these masculine roles have the effect of deferring the emergence of any kind of paternal hegemony within the world of the nationalist dramas. Just as the relationship between the nation and its people crystallizes in opposition to the avaricious and monopolizing intentions of the colonial state, so it would seem that the gender differences between women and men do not coalesce around a paternal figure of authority.[34] Instead, these differences come up against and before the persistent figure of the motherland. This is not to say that men and women were considered equal; only that the inequality inherent in gender formations was called into question, cast as provisional and conditional under specific historical circumstances. Gender in these plays does not come across as a series of fixed and natural categories but as a set of negotiable positions in the articulation of nationhood. In the absence of a symbolic father that would serve as a point of reference in the gendering of social relations at a time of intense turmoil and uncertainty, it is conceivable that the association between woman and nation in the dramas did not simply reproduce gender stereotypes; it suggested alternative roles as well, enabling women to speak and act in the defense of the body politic against the designs of colonizing others. Small wonder, then, that "the women are as ardent theater-goers, even in times of political stress, as their husbands, brothers and sons" (Riggs, 46).

Nationalist melodramas indicate that the imaging of the nation as woman did not invariably translate into a reified gender hierarchy. Rather, the ambiguous construction of gender categories in the plays arose from the specificity of Filipino notions of kinship historically articulated in relation to the turbulence of war, the revolutionary expectations of freedom (kalayaan), and the absence of a stable patriarchal state between 1899 and 1905. What made the plays significant was that by imagining the nation as woman, they projected a notion of the nation as *distinct* from the state. And such was indeed imaginable at that particular historical moment, when the structures of authority—colonial as well as familial—were up for grabs. Thus did nationalist dramas allow for a certain play on the meanings of male and female. The unresolved status of gender roles (where, for instance, a display of utter weakness rather than confident mastery can be a male attribute as much as it is a woman's) underscores, once again, the differences between the representational operations of the census and plays. Where the former was organized around the production of a stable state apparatus that would rule paternally over a racialized and gendered people, the latter were far more concerned with imaging the nation as an extended family predicated less on a patriarchal principle of authority than as a general economy of reciprocal obligations freed from the violence of colonial rule.

Unlike the census, then, nationalist plays did not seek to represent the population as implacably bound to gender and racial categories subject to the continuous gaze of white benevolence. Their seditiousness consisted precisely in providing alternative sources of knowledge and power—sources into which colonial agents were assimilated, but as figures disruptive of reciprocal obligations. As melodramas, they depicted social desires in motion, thereby reintroducing a deep sense of contingency into the narrative of recent events on the levels of language and gender. For where white love prescribed manly discipline, the love of nation postulated a different kind of bondage, one where a network of supervision gave way to a spectacular commerce in tears.[35] As Tolentino writes in dedicating his play *Luhang Tagalog* to the motherland:

Weeping without ceasing for your children,
    And weeping always for your sorrows.
I have taken care to write this piece
    So that my tears should flow
    Together with the tears from your eyes.
To you I offer this: it is so very fragile
    Because it is from me;
    Still accept this
For I have nothing more valuable to give. (Riggs, 352)

2 Colonial Domesticity
Engendering Race at the Edge of Empire, 1899–1912

"I began to love the tropical nights and to feel that I had never before known what night can be like," wrote Helen Taft, wife of then Governor-General of the Philippines William Howard Taft, in 1902, of the view from her veranda at the Malacañang Palace. "The stars were so large and hung so low that they looked almost like raised silver figures on a dark blue field.... The wonderful sunsets and the moonlit nights have tied more American hearts to Manila and the Philippines than all other charms combined. And they are both indescribable."[1]

To say that the Philippines is "indescribable" is, of course, already to describe it as sublime. Composed into a view, the space of empire becomes available for private consumption and sentimental regard. Performed on the threshold of the colonial home—in this case, the governor-general's palace forcibly taken from the Spanish colonizers and later deeded to the postcolonial Philippine government—the consumption of that view becomes a feat of domesticating what is seen as native and natural into aspects of the colonial, which is at once also national. The "charms" of the tropics thus become signs for the benevolence of conquest: part of a complex of imperial aesthetics that allows Taft to feel at home while she is away from home.

Helen Taft's remarks are not unlike those of other women from the United States writing on the Philippines during the first decade of U.S. rule: they invest colonialism with a sense of both the domestic and sentimental. This chapter explores the nature of those investments. Integral to the construction of colonial modernity in the late nineteenth and early twentieth centuries, colonial domesticity in the tropics heralded the conjugation of *whiteness* with *femininity* as a sign of public entitlement as well as a source of private ambivalence.² Colonial sociality in this period reflected and refracted the globalization of Western bourgeois notions regarding the gendered and racialized embodiments of both rulers and ruled. In the notion of the domestic, U.S. imperialism in the Philippines, like its European counterparts in Asia and Africa, furnished a public idiom for representing as well as containing the private lives of its most privileged agents. Domesticity as an idiom of colonial modernity assumes that the structures of public and private are mobile and indefinitely reproducible, capable of translation across cultural and bodily spaces. By focusing on U.S. formations of colonial domesticity in the Philippines, I ask about some of the conditions that alternately enabled and disabled the construction of the uneasy divide between the public and private in the empire, and the ways in which this ambivalence generated phantasms of home that were at once in and out of place.

Much of the available scholarship in the United States on white women and imperialism has tended to focus on British, French, and Dutch colonial societies, often evading the presence of Euro-American women in U.S. possessions. Such an evasion is, in part, a function of the myth of the exceptionalism of the United States: that is, of the general tendency to regard U.S. imperialism as an aberration from the otherwise democratic trajectory of the nation, or in any case, to see the imperial interventions of the United States, especially in the Philippines, as far more benign and progressive than its European counterparts.³ This chapter seeks to question those assumptions, situating its critique of colonial domesticity in relation to both past and current inquiries into the constitutive role of empire in the formation of U.S. nationhood.⁴ In so doing, it tries to specify the ways in which gendered and racialized ideas about national agency became instrumental in the elaboration of globalized relations of power on the level of individuated, localized bodies.

Here, then, I examine the writings of a number of women from the United States to see how assumptions about domesticity were put to work in the Philippine colony. Such assumptions, I argue, had the effect of lending a double identity to these women. They appeared as subaltern (and thus akin to natives) yet privileged (hence, in closer proximity to white men and creole/mestizo elites). As such, they were both captive to and empowered by the structures of empire. Given their ambiguous position, North American women in the Philippines could engage in the simultaneous enactment and disavowal of the everyday inequalities of colonial rule. In tracing their remarks about the natural landscape, colonial house, and bodies of native servants, we can see how they dealt with the imperatives of domesticity outside the domestic sphere they were used to; how such dealings relied on a language of racialization; and how such a language proved problematic, now managing, now failing, to stabilize social identities—both their own and that of the natives they encountered—in a colonial setting. Finally, in drawing attention to the recurrence of an idiom of sentimentalism in women's accounts, I suggest how the novel and endlessly ironic conjunction of colonialism with domesticity resonates with the tensions endemic to the colonial enterprise.

Engendering Empire   Disavowing the catastrophic consequences of the Filipino-American War, the U.S. colonization of the Philippines was predicated, as we saw in the previous chapter, on a policy of benevolent assimilation. The earlier notion of manifest destiny had disclosed the frontier as a divine gift to a chosen people, the taking of which was sustained by what Richard Drinnon has called a "metaphysics of Indian hating."[5] Benevolent assimilation, in contrast, amounted to a sentimental reworking of manifest destiny. Instead of annihilation, it called for the domestication of native populations and their reconstruction into recognizably modern political subjects. Rather than conquest and enslavement, Filipinos were infantilized as racial others in need of nurturance and tutelage in the fundamentals of Anglo-Saxon democracy to turn them into a self-governing people, separate from but equal to white civilization.

Hence, where the continental frontier had appeared as a gift bestowed to a putatively pioneering race, the colonial frontier was now construed as a site for the return of that gift through the workings of colonial administration. Imperialism as a form of good housekeeping was meant to forge a sentimental affiliation or "special relation" between colonizer and colonized—the bond between parent and child rather than master and slave. Imagined as the restoration of a moral economy, sentimental colonialism established the United States as the solicitous guardian of a culturally deprived race, setting conditions that would—in some preordained time—allow them to become individuals in full possession of themselves and their own national household.

Benevolent assimilation as an allegory of the domestication (and therefore nationalization) of imperialism reveals something about the imperialization of domesticity as well. Recent works by a number of feminist scholars have pointed out gendered aspects of the U.S. imperialist imaginary.[6] Empire building historically has been associated with popular projects for the reconstruction of manhood in the United States. The tropics opened up a terrain for the testing and validation of white masculinity at a moment of fantasized crisis stemming from the proximity of "contaminating" nonwhite and nonmale others. The romance of empire was thus a means for shoring up an endangered white masculinity at home by spectacularizing the aura of its sovereign virility abroad.

This formation of imperial masculinity, however, required as its enabling context the deployment of an imperial femininity. The colonial order was inextricably bound to a domestic one. As Ann Stoler has shown, the chief agents for constructing colonial domesticity in the tropics from the early twentieth century on were white bourgeois women. In the British, Dutch, and French colonies of Asia, for example, the inception of white women was meant to protect white men from the dangers of racial corruption symbolized by the native concubine. In providing a semblance of domesticity, white women were charged with the patriotic duty of upholding middle-class morality and respectability amid the barbarism of a colonized people. Colonial officials considered the presence of such women to have a prophylactic effect vis-à-vis the threat of miscegenation and the moral degeneracy it was thought to cause. By domesticating the desires of white men, white women were seen as vital agents in the reproduction of a bourgeois imperialist ethos.[7]

Where the Philippines was concerned, Euro-American women who celebrated rather than opposed colonization did so as a logical extension of their support for domestic reform.[8] The language of benevolent assimilation called many of them into the public sphere of empire as patriotic participants in a civilizing mission. Charged with the task of manufacturing a sense of the everyday amid the eruptive contingencies of colonial expansion, these women sought to establish a domestic realm from which social relations would be cleansed, as it were, of political entanglements. This process of fashioning colonial domesticity as a realm for rehearsing and containing the quotidian crisis of empire can be read in their writings on the Philippines.

Mobilizing the Home Coming from different regions of the United States, the women whose writings I am concerned with here did not form a homogeneous group. Numerically, they were a minority within a largely male white community that was itself a minority among the overwhelmingly "native" population of the Philippines.[9] A number of these women came in the capacity of official wives; some arrived as professionals, mostly teachers; and a smaller number were single while at least one was widowed. A few, like Helen Taft and Edith Moses, came from fairly influential backgrounds and tended to remark on the more common upbringing of other white women, such as the teachers and nurses they came in contact with. And relations between military and civilian wives were at times strained.

Yet once in the tropics, these class, regional, and other social differences tended to give way to a shared and seemingly unquestioned attachment to a specifically U.S. national identity: that is, they all had a sense of acting as representatives of white middle-class femininity in the colony. Caught in the novel and masculinized terrain of colonial society, women from the United States sought in their writings to articulate a defensive and acutely ironized sense of their position of relative and shifting dependence on both white male figures and native male and female servants. In doing so, they came to grasp the mutually constitutive relationship between imperial rule and domestic ideology. By making a home away from home, the women assumed the role of active agents in the politics of colonial reproduction, erecting domestic outposts of "beneficial republicanism" on the imperial frontier.[10]

Nearly all the women's accounts between 1900 and 1910 consist of letters written back to the United States from the colony or memoirs written in the United States but culled from letters written to family and friends while living on the islands. Composed on the edges of empire, such writings traced a circuit between one domestic scene and another. Most were published within or shortly after the lifetime of their authors, often as ways of providing a U.S. readership with "personal" firsthand accounts of life in the Philippines.[11] As part of a larger archive of colonial knowledge, such texts straddle the divide between the official and anecdotal, the public and private spheres of colonial society. As such, these documents share in the liminal status of their writers, marking out discrete zones of contact between the political and symbolic economies of U.S. rule.

Indeed, the epistolary and autobiographical nature of women's writings seemed hospitable to the dramatization of a recurring sense of alienation in the tropics. Letters and memoirs recast women's displacement, emplotting their travels as a series of episodic, multiply mediated encounters with the otherness of empire—an otherness that included not only the land and peoples of the islands but also the very colonial machinery that governed their lives. Subject to interruptions, accidents, and abrupt beginnings and endings as well as arbitrary shifts in topical interests, women's accounts repeatedly staged the everyday processes involved in the domestication of the colonial. They performed the representation and containment of what appeared foreign and contingent within the confines of what felt familiar and obvious.

How did these women seek to negotiate between the pressures of a masculinized realm of colonial administration and the novel appearance of native peoples and places? One strategy was to ironize their sense of estrangement. In their accounts of traveling, for example, women's texts differed from men's in the decidedly nonheroic, even half-mocking tone they assumed. Mary Fee, a schoolteacher who taught in the Philippines from 1901 to 1908, describes her experiences as "singularly unadventurous."[12] Edith Moses is not atypical when she writes in 1901, "I find that in the Philippines the dangers are generally exaggerated. We had been told that the Benguet trail was impassable for women, but we had come down not only in safety but enjoyed every minute of it."[13]

Unlike their male counterparts' accounts, the experience of traveling among women writers is told not in terms of epic undertakings that entail placing oneself in situations of danger so as to test one's strength and character and restore a sense of mastery over one's body.[14] Neither do they dwell on triumphal scenes of arrival whereby the traveler is celebrated at the expense of erasing the presence of his or her companions and servants. Instead, women's accounts highlight the mediated nature of colonial expeditions and their dependence on native others. "In fact," Moses explains, "without our guides we could never have made this trip" (319). Travel is figured as a collaborative and contingent affair rather than an individual undertaking.

Ironizing colonial authority, however, did not amount to the subversion of colonial rule. Relativizing white men's claims to speak for the empire, these women's accounts call attention to a feminized sphere of influence that is distinct from, even as it necessarily accompanies, the reproduction of colonial authority. They reinscribe the domestic as apart from and yet a part of the colonial. As such, they show colonial domesticity to be a mobile and highly flexible apparatus for the reproduction of the rhythms as well as disruptions of everyday life predicated on securing social hierarchy. More significant is the fact that the narrative of the domestic, insofar as it turns on the quotidian, tends to come across as self-evident and innocuous. For instance, from the mountains of Bontoc, Nona Worcester, wife of colonial official and ethnologist Dean C. Worcester, enters the following in her diary: "This morning, being less than three hours from our destination, we did not have to make a very early start but got up comfortably at five o'clock and were off at half past six after a most satisfying breakfast of eggs, potato balls, rice, beef stew, chicken and coffee. There is no danger of starving on this trip."[15]

Travel itself in Worcester's diary is converted into a sign for the domestic. The routine of daily meals along with sleep and leisure measured in clock time organizes the experience of travel into discrete temporal units. These units, in turn, coordinate and shape the labor of native servants, determining the pace and nature of their activity in order to sustain the daily needs and expectations of their masters. From the American woman's point of view, then, the empire becomes the site of mobility *and* predictability, where the authority to map, inspect, and survey colonial space intersects with the management of servants and the ordering of bodily functions and comforts. Imperialism comes across as domesticity on the move, embodied by the supervisory presence of the white woman and collaborative work of her servants:

And we had a tablecloth, napkins and pretty dishes for the first time since leaving Baguio. It seemed like perfect luxury. Eduardo had a real stove to cook on and evidently took the keenest delight in showing us what he could do. We had delicious soup for luncheon, stewed chicken and dumplings, roast beef, potatoes, peas, and two kinds of pies. In the afternoon, we had hot doughnuts, and tea, for dinner a chocolate layer cake, besides all the rest of the good things. . . . We rested and wrote until five when we decided it was time for bridge, which we played until dinner was announced and after dinner until nearly nine o'clock. (N. Worcester, 14–15)

The banality of Worcester's narrative is the trace of a certain triumph. Though far away from home, she is able to draw those things associated with it close by. Tablecloth, napkins, and pretty dishes: everything appears in its proper place and so mitigates her sense of displacement. Here, what appears is not only food but the particular context for its production and consumption. What Worcester records is an accomplishment: the reproduction of bourgeois conventions that map and secure the borders of colonial domesticity. The home in the empire is the movable site for the reproduction of privilege through the avid collaboration of servants. Enumerating the kinds of food prepared by her cook, Eduardo, Worcester marks out the sphere of her authority in a foreign world. One reads this account and senses Worcester's quiet delight. Her pleasure comes from the ease with which she establishes her mastery over native labor, the readiness by which the latter accommodates itself to every demand from above, and the smoothness with which its products are transformed into the signs of its recognition of its proper place relative to that of the mistress. Recalling the stretch of time leisurely filled in between meals with bridge playing, resting, and letter writing, she conjures the results of such recognition: an ordered realm of private pleasures that include the joy of privacy on the fringes of empire; indeed, of empire itself as the context for the re-creation of the pleasures of home.

However common these evocations of the pleasures of domestic agency were, it is important to note that they comprised only one aspect of colonial women's writings on the Philippines. Such pleasures were contingent on something else. The sense of privacy and the resulting feeling of mastery were apt to produce periodic moments of unease. For in their descriptions of the land, native populations, and their households, especially their servants, these women's texts are also traversed by recurring tensions. Most pressing among these is the sense of the writers' structural and physical proximity to those "foreign" bodies from which they nonetheless sought to distinguish themselves.

The Colonial Picturesque   One of the most common sites for the production of colonial domesticity is found in women's descriptions of the tropical landscape. As in the passage cited earlier from Helen Taft's memoirs, there is a persistent link between the composition of the land as a set of ordered appearances and the domestication of differences amid colonial displacement. The move to conceive of the landscape as a picture to be seen rather than the setting of unequal social relations characterizes, for example, Mary Fee's description of arriving at Capiz in the Visayan Islands south of Manila, on a provincial steamship:

Here at last was the tropical scene of my imagination—a tide-swollen current, its marshy banks covered with strange foliage and innumerable water lanes leading out into palmy depths....

Though subsequent familiarity has brought to my notice many details that I then overlooked, that first impression was the one of greatest charm, and the one I love best to remember. There were great, square, white-painted, red-tiled houses lining both banks to the river; the picturesque group of women beating their clothes on the flat steps which led down to the water. On the left of the bridge was a grassy plaza shaded with almond trees, a stately church, several squat quarters, and a flag staff with the Stars and Stripes whipping the breeze from the top. Over all hung a sky dazzlingly blue and an atmosphere crystal clear. Back of the town a low, unforested mountain heaved a grassy shoulder above the palms, and far off there was a violet tracery of more mountains.

I knew that I should like Capiz. (72)

The tropics here is no heart of darkness but a collection of scenic spots where culture and nature harmoniously coexist. As Fee's vision matches her imagination, the scene of arrival unfolds as something she has already seen, as if the landscape existed all along simply to fulfill her intentions and arrange itself for her benefit. The view positions the writer as a spectator and collector of colonial impressions with which to fill her account, like a tourist filling an album with photographs of her trip.

The conversion of the land into a set of appearances allows Fee to pass herself off not as an agent of colonial intervention but an individual traveler innocently recording what passes before her. That pose of innocence is, in fact, a gesture of disavowing the social—a gesture that, as we have seen, is a crucial moment in the formation of the domestic. Indeed, Fee notes with satisfaction that from the windows of her house in Capiz, she "commanded a fine view of the bridge, the plaza, the gray old church, and the jail, with the excitement of guard mount and retreat thrown in" (74). Afforded a room with a view, Fee takes pleasure in grasping the empire as a benign spectacle. From the interior confines of the domestic, she is able to distance herself from the exterior space of colonial society, yet have ready visual access to it. Colonial society, rendered as a scene of "greatest charm," is conflated with the tropical landscape resonating with the fantasy of benevolent assimilation. From her window, domination takes place without coercion, possession without the complications of contact or contamination.

That the picturesque view was such a source of pleasure to women writers in part had to do with what they feared might lie behind the scenes of tropical repose. There lingered the possibility that the landscape could look back, returning the gaze that fell on it, shattering the distance between seer and seen, and confounding the imagined space of privacy of the colonial viewer. Nona Worcester, for example, writes about the "fine appearance" of the rice terraces while traveling through the mountain province, admiring their colors and shapes in relation to the textures and hues of surrounding native houses (32). As in the previous accounts we saw, the move to aestheticize the land has the effect of erasing the marks of native labor. The rice terraces exist as a panorama for the traveler's gaze, dissociated from the workings of native intentions. Hence, Worcester in admiring the handiwork of native farmers remarks, "One would think the people really had an idea of the picturesque" (32), as if the picturesque was something only Americans were capable of perceiving. In an earlier letter, she writes of looking out from a trail to see Igorot villages: "They are really so picturesque to look at from a distance—it is the old story, 'distance lending enhancement,' though I do not doubt the inhabitants are just as dirty as other Igorots" (28).

Here, to see the view is to imagine the possibility, however tentatively, of other points of view. That Igorots may have a different, though purposive, relationship with the land momentarily invades Worcester's thoughts, pushing her toward disavowal: the Igorots could not possibly have an aesthetic sense; and that the sign of that absence is inscribed on their bodies.

The disjunction between the pristine view of the tropics, on the one hand, and the thought of seeing "dirty" natives, on the other, is symptomatic of the instability that haunts the discourse of colonial domesticity. For what emerges in such moments is the fundamental—and I shall try to argue, *enabling*—ambivalence of the colonial encounter whereby the colonizer imagines herself sliding into the position of the colonized. We can see such moments in the letters of Caroline Shunk, wife of an army lieutenant assigned to Camp Stotsenberg (later to be known as Clark Field) in Pampanga Province in 1909. Not surprisingly, she begins by situating the Philippines as part of the expanding topography of the United States:

After twenty years of our own Indian frontier, from Dakota blizzards to Arizona's burning sands, in adobe houses in Texas, in tents, and on rolling prairies, here we are in the tropics, making a home in the shadow of an extinct volcano, with the Southern Cross above us, but still under the Stars and Stripes.[16]

The task of making a home in the wilderness conceives of the domestic as a movable entity positioned on the edge of a mobile frontier. Shunk's letter constructs a map of these movements where "home" serves as a relay point in the construction of empire. As with the view of the landscape, this map of the empire as the site of home subsumes the Philippines into something already known, as a node in a network of colonial outposts. It is no different than other points on the map—from Dakota to Texas—that she has already seen. To be in the Philippines, for Shunk, is already to be at "home": displacement for her becomes a mode of habitation insofar as the same Stars and Stripes makes visible the terms and limits of that displacement.

The domestication of displacement, however, enters into a crisis as

Shunk finds herself waiting for her husband on a crowded platform at the train depot en route to the army camp:

> I stood, with eight boxes, bags and bundles about me as all the benches were occupied, or had been, by smokers of both sexes, and all of them champion spitters of the world. A circle of Chinamen, Filipinos, Hindus, men, women and children closed me in. They were all smoking and chewing, and I was in the midst of the "firing line." My freshly pressed white linen suit and white shoes seemed an irresistible target. (20)

Confronted with the view of racial others, Shunk's whiteness suddenly appears to her. The image of a white woman besieged by foreign bodies in effect interrupts the colonial fantasy of a benevolent white presence in the scenic tropics. Rendered all too visible in her newly pressed white linen suit, Shunk is seized by the fear of being contaminated by the bodily excess of nonwhite others. Her sense of vulnerability, like the pose of innocence in Fee's account, is derived from disavowing the violence of the colonial context within which her presence occurs. But rather than producing the distancing effect of confinement, disavowal simply places her in uncontrolled proximity to the undomesticated bodies of smokers and "champion spitters." Rather than mapping her place in the scheme of empire, Shunk finds herself mapped as the target of unknown intentions.

It is only when she and her husband finally make it to the first-class section of the train, safe from the "Filipinos with chickens in their arms and Chinamen with bundles," that she regains her composure. She looks out the window and sees the sight of "natives pulling or planting rice . . . the little rice-paddies looking like a large green chess-board with brown pawns bending over squares" (20). This "fine view" (20) offers Shunk a sense of relief from what she regarded as a scene of racial chaos at the station. Composing the view, she composes herself as the unseen beholder of the scenery where native bodies are reified, put back in their place as objects for her contemplation.

Such passages indicate that one feels most at home with one's identity when it need not be reproduced and performed, made visible by being reattached to the materiality of the body caught in a web of contingent relations. Here, whiteness is at its most secure when it seems disembodied and distant, distinct from the appearance of the native others. Native bodies appear only as accessories, reinforcing the link between whiteness and domesticity that informs the identity of American women in the colony.

This sense of relief from the demands of identity was always tenuous, however. As women, these writers invariably stood in an uneasy relationship to the masculinized sphere of empire. They found themselves reminded again and again of their paradoxical status as embodiments of that which claimed to transcend sheer embodiment: white men. As such, they were placed in the odd role of representing those whose claim to power rested precisely on administering the terms of representation. Charged with disclosing the surface of that very power that eluded full disclosure, white women were acutely conscious of becoming spectacles themselves.

Presbyterian missionary Alice Byram Condict recalls, for example, how her presence in the provinces attracted "all sorts of Filipinos. . . . [T]hey were so eager to get a close look at us American ladies that as soon as I began playing the organ, I found myself quite shut in by the crowd."[17] Shunk notes the anxiety she felt at becoming the object of unsolicited attention from natives leaning out of their windows and children running up to her "hailing us as 'Americanos' " as she walked to the marketplace (73). While traveling with her husband and other members of the Philippine Commission on a series of inspection trips to the provinces, Helen Taft writes of going to places where "white women were still a novelty . . . and I'm sure we looked much more peculiar to them as they looked to us" (187). In many areas, Taft adds, "we created a sensation. . . . [T]he people gathered around us in hordes" (193–94). And Edith Moses, on the same trip with Taft, relates riding on a "rickety old ambulance" used by U.S. military doctors through the streets of Apalit as "staring, black-eyed, round-faced, dark-skinned natives; . . . parents, children, and elders crowded to the front windows to catch a glimpse of the strange white women" (53).

In these passages, women find themselves becoming the irresistible objects of native curiosity. From being the distanced viewer of images, they become immediate objects of others' imaging. Here, their whiteness suddenly betrays them, revealing rather than concealing their presence. As spectacles, the "strange white señoras from America," as Moses refers to her party, are seized by their own alterity, redoubling rather than resolving their sense of displacement and exposure in the tropics. Through the avid gaze of the natives, white women find their bodies mirrored back to them, returning as uncanny and therefore undomesticated figures available for public and promiscuous solicitation.

Whiteness as that which is predicated on rather than freed from difference becomes most apparent when yoked to a feminized body subjected to the gaze of colonized others. Yet such a predicament turns out to be provisional. In Moses's account for example, we see the workings of a strategy for containing the force of native interest. The looks she receives are invariably described as originating from racialized bodies. "Black-eyed," "dark-skinned," and "round-faced," these native bodies have already been marked and categorized as subordinate to and dependent on the constituting force of a prior look. Thus, the natives look on white female bodies, but never from a position of safety and invisibility. In seeing, they are already seen, exposed unremittingly to the racializing depictions of a colonial narrative. Indeed, though white female bodies come into view, they remain beyond narrative description in women's texts. Instead, it is the bodies of natives that leave their traces in the text as "staring" but "dirty bare-legged men, women and girls clad in rags" who, like insects, "swarm about the place" (Moses, 62–64).

In those texts, then, one encounters a rhetoric of displacement whereby white women's recurring sense of embodiment is shifted onto natives. Reconstituting their identity as both white and feminine, American women enact a reversal of positions so that it is the native that now appears foreign and unsightly. Displacing their sense of displacement, they regain control of the circulation of sight. In doing so, they re-mark native bodies as resources for the material and symbolic reproduction of colonial difference. As with the sublation of the landscape into a "view," narrative processes of disavowal and reversal convert native bodies into a set of appearances or impressions. Located as the excessive traces external to the observing self, native bodies become objects that occasion the emergence of a white female agency capable of representing itself amid the dislocating force of imperial history.[18]

Caught in a chain of inversions, displacements, and disavowals, colonial domesticity could not but be conflicted and unstable. Indeed, ambivalence, as I have been arguing, was (and undoubtedly still is) constitutive of the domestic. And nowhere was the productive workings of ambivalence more evident than in the very space of interiority, the zone of privacy for the re-collection of white femininity: the colonial home.

Domesticity in and out of Place Designed to counterpose the pressures of the public sphere and marketplace, the architecture of domesticity in the United States has historically consisted of "private views and protected access."[19] The interior space of the bourgeois home was meant to be the site of leisure and recuperation, where walls insulated the inside from the outside, and windows and doors restricted and privatized access to and from as well as within the house. Interiors of homes were divided and arranged to conceal and segregate the spaces of leisure from the sites of domestic labor. Thus did they announce the work of domesticity by concealing its traces. The bourgeois home, in this sense, was thought to be distinct from the open and fluid spaces of the marketplace or public square, where display and the circulation of looks, words, and commodities reign along with the unsolicited attention of anonymous others. Connoting durability and stability amid the impermanence and uncertainty of market forces and political changes, the home would serve as an outward sign of the private life of its owner, a tribute to the fact of ownership itself, and hence, a monument to the ideal of possessive individualism.

These Anglo-American bourgeois notions of domestic space tended to be undermined in the Philippine colony. From the late nineteenth century through most of the first half of the twentieth, houses built for Filipino elites in urban centers had a kind of hybrid Spanish colonial/island Southeast Asian design built to maximize ventilation due to the humid climate. Rather than solid walls, the wooden living sections of the house had large windows made of capiz shells that would filter the harsh sunlight. Such windows and the baseboards underneath could be drawn aside so as to reveal the inside of the house to the street. Similarly, the construction of the interior of the living quarters allowed for the circulation of air, light, and sound by virtue of the grilled partitions on top of the doors and the light materials used for walls. A large veranda, or *azotea*, functioned as an all-purpose space for drying clothes as well as fish and storing water; it also served as a gathering place for family members, especially on hot summer nights, and an occasional sleeping area for servants. In such houses, space did not seem "enclosed or contained and ... public and private rooms, *bulwagan* and *silid* form[ed] a continuous whole."[20]

Those who came to the Philippines from the United States found themselves living in such houses in Manila and the provincial cities. Only later on, in the 1920s, would they construct new ones of their own. Many were struck by the open construction of spaces and the porous boundaries between rooms, all of which amounted to what felt like an absence of privacy. Edith Moses, for instance, contends that "one can hear every sound in these houses, for in order to have a circulation of air, there are open spaces over all the doors.... This is another feature of Manila houses to which I object" (16). And Mary Fee recalls her discomfort with using bathrooms since the floors were made of bamboo strips, "which kept me constantly in agony lest somebody should stray beneath" (75). As with many parts of the house, bathrooms did not afford total enclosure from the outside but shared in the overall permeable construction. The interior seemed to exist in constant commerce with the exterior so that the space of privacy was never wholly sealed off from the sudden intrusions of the public. In the colonial house, the white female body felt as if it was always on the verge of exposure.

The prospect of indiscriminate and sudden exposure was, at times, registered in terms of the fear of bodily invasion by alien forces and creatures. At such moments, the phantasm of domesticity is punctuated by an acute sense of dislocation and panic.

Echoing the remarks of other American women, the Englishwoman Mrs. Campbell Dauncy, whose husband managed a large sugar mill in Iloilo between 1904–1905, vividly conveys white dissipation under the influence of the tropical climate within the confines of her room:

When the wind was off me, I burst into perspiration, my face dripping on to the paper, my clothes soaking and my head beginning to ache and throb.... It gets on one's nerves not to be able to move a chair, to walk yards without dripping at every pore, and one's clothes feel so irksome and heavy. If one takes exercise, it is acute discomfort, and if one does not, one is ill![21]

Rather than conserve the body and conceal its traces, the interior of the colonial home is permeated by its exterior, beginning with the overbearing pressure of the climate. The tropics here dismantles the white female body so that it seems excessive and uncontained. It perspires constantly and seems restricted even in its most rudimentary movements. Her sweat-soaked clothing intensifies her sense of immobility, betraying rather than concealing her body. Dauncy's sense of self-possession is thus disrupted by an anguished body that, thanks to the climate, feels fragmented, bound to the limits imposed by its surroundings. In this sense, she begins to bear an uncanny resemblance to the image of the overembodied and shiftless natives described in earlier accounts.

The colonial house as the site for discomfort and disorder also comes across in Caroline Shunk's letters. At home, she feels under constant siege. "The insects increase with the heat. The worst of the pests are flying ants. They are so tiny they get in the hair, eyes, ears and crawl up short sleeves and down on your neck" (80). She complains about the humidity that renders clothes damp and "sticky," the typhoons and rain that cause such noise "that we cannot make ourselves heard without screaming!" and the occasional earthquakes that occur unexpectedly (86–87). And caught in the middle of one of the worst cholera epidemics in the country's history, Shunk is repulsed by the odor of the lime and carbolic acid associated with the sanitary measures to control the disease. Such smells give rise to thoughts of multiple and indiscriminate deaths, of loss both out of place and anonymous (90).

Colonial domesticity thus projects the tropics not simply as a pleasurable view, a set of ordered appearances to be apprehended at a secure and confined distance. It also induces the fear of feeling the limits of that confinement. The climate and insects work to erase the borders between the white body and its surroundings, reinscribing its materiality and contingency. Robbed of its fantasized sense of sovereignty, Shunk begins to feel as if she were other than herself. The compulsive quality of her complaints is symptomatic of a kind of involuntary mimicry otherwise ascribed to the natives. As such, she comes to approximate the very objects against whom her identity as a domestic subject in the empire is constituted. In her proximity to the exterior sources of her identity, she conceives of the domestic as the site of recurring dislocation.

Domestic order is conceivable only in relation to the repeated threat of disorder characterized by the confusion of inside with outside, just as middle-class whiteness is predicated on gendered notions of self-possession that entail the repeated containment of bodies, one's own as well as that of others. Such reminds us, once again, of the intimate link between whiteness and domesticity. In a bourgeois-colonial setting, both are dramatically articulated under conditions of pressure experienced as the potential subversion of the interior, private, and sovereign self by the exterior, public, and contingent other. Poised on the frontier between civilization and barbarism, colonial domesticity shelters the sense of whiteness as constitutive of a gendered agency forged in crisis and displacement. For this reason, it can claim to reorder differences and regulate the representation of oneself and the other. Securing this order, however, would prove to be an endless task. This is because colonial domesticity was also predicated on the mastery of servants. And such mastery, as we shall see, periodically entailed the wilful mimicry of the native other.[22]

Servants and Sentimental Segregation   We can see the dialectic of domesticity at work most vividly in these white women's relationship with what was clearly the most vital part of their household: their servants. "Naturally," Edith Moses notes, "the servant class is the one with which we come in closest contact" (346). Circulating within the most intimate spheres of the home, servants were simultaneously consigned to the most marginal of status, often spoken of in the same breath as household appliances and pets. Decidedly distinct from those they served, they were nonetheless crucial in the reproduction of the rhythms and routines of privacy constitutive of white identity. Indeed, the very possibility of a domestic order relied on the labor of servants, without whom white female agency in the tropics would remain unrealized. Yet the formation of domestic subjectivity, as we have seen, is idealized in terms of sovereign control over the household. Caught between dependency and disavowal, white women confronted servants' bodies as both promise and threat, as subagents in realizing their will-to-domesticity and as sources for the frustration of that will.[23]

By way of background, it is useful to point out the heterogeneous composition of domestic workers in the Philippines at the turn of the century. Colonial households employed predominantly male servants, both Chinese and Filipino, usually obtained through the intercession of a relative already attached to the household or passed down, as it were, from one employer to another. Unlike the United States at this time, where the majority of domestics were females, in the Philippine colony over three-fourths of the live-in servants were males, with a smaller number of females working as day laborers, usually doing laundry.[24] Hired as wage laborers rather than indentured servants, those who lived in the house were referred to by the infantilizing and desexualized Spanish term muchachos, or "boys" in English, regardless of their age. In the house, they slept on whatever floor space existed for the night: the *sala* or living room, the *volada* or corridors, the basement, or the azotea or veranda. And given the meager wages they pulled in—one account by a Mrs. Winnifred Hubble in 1907 placed it as low as ten centavos (five U.S. cents) a day plus an allowance of bread, brown sugar, coffee, and rice—such boys could not conceive of accumulating property of their own.[25] Devoid of privacy and property, servants were the antithesis of the possessive individual, often left only with their bodies as tokens for transacting with their U.S. employers.

In the accounts of women from the United States, the complexities of the ethnic, gender, generational, and class composition of domestic workers, while occasionally glimpsed at, tends to be elided in favor of conceiving them in terms of a polarity between bad and good servants. This restructuring of differences among servants into a binary works to position white women as guarantors rather than merely the effects of a domestic order—an order whose appearance is produced through the systematic erasure of the traces of domestic labor itself.

"Your first impression," writes Moses, "will be that we keep trained baboons to do the housework, for the probability is that a half-naked, dark-skinned creature is rushing up and down the hall on all fours, with big burlap sacks under his hands and feet. He is only the monkey-like coolie who polishes the narra floors" (14). The comparison of native servants to simians is a typical and by now unsurprising move in construing the other as all body and motion emptied of conscious intention. Domestic work looks to Moses like a series of purely mechanical gestures, its repetitiveness blurring the distinction between the body that works and the results of its labor. Wholly indistinguishable from its labor, the native body appears less like it is working than mimicking the idea of work, as if it were an ape.

It is this animal-like and therefore always-yet-to-be-domesticated semblance of servants that Caroline Shunk's letters similarly portray. She writes of her new servant, "He stalks stolidly about in shirt-tail, short drawers, and bare feet, smoking enormous cigarettes. He speaks not a word and looks an *insurrecto* of the deepest dye" (9). Insolent and almost criminal, the servant is far from being a boy, much less a good one. His silence, linked to his appearance, brings to Shunk's mind the undoing rather than the collaborative production of domestic order.

That silence is indicative of a certain linguistic economy that figures significantly in distinguishing a bad from a good servant, one that allows for the conversion of the former into the latter. Maude Huntley Jenks caps her litany of complaints about her new cook by saying, "He can't understand a word of English, and to everything we say to him, he says, 'hayz,' in the most idiotic fashion. So far as I have been able to learn, that expression means nothing to anyone except the cook, and he can't explain it."[26] The cook's incompetence occurs in relation to his inability to recognize the mistress's speech. He proffers a kind of unintelligible language, and for that reason, is unable to acknowledge his place as well as that of his mistress. What he communicates instead is his failure to communicate in the language of authority. The cook is doubly culpable as such, undermining both his and Jenks's position within the home.

The limits of domestic order are thus predicated on the workings of a communicative order without which any sort of sympathetic exchange and mutual recognition of one's proper place in the household would be impossible. As Mary Fee relates, the communication of the failure to communicate results in "bad boys" provoking the white mistress to take violent measures, occasionally hitting, under the guise of disciplining, the erring servant, or firing him. At times, as if to confirm his undesirability, the servant steals from the mistress in retaliation for her actions. The failure of domestication results in the loss of the mistress's identity and even property, the recovery of which is possible either through the expulsion of the servant or his reincorporation (Fee, 228–31).

The reincorporation of the servant, however, requires finding a way of getting to and through him. Inasmuch as servants were in most cases unable to speak up coherently in English, the language of authority, white women often found themselves speaking down, as it were, to servants by miming their speech. Moses, for one, explains to her Chinese cook the need to stave off the threat of cholera by keeping the house clean in a language that she thinks approximates his: "I told Lai Ting: 'Cholera all same cockroach, ally velly small. He hide in dirt, and jump to kill "China" boy and Filipino. If "China" boy keep house clean, no die'" (222). Likewise, Fee is forced to communicate her orders for dinner to her servants in a "mix of Spanish and Visayan," miming what she thinks is their language. And Shunk, in struggling to convey to her Chinese cook that "we could not eat the queer things he served," finally confronts him in the following manner:

"You good cook, Ah Yan?"
"Oh yes, he velly good."
"No you are not," I declared firmly. "You velly bad cook. You cook *good* now or go pronto!"
I retreated with dire visions of Chinese wrath in store, but at luncheon we could scarcely credit our eyes or mouths. Such a perfectly good meal! . . . And from that day on, every meal has been a culinary dream. (40)

White mimicry opens the door to the restoration of a communicative and domestic order. Such mimicry consists of repeating the servant's speech, which to begin with, comes across in the accounts as failed attempts at copying English. The white woman confronts the male servant by way of a calculated repetition and parody of native mimicry. Only through the mistress's ventriloquizing of the servant's mimicry is the latter ever given voice in colonial texts. The servants in these accounts can speak only within quotation marks, as it were, borne by the narrative and mimetic intervention of the mistress. Unable to represent themselves except as figures that are unable to represent themselves, servants can only be represented: first, as undomesticated and unintelligible figures analogous to apes, pets, criminals, and children, linked metonymically to dirt and disease; and second, as imitative subjects available for imitation and recuperation by the white mistress. In citing the servants' mimicry, white women can reclaim communicative authority in framing and thereby domesticating their encounters with them. In so doing, white women set themselves apart from the intimate presence of servants even as they ironize and so render benevolent their authority over them.[27]

Once enveloped within the representational order of the colonial home, servants can be enlisted as collaborators in the production of a colonial domestic order. Shunk writes about her favorite servant:

Houseboy No. 1 is a treasure. At seven o'clock, our dinner hour, he comes softly to the porch corner from which we watch the sunset and announces something which means "Señora, dinner is served!" He looks like a hired mourner at a funeral, dressed in crisp, white clothing. We go out with all the ceremony attending a state banquet and Vicente stands at "parade-rest" behind my chair. He serves quietly and well. Our table looks pretty, red-shaded candles, and a bowl of vivid red lillies. . . . Lizards run down the walls to catch the insects attracted by the lights, great June bugs buzz noisily about and coming too near the table are deftly caught by the "boy." (41)

Good servants make possible the emergence of the ideal domestic sphere, here understood as the unobstructed recognition of authority and flawless enactment of social hierarchy. Unobtrusive and barely palpable, the ideal boy is one who labors at serving *and* rendering the labor process itself inaudible and invisible. The temporal and spatial ordering of the home simply appears, as if by magic. And the servant's body is itself rendered continuous with this order, "crisp" and clean, dressed in white and standing erect. The boy becomes a copy of the domesticated white body while at the same time appearing radically different and distant from that body. Orchestrating the relationship of domestic objects to include even the movements of insects, "Houseboy No. 1" secures the zones of white comfort even as he conceals the signs of the labor necessary for this accomplishment.

As with the landscape becoming a view, housekeeping is converted into an aesthetic experience for the private consumption of white masters. "Ah Yan," Shunk remarks elsewhere, "is as solemn and immovable as a bronze statue and Mrs. G., who admires him, whispered, 'Isn't he a picture?' And he is indeed in a linen coat, white trousers and white linen cap" (76). Depicted as a "bronze statue," the good servant becomes an object of contemplation for white women, deriving his agency in and through the reproduction of the domestic order. He literalizes on his body the allegory of benevolent assimilation. Silent and self-contained, he is valued for his ability to efface the traces of his labor. And in his modulated obsequiousness, he produces for the white female observers the thrill of witnessing differences reordered into a sanitized hierarchy amid the unruly frontiers of empire. Masters thus reap a surplus of benefits. They gain access not only to the servant's labor power with which to secure their material needs; they also acquire symbolic purchase over the servant's body now abstractable from its labor and converted into an aesthetic possession, which like the view of the tropics, reiterates the fantasized benevolence of colonial rule.[28]

The good servant is one who seems able to represent domestic order by repressing the historical contingency of its formation. S/he begins to mimic the role of the white mistress, acting as the mute representative of the white woman's will without, however, displacing or subverting her authority. As such, the servant furnishes the signs for a sentimental commerce that removes the political from the realm of the domestic. Hence, in Nona Worcester's letters, we read, "Anna, Santiago's wife, has been a jewel in Baguio this season. She washed and ironed the best napkins, has done any little extra washing there was to do, has shampooed Alice's hair and mine. . . . Gregorio was a perfect servant on the trip, turning his hand to anything" (92). Mary Fee ends her account with a series of tender portrayals of good servants, one of whom risks her life in order to save the mistress's belongings from being consumed by a fire. Indeed, Fee waxes nostalgic about her life in Capiz, where the "noiselessness of the Oriental" (as against the "rudeness of colored porters" thanks to a "new confidence born of democracy" in the United States) allows her to return to a "well-ordered" house and lead an independent life in the tropics difficult to attain at home (246, 291). Maude Jenks, on the eve of her departure from Bontoc, writes, "I cried yesterday when our boys left. . . . Bert nearly cried, too. We think a great deal of them; they were such good boys" (134). And Caroline Shunk recalls her departure from the Philippines, speaking wistfully of her servants and the outpouring of affection between white mistress and Houseboy No. 1: " 'Who make Señora's room clean?' he asked, and tore my heart by handing in the shoe-polish, saying, dolefully, 'The Commandante's shoes" (176).

These tender scenes of parting are remarkably common in white women's accounts. They reiterate the fantasy we already saw at work in the notion of benevolent assimilation: that is, the exchange of white love for brown affection. The phantasm of colonial domesticity culminates in the melodrama of mutual recognition: of native servants coming to desire their subservience, thereby affirming white women's desire for sentimental mastery. Like valuable possessions, native servants furnish the means with which to romanticize the inequality and celebrate the consequences of conquest. Mystifying the hierarchy between mistress and servant, these moments of imperialist nostalgia commemorate domesticity as the affectionate regard for the ordering of differences held in a state of sentimental segregation.[29]

3 The Undead
Notes on Photography in the Philippines, 1898–1920s

Photography evades me.—Roland Barthes, CAMERA LUCIDA

One of the more visible legacies of the wars of 1898 was the explosion of photographic images, especially those of the lands and peoples that came under U.S. rule. Lighter and more mobile cameras allowed the photographing of sites and populations at greater distances, bringing these up close to a consuming public curious to see the recent "beneficiaries" of imperialist intervention. Photography transformed native peoples into images that could be wrenched from their origins and made to appear in novel contexts. Such images gave metropolitan viewers an acute sense of the technological and material expansiveness of the state and the mechanically reproducible proximity of its new subjects. Yet, photography as a means of expanding the aura, as it were, of the imperialist state, was also put to other uses productive of other effects in the colonies. In this chapter, I look into some of the ways in which photographic images as historical documents both confirmed and confounded the modernist vision of an imperial nation in one of its new possessions, the Philippines. For not only did photographic images reflect a tendentious notion of progress through disciplinary intervention; they also suggested the workings of a force that, as I shall try to show, eluded the demands of colonial and national ways of seeing.

Dead Images of the Living Many of the recent writings on colonial photography have tended to focus on the expropriative nature of the photographic enterprise. For this reason, they are often infused with a desire for revenge: the wish, as expressed in Malek Alloula's study of French photographs of Algeria, for example, to return the colonizer's gaze that had left its traces on the images of colonized natives.[1] In part, such projects have the effect of stirring anger, guilt, and embarrassment among contemporary readers. They remind us, whoever "we" are, of the violence that underlay the production and distribution of such images. They show the complicity of photographic representation with colonial policies as well as the ethnological and military means with which these were formulated and realized. Again and again, such approaches have demonstrated the tendentiousness of the eye that sees but remains unseen, resting on bodies that it both fixes and consumes for purposes alien to the lives of those it photographs.[2]

It is this capacity to convert the colonized into objects of foreign interests and subjects of colonial accounts that historically has lent to photography a predatory and cannibalistic quality. And it is all the more problematic, as critical studies have suggested, for its ability to provide an alibi of objectivity so that a photograph seems only to record what is in front of it while masking intentions, concealing selections, and rendering invisible the various frames that determine what is seen, how it is seen, and by whom. Photography has thus functioned as an apparatus of disavowal. Small wonder, then, that present-day discussions of colonial photography tend to incite an undercurrent of unease. They expose us to the relentless voyeurism that animated late imperial projects. In studying and, especially, looking at such photographs, we come into association with imperialist ways of looking and so feel unwittingly implicated in their workings. Like the gun, the camera has been part of the technology of subjugation, furnishing images to relay the workings of a prior and seemingly unassailable will. Colonial photographs seem like trophies of conquest. And to see them—even today—is to come in contact with this violence.

Looking through the photographic archive of U.S. colonial rule in the Philippines, it is not difficult—indeed, it would seem too easy—to confirm such arguments. One sees such photographs and feels compelled to respond.[3] Far from rendering Filipinos "invisible," colonialism instigated the proliferation of images of Filipino bodies. As part of a

Fig. 8. "Negritos in the island of Luzon" (William S. Bryan, ed., *Our Islands and Their People as Seen with Camera and Pencil* [New York: N. D. Thompson and Publishing, 1899])

colonial regime of "compulsory visibility," photography was crucial in the depiction of a plural society as a target of imperialist reform.[4]

Particularly instructive in this regard are what might be called ethnological photographs: pictures that construct natives into distinct types. Appearing in a variety of texts, from popular magazines to academic studies, these sought to divide and classify the population into a hierarchy of ethno-racial differences.[5] As we saw in chapter 1, each group was situated in relation to its distance from or proximity to what was thought to be the norms of Anglo-Saxon civility. At one extreme were the non-Christian "tribes," such as the Negritos. They were routinely regarded as the most abject group because of their dark skin, short build, "nomadic" lifestyle, and lack of clothing (fig. 8). The more Malay-looking Igorots, the generic name for ethnic groups in the mountain

Fig. 9. "An elaborate tattoo" (Albert E. Jenks, *The Bontoc Igorot* [Manila: Bureau of Public Printing, 1905])

regions of northern Luzon, elicited intense curiosity among white ethnologists, who often compared them to the Indians of North America. The Igorots—with their history of resistance against Spain, violent practices such as head-hunting, and muscular physique adorned with intricate tattoos—evoked fantasies about "noble savages" as natural allies of white colonizers on the tropical frontier (fig. 9).

Other groups on the southern island of Mindanao, both Muslim and non-Muslim, were regarded as slightly better-off in the ethno-racial hierarchy, given the allegedly improved nature of their material culture, but still requiring close colonial supervision (figs. 10 and 11). Finally, at the top of the hierarchy were the Christianized lowland groups, especially the Tagalogs. Thanks to centuries of Spanish rule, they had managed to come closer to the norms of civilization. But a history of racial mixing had supposedly weakened these groups, producing social divi-

Fig. 10. "Bagobos, island of Mindanao" (*Annual Reports of the Philippine Commission, 1901–1908* [Washington, D.C.: U.S. Government Printing Office, 1902–1909])

Fig. 11. "Native chiefs of Mindanao, Philippines" (Marrion Wilcox, ed. *Harper's History of the War in the Philippines* [New York: Harper and Brothers, 1900])

sions that installed an ambitious and corrupt mestizo upper class over a helpless lower class. These conditions made for a society that was as exotic as it was in need of discipline and reform (figs. 12, 13, and 14).

Distinguishing between "uncivilized" and "civilized," "pure" and "mixed," "lower," "middle," and "upper" classes, such photographs reproduce a typology of native societies that had become commonplace in North American and European ethnology, one that viewed the world's people in social evolutionary terms. Fixing their subjects into timeless settings, these photographs effect the isolation and dissection of native bodies, converting them into specimens of colonial knowledge and reform. Rendered as dead objects, images of natives were cataloged as discrete items and made part of what I earlier termed a diorama of white love, better known as benevolent assimilation. That is to say, they were meant to represent less the particularities of native societies as the intentions and interests that posited their poses beyond and outside the photographs' frames. Looking at them from the standpoint of the present, we cannot but be aware of a presence exterior to the images that sets out to measure, calculate, and mummify, as it were, the bodies we see.

Ethnological photographs, then, had a kind of totemic significance. They served as supplements to a national identity in the United States that was suddenly expansive, and hence, coming under pressure throughout the late nineteenth century, but especially after 1898. Photographs of native bodies provided visual referents to the expansion of an imperial body politic in at least two ways. First, they signaled a frontier to be crossed and conquered, and second, they posed a limit to what could be assimilated into the nation. Put differently, these photographs of tribes, whether assumed to be savage or halfway civilized, functioned as fetishes of U.S. nationhood. Like the mass-produced images of Indian and African tribes on the North American continent itself, they were invested with the ability to incite phantasms of manifest destiny.[6]

For imperialist apologists, fulfilling this destiny meant not only the taking of lands and labor but also the giving back of civilization. U.S. colonization, as previously discussed, was conceptualized like other late European colonial projects as a modernizing and benevolent mission. As with any missionary undertaking, the key to success was securing the collaboration of converts and their disciplined adherence to the state.[7] Again, photography registered the circulation of colonialism's gifts.

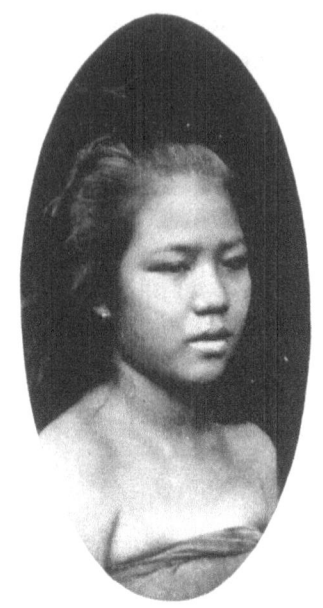

Fig. 12 (above). "A pure Tagalog type of the lower class girl of Manila" (William S. Bryan, ed., *Our Islands and Their People as Seen with Camera and Pencil* [New York: N. D. Thompson and Publishing, 1899])

Fig. 13 (above left). "Filipino Boy—Upper Class" (William S. Bryan, ed., *Our Islands and Their People as Seen with Camera and Pencil* [New York: N. D. Thompson and Publishing, 1899])

Fig. 14 (left). "Type of high-class woman of Manila. The women of the Malay tribes are delicate of form and feature and more attractive than those of the Mongolian type, of whom many are found in the Philippines. The one whose portrait appears herewith has an admixture of Chinese blood." (William S. Bryan, ed., *Our Islands and Their People as Seen with Camera and Pencil* [New York: N. D. Thompson and Publishing, 1899])

Government reports, travel accounts, and historical narratives were generously illustrated with photographs of the natives' inevitable transformation under U.S. tutelage. For example, there were pictures of savages turned into soldiers (figs. 15, 16, and 17); prisoners turned into obedient citizens (fig. 18); lazy natives turned into productive laborers (fig. 19); and local elites turned into national politicians already destined for monumentalization by future generations (fig. 20).[8]

As with ethnological photographs, these images convey the workings of an order outside their frames. We see individuals whose individuation seems to come from processes beyond what is visible. They appear as if composed by a power that is dispersed throughout the colony, inhabiting every aspect of everyday life and manifesting itself in and through the bodies of each subject. Their poses suggest their internalization of such a power. They come across as if they were recipients, and therefore also carriers, of promises that emanate from a hidden and distant elsewhere.

Living Images of the Dead So far, so obvious. What I've said about colonial photography in the Philippines could perhaps be said about photographic practices in many other colonial societies at the close of the nineteenth century and through the first half of the next one. That photography has been used to typify the relationship between colonizer and colonized, expanding the purview of the former while constraining that of the latter; that it has yielded images for the sake of compiling an encyclopedia of colonial visibilities; that it has served as a medium for the generation of imperialist desires and nostalgia: all these are true, and thus only partially so.

We might ask: what are the other sides of photography's truth? In treating colonial photographs as historical documents, to what extent do we find ourselves sliding into the temptation of seeing them as transparent emanations of the photographer's will? In insisting, as perhaps we must, that such images are conveyors of ideology chained to the determinations of sociopolitical contexts, do we risk reducing photographs to their frames, seeing them only to the degree that we look away, behind, or beyond that which appears in front of us? Seeing them by looking away from them, regarding them as mere appearances that carry messages whose meanings are already laid out in advance, do we

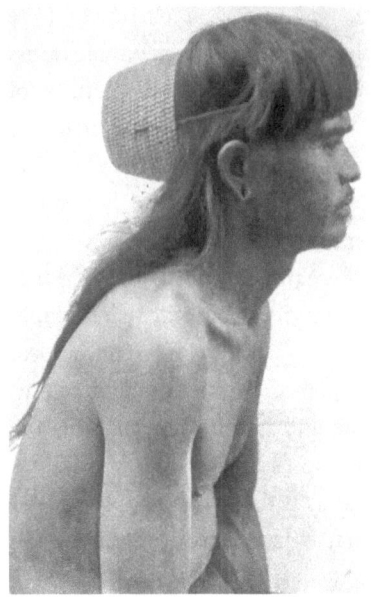

Fig. 15 (above left). "Evolution of a Bontoc Igorot constabulary soldier—1901, when he was a head-hunting savage" (Dean C. Worcester, *The Philippines Past and Present* [New York: Macmillan Publishing Co., 1914])

Fig. 16 (above right). "Evolution of a Bontoc Igorot constabulary soldier—1902, after he had been for a year in contact with Americans" (Dean C. Worcester, *The Philippines Past and Present* [New York: Macmillan Publishing Co., 1914])

Fig. 17 (left). "Evolution of a Bontoc Igorot constabulary soldier—1903, when he was a well disciplined and competent sergeant of a company of Philippine constabulary made up of his fellow tribesmen" (Dean C. Worcester, *The Philippines Past and Present* [New York: Macmillan Publishing Co., 1914])

Fig. 18. "The prison band 'sounding off' at retreat, Bilibid Prison" (U.S. Philippine Commission, *Annual Report of the Philippine Commission, 1901–1908* [Washington, D.C.: U.S. Government Printing Office, 1902–1909])

Fig. 19. "Typical scene in a trade school. In institutions like this, young Filipinos are being taught the dignity of labor and are learning useful trades" (U.S. Philippine Commission, *Annual Report of the Philippine Commission, 1901–1908* [Washington, D.C.: U.S. Government Printing Office, 1902–1909])

Fig. 20. Filipino elites in the colonial legislature, 1918 (U.S. Bureau of the Census, *Census of the Philippine Islands, 1918*, 4 vols. [Manila: Bureau of Printing, 1920–1921])

not also submit to the force of a colonial reading practice that we might have wanted to expose and negate? And arriving at this moment of virtual complicity with colonial ways of seeing, as in fact nationalists tend to do, could the urge for a kind of violent separation not arise, fueled by the phantasms of humiliation and revenge, embarrassment and anger, critical smugness and moral superiority?

Perhaps there is no definitive way one can avoid turning to and returning the imperial gaze. It arguably continues to inform modern ways of seeing.[9] Nevertheless, it may be possible periodically to see otherwise. Images emerge at times from the archives that contain certain intractable elements, peculiar details, or distinct sensibilities that do not easily fit into the visual encyclopedia of colonial rule. Seeing them, one tends to linger, as I do, over those things that seem to peel away from one's expectations. Detaining one's eye, they give one pause about the nature of their illustrative function in narratives of various sorts. One looks, but isn't sure what one is looking at exactly. One feels the call to respond, but to what and to whom remain in doubt. As with

Fig. 21. "Dead insurgent officer and soldier on the road to San Pedro Macati, after the charge of Gen. King's brigade" (Marrion Wilcox, ed., *Harper's History of the War in the Philippines* [New York: Harper and Brothers, 1900])

all photographs, one senses a message. But not knowing what it might be, one is left with a communicative force suspended in the world.

There are, for instance, a number of arresting images from the Filipino-American War of 1899–1902. The most problematic—that is to say, persistently inconclusive—of these are the numerous photographs of Filipinos killed in battle. Images of death pervade photographs of the war. There are pictures of corpses left on the roadside (fig. 21), corpses lined up for mass burial (fig. 22), corpses on hillsides (fig. 23), and corpses dumped in mass graves (fig. 24). The circulation of these photographs was fairly widespread. They appeared in the private albums of colonial officers, newspaper accounts, and popular narratives of the war as well as historical studies of more recent years.[10] And at one point, anti-imperialists in Boston were given to displaying these photographs as a way of decrying the brutality of the war.[11]

Photographs of war dead date back to the American Civil War with

Fig. 22. "Burying the Filipino dead" (photo by J. D. Givens in General Oscar Fitzhalan Long's photographic album, "Our New Possessions in the Philippines," 1900, Bancroft Library, University of California, Berkeley)

Fig. 24. "The American Artillery did wonderful execution in the battles with the insurgents. In a trench at Santa Ana the Tagal [sic] dead lay in piles. The group shown in the picture consisted of thirty eight bodies" (Marrion Wilcox, ed., *Harper's History of the War in the Philippines* [New York: Harper and Brothers, 1900])

Fig. 23. "At the battle of Caloocan some shots were seen to come from a trench, and a single shell was sent toward it by the Utah Battery. When our troops advanced they found no less than ten men dead at this point" (Marrion Wilcox, ed., *Harper's History of the War in the Philippines* [New York: Harper and Brothers, 1900])

the work of Alexander Gardner, Timothy O'Sullivan, and Matthew Brady. Most of their images did not see publication until after the war, and did not become widely available until the end of the nineteenth century. By then, such photographs—usually labeled as the "harvest of war"—had come to signify, at least to a public two generations removed from the horrors of the Civil War, the "unimpeachable witness and irreducible essence" of the war's horrible truth.[12] Photographs of the dead in the Filipino-American War, however, to the best of my knowledge do not depict the American (or for that matter Spanish) dead lying on the battlefield. That photographic fate solely is reserved for Filipino bodies. One might think that in such a case, a different truth was at stake.

How is it possible to understand, much less look at these photographs? We might begin by speculating that such images of dead Filipinos were supposed to certify the mastery of the United States over death. Guerrilla warfare based on sporadic engagements, hit-and-run tactics, and techniques of camouflage rendered Filipino fighters relatively invisible, much to the frustration of U.S. soldiers. Photographing them dead meant making visible what could not previously be seen, fixing their once-mobile bodies into a set of unchanging images. Such images consolidate the memory of a prior confrontation. They were meant to prove less the skill of Filipino fighters as the courage of North Americans, who in setting aside their fear of death, showed themselves capable of risking their lives as well as taking the life of an other. But such risks in order to enter into history had to be acknowledged. Photographing the dead was a way to secure such recognition from those who survived the war. The captions that accompany each picture suggest as much in their description of each scene, accounting for Filipino deaths as if these were the natural outcome of U.S. superiority—moral, technological, and military. Unlike the American Civil War photographs, those of the Filipino-American War could then be read in triumphalist terms, whereby images of dead natives stood in stark contrast to those of living U.S. soldiers now united in a common cause on the other side of the world.[13]

But to photograph corpses also meant to keep them alive, after a fashion. It entailed preserving their death as a living legacy, beyond even one's own death. Thus the ghastly quality of these images. Where the ethnological photographs of natives could be understood as the dead images of living beings, images of corpses are what Roland Barthes would call "living images of [the] dead."[14] As the living dead, they refuse to be buried. Tendentious captions, colonial accounts, nationalist responses, and sociopolitical analysis can explain the conditions that may have led to such images but they cannot in the least bit transform them. For what appears in these photographs are neither individual bodies nor a body politic but a jumble of body parts that resist recognition and classification. They cannot be identified—that is to say, they cannot be read as signs or documents of a particular person or event. (In fact, calling them Filipino is itself freighted with a certain anxiety about their visibility and a wish to set them apart and put them in their proper place, or at least a place that might have some sociological depth.)

Pictures of corpses were taken shortly after military encounters by professional photographers working for U.S. newspapers or hired by the U.S. military as well as by U.S. soldiers who had cameras. They thus preserve the shock of contact. They are less the signs of war's traumatic effects so much as they are those effects themselves. They do not serve merely as representations of the past but relay a past event that cannot be assimilated into the present. The bodies that are scattered about are dead in a biological sense, or so we might assume, yet their status vis-à-vis the living remains in doubt. This is the source of their horror. Thanks to photography, they appear unchanged and therefore hopelessly out of place. Photographs capture their relentless dislocation and so make visible their scandalous presence. For after all, what sort of sociality could exist that did not have a place for the dead? What aesthetic practice would be possible that could not contain death but could only transmit what seemed like its unalterable and untranslatable thereness?

As enduring traces of the scandal at the heart of war, such images are eventful in their capacity to assail our present and convey the sense of something unreadable. In doing so, they act to limit not just the stretch of imperial vision and its narrative purchase over the interpretation of events; they also frustrate critical commentaries that might seek to reframe and thereby bury them in the discursive graveyard of the archives. Thus do these photographs of corpses—what we might regard as the undead—resist the closure of mourning. Unburied, they seem to have no place in the world and so cannot be put out of mind. Inhabiting the world of the living, images of the dead remain radically obscene to the viewer. Looking at them, our vision falters as we apprehend far more than we can ever comprehend. We cannot close a circle, square accounts, determine blame, much less seek revenge. Rather, we feel ourselves in the midst of spectral wanderings that recall, if that is the word for it, the trauma at the foundation of empire, the unaccountability of deaths in the course of war, and the inevitable failure to narrate the truth of a history that exceeds our capacity to see.

Photographic Survivals Photographs of the dead haunt the colonial archives precisely because they seem so excessively visible. They suggest that the dead did not have a place in a society that was violently moving from one colonial regime to another. It is as if such images communicate too much, and hence, fail to stabilize the communication between the living and the dead. Indeed, they bring up the recurring inability of the living to respond and distinguish themselves from the dead. Images of the dead come across as messages whose meanings have forever been detained. It is this failure and the deferral of meaning at the inaugural moment of U.S. colonial rule that provides us with a context for inquiring into the photographs of the living in the years that followed. Those who survived the war, how did they take to photography? How did Filipinos, or at least those among them who could afford it, picture themselves while alive and so preserve themselves from the claims of death? Were there ways in which they sidestepped these two photographic fates: on the one hand, that of ethnological imagery—the prospect of the living affixed to dead images of native typicality; and on the other hand, that of the visibly decomposing corpses—the dead who live on, eluding mourning and memorialization?[15]

One of the most common ways in which Filipinos used photography was to have their own portraits taken. The popularity among the Filipino middle class of portrait painting, especially miniatures from the latter half of the nineteenth century, had doubtless paved the way for photographic versions beginning at least in the 1860s.[16] Photography expanded and altered the nature of portraiture, making it available to a wider number of people. As with the bourgeoisie in many other areas of the world from the late nineteenth century on, Filipinos who belonged to or sought to identify with this class posed in studios.[17] There, they had their choice of backdrops that, as one writer put it, "ranged from gardens, sweeping staircases . . . [to] cardboard sailboats and . . . crescent moons," as well as costumes that might include "Japanese kimonos with matching parasol and fan, an Igorot outfit with a matching basket of everlasting flowers . . . or a coat or *Americana* for a small extra fee" (figs. 25 and 26).[18]

These portraits served as tokens of affection among friends and family. As elsewhere in the world, photographic portraiture was meant not only to convey the person's likeness but to situate it in relation to the viewer. Such was the function of the dedications. Written either in Spanish, English, or Tagalog, these were addressed to specific recipients, evoking a sense of intimacy between the sender and receiver. "A Mi Amada Cristeta," reads one, "Dedico este retrato en prueba de nuestra cariño, Teang" (To my beloved Cristeta. I dedicate this picture as proof of our love, Teang) (fig. 27). "To Chimang," another says in English, "To prove once more the sincerity of my true love. Otelio" (fig. 28). And in Tagalog, "Kay Genoveva—Ala-ala ko ito sa iyo tanda ng di ko pagkalimot. Ang iyong kaibigan, Luming" ("For Genoveva—A souvenir of me, a reminder of my never-ending memory of you. Your friend, Luming") (fig. 29).

The printed captions that accompanied ethnological and war photographs, such as those we saw earlier, were meant to turn pictures into representations of a prior thought. In so doing, they were supposed to organize the drift of associations that such images gave rise to. Inscriptions, in contrast, carried with them the force of a desire to communicate. They transformed the photographic image into a gift whose circulation traced the reciprocal bond between viewer and viewed. Such dedications mark the movement of affect from source to recipient, and so move the recipient to respond in turn.[19] The history of such exchanges is difficult to date with any precision. Nationalists in the late nineteenth century were fond of exchanging photographs among themselves and their families, as if to dwell in the daily commemoration of one another's absence.[20] Such practices continued through much of the twentieth century. Photographs as gifts furnish evidence of thoughts that reach past the space and time of their circulation. They speak beyond the mortality and forgetfulness of their particular senders and receivers.

To speak beyond life and death: what could this possibly mean? How is it that portraits were thought to convey something beyond themselves? In the dedications above, the senders speak of photographs as proof (*prueba*) and memory (*tanda*) of one's love, even and especially in one's absence. The inscription and picture substitute for the persons speaking even as they extend the reach of their speech. They supplement the "I" or "we" who cannot be present in their image and words; but equally significant is the fact that such portraits and words survive beyond the lifetimes of those they were meant to supplement and address. Herein lies the power and persuasiveness of the proof they provide. For what they indicate is a certain communicative force at work: that at some point in time, someone speaking in the first person as an "I" or "we"—Teang, Otelio, or Luming—said something to a second, a "you"—Cristeta, Chimang, or Genoveva—in such a way as to surpass both; and in doing so, connected with some other, third receiver. What is transmitted in these photographs, then, are two messages: first, that there occurred an exchange of affection between the sender and receiver in and through their absence; and second, that such a transaction had

Fig. 25 (above). "Tating dear, Let this picture of your friend remind you of our companionship. With love, Apolinar" (E. Aguilar Cruz, "Vintage Photographs," in *Being Filipino*, ed. Gilda Cordero-Fernando [Quezon City: CGF Books, 1981])

Fig. 26 (below). "Heartily dedicated to my dearest Enchang as a sign of everlasting friendship. Lovingly yours, Cleofe" (E. Aguilar Cruz, "Vintage Photographs," in *Being Filipino*, ed. Gilda Cordero-Fernando [Quezon City: CGF Books, 1981])

Fig. 27 (above). "A Mi Amada Cristeta, Dedico este retrato en prueba de nuestro cariño, Teang" (E. Aguilar Cruz, "Vintage Photographs," in *Being Filipino*, ed. Gilda Cordero-Fernando [Quezon City: CGF Books, 1981])

Fig. 28 (below): "To Chimang, To prove once more the sincerity of my true love. Otelio" (E. Aguilar Cruz, "Vintage Photographs," in *Being Filipino*, ed. Gilda Cordero-Fernando [Quezon City: CGF Books, 1981])

Fig. 29. "Kay Genoveva—Ala-ala ko ito sa iyo tanda ng di ko pagkalimot. Ang iyong kaibigan, Luming" (E. Aguilar Cruz, "Vintage Photographs," in *Being Filipino*, ed. Gilda Cordero-Fernando [Quezon City: CGF Books, 1981])

the capacity to reach beyond them toward some other third term who is likewise absent from the scene of exchange.

Who might this third person be? Where the ethnological photographs were concerned, we can assume that this third party was the colonial state under whose authority such pictures were taken and circulated as well as a metropolitan audience in the United States eager to consume such exotic images. In these portraits, however, the identity of the third person is persistently uncertain. That is, he or she is a viewer whose identity is always yet to be disclosed; who, unknown to the sender and receiver, arrives from the future and anticipates the reception and recirculation of the photograph. What is indeed so compelling about these photographs is the way they leave open a position for an unknown and contingent addressee at some indefinite place and deferred time— us, here, today, for example—a viewer who acts to register the force of a desire that speaks before and beyond the moment of its photographic expression.

Fig. 30. "A mi distinguida y buena prima Agueda, Mi mas humilde recuerdo. La Original" (E. Aguilar Cruz, "Vintage Photographs," in *Being Filipino,* ed. Gilda Cordero-Fernando [Quezon City: CGF Books, 1981])

The sense that photographs were meant to survive the particular moment of their taking comes across even more acutely in the next set of portraits. In the first, we read, "A mi distinguida y buena prima Agueda, Mi mas humilde recuerdo. La Original" (To my distinguished and good cousin Agueda, A very humble remembrance from me. The Original) (fig. 30). And in another, "To my dear Estrella, When rocks and hills divide us / And you no more I see / Just take a pen and paper / And write a line to me. The Original" (fig. 31). Following a convention, the senders sign themselves as "The Original" as though to let the receiver know that the words come from someone who exists apart from the image. Through the photograph, "The Original" herself speaks to an other, in these cases "Agueda" and "Estrella." The recipients presumably know the name of the sender and so can read in the original a particular identity. Yet this identity is already other than itself. For what the recipients read are formulaic greetings, words whose origins reach beyond the actual sender. The sender, "La Original," is not the author of these words in the sense of having originally composed them. Rather, the

Fig. 31. "To my dear Estrella, When rocks and hills divide us / And you no more I see / Just take a pen and paper / and write a line to me. The Original" (E. Aguilar Cruz, "Vintage Photographs," in *Being Filipino*, ed. Gilda Cordero-Fernando [Quezon City: CGF Books, 1981])

formulaic nature of these inscriptions suggests that she's heard them before from someone else who, in turn, has heard them from others. What she sends is a chain of repetitions affixed to her mechanically reproduced image. She passes on what does not originate from her: a photographic image taken by a camera and a formulaic inscription. She constitutes herself as both a first person—the "I" that has her photograph taken and intends the words that appear on it—and a third person, the "she" who has heard these words from someone indeterminate and anonymous (hence their conventional nature) and has taken them for her own. The second person that receives the photograph receives a surplus as well: not just the intentions of the first person, the sender, but also the words of an indeterminate third person that infuse the latter's image and words.

For our part, we receive the photographs as their unintended addressees. Our relationship to them is like that between "The Original" and the formulaic words she's heard. The photographs were not intended for us, yet we feel compelled to look and linger on them. What we see of "The Original" is only its copy. For us, the distinction between the original and the copy has been lost. Or better yet, the copy seems to have absorbed the sense of the original so that it appears not only as a representation but as an extension of the subject.[21] The photographs are like the words that are inscribed on them: they transmit a message about their ability to transmit messages. They hold our interest precisely because of their power to cross the "rocks and hills [that] divide us," past the deaths of both the "I" and "you." It is a power of transmission that breaks the portraits off from the particular origins and contexts of their circulation, conveying memories that drift away from the specific time and place of their memorialization.

Here, the function of photography differs from the needs of colonial authority. Rather than serve as receptacles for colonial intentions, such photographs suggest the existence of another world that existed within but was not wholly absorbed by colonial representation. Like dreams or secrets, such photographs unhinge identities from their received contexts, expanding the terrain of possible identifications beyond what could be surveyed and disciplined. They thereby introduce an element of playfulness and indeterminacy into the formation of Filipino identity. Now ironic, now melancholic, such poses as we see here seem all the more remarkable when considered against the grain of the encyclopedic ambitions of colonial representation. They reiterate the sense of contingency that underlies appearances and the mechanically reproducible fantasies of identification that evade ascribed categories. Filipino portraits indicate another path for the recognition of native remains. They constitute a kind of anti-ethnology in their insistence on an empirically unassailable subjectivity and the evidence of their indeterminate and unknowable reception in the future.

Dialectical Images To give a photograph of oneself to someone constituted a kind of demand: that the viewer keep one in mind in one's absence. In evoking absent presences, portraits called forth affective ties across spatial and temporal divides, intimating the survival of figures beyond death. Whereas photographs of corpses kept alive disfigured bodies and so brought back the disfiguring experience of war, portraits as gifts refigured native bodies as sovereign entities. Thus did these portraits appear as the bearers of messages about the afterlife of colonialism already palpable within the discrete domains of colonialism's subjects. We might think of these portraits then as theaters for the domestic staging of phantasms of independence. Eluding the need to be recognized by the state, they sought acknowledgment instead from within a network of reciprocal intimacies. And addressing themselves to an absent third viewer, portraits anticipated their afterlife in a future beyond any present reckoning.

But there is, I believe, another twist to these views. It is important to keep in mind that photographic portraiture was limited to the Filipino bourgeoisie and those who aspired to such status. Historically, they had come to regard themselves as the vanguard of nationhood. Having alternately fought against and collaborated with Spain in the revolution of 1896–1897, and fought against then collaborated with the United States afterward, the bourgeoisie never doubted their ability and privilege to speak for the nation. They saw themselves as its very embodiment.

If one were to see photographic portraiture as a practice that seemed to resist the genres of colonial representation, one would have to qualify the limits of such resistance. For not only did this practice leave the colonial order relatively undisturbed; it may well have contributed to entrenching and rationalizing Filipino collaboration with U.S. rule. In providing the nationalist bourgeoisie with the fantasy of an autonomous space, it furnished what we might think of as the aesthetic equivalence of independence. Indeed, there is more than enough evidence to show that Filipino nationalism as it developed under U.S. rule tended to aestheticize the politics of independence—in public education, in the work of the Institute for National Language and the University of the Philippines, to cite some examples—and hence, remained deeply complicitous with colonial rule. There will always be an element of wishfulness if not error, then, in treating Filipino portraiture as an instrument of resistance.

But this is perhaps what makes such photographs all the more compelling: they seem to escape instrumentalization and reduction into either colonial or anticolonial narratives. They do so by bringing with them a certain force that enjoins a different politics of seeing. Unlike paintings, photographs evacuate their subjects of their presence and allow images to slide away from their original moorings. Such pictures convey the past as a series of moments that are detachable from any single appropriation in the present and are thus available for future reproductions (such as, for instance, in this book). The richness of their details, the expressiveness of faces, and the intricate precision of their surfaces give each photograph a particularity that exceeds generalization. To the extent that such photographs allow only for their mechanical reproduction, they refuse transformation short of their destruction and so elude the demands of imperialist pedagogy, on the one hand, and the domesticating pull of nationalist mourning, on the other.[22] Destined for daily and private commemoration, they instead awaken in us, the unknown viewers who arrive from the future, a flood of associations that can barely find expression. Conceived from fantasies about identity, they propel their recipients to follow further identifications. They refuse to stay fixed within the circle of the private, subjective remembrance just as they seem to say more than what can be contained within a sociohistorical frame. For these reasons, they evade the work of mourning. They share instead in the haunted qualities of the corpses. Consider this: the subjects of these photographs are now all dead; yet they remain, here, in our midst, alive, preserved by the chemical action of the photographic process. We see in them the eyes of those who have seen what ours cannot: the particular moment of a past now held at a standstill.

As dialectical images, such photographs bring the past forward into our time. But in their unyielding particularity, they inhabit our present like unburied corpses. In this sense, they arrive as foreign presences, lodging themselves in the archives of our daily lives. We, the alien because unexpected recipients from the future, encounter them as images irrevocably alienated from their original contexts. Hence their affecting strangeness: they are the materializations of an unassimilable memory as much as they are that memory's eerie envoys. As material memory, portraits of Filipinos confound in their own modest way the temporality of colonial and nationalist modernity. The latter, as we saw, entail notions of progress that while abolishing the materiality of the past, conserves it as a collection of "primitive" images to be reformed and disciplined in the present. Used as documents of a colonizing or nationalizing regime, photographs are tied to the task of keeping the past in its place in the same way that rituals of mourning keep the dead segregated from, yet symbolically available to, the living.

However, we have also seen the ways in which certain photographs put forth an alternative temporality. Neither past nor present, we might think of them as taking place in a future anterior, the sense of "this will have been." It is for this reason that we can conceive of such photographs as always timely. Furthermore, their timeliness contains intimations of a boundless generosity: that in their having been gifts for and from someone in the past, they continue to circulate and transmit messages, soliciting responses from those who feel the pressure of their call. They make themselves available for indeterminate and contingent receptions and returns. Herein lies their historicity. They relay the force of a transmission that seems to surpass colonial and nationalist modes of surpassing. Thus, they put us within the ambience of a certain fantasy: that of a kind of freedom that defers the need for recognition and thereby always leaves open the possibility for future circulation.

4 Anticipating Nationhood
Identification, Collaboration, and Rumor in Filipino Responses to Japan

Writing from Yokohama to one of his fellow nationalists in 1898, Mariano Ponce—then ambassador to Japan of the short-lived Philippine revolutionary government engaged in a war with Spain and shortly thereafter the United States—typifies Filipino attitudes toward the Japanese at the turn of the century:

We ask the Japanese for help because they are the only nation in the world with whom we can have common interests to defend, and with whom we are linked by affinities of race [*afinidad de raza*]. And geographical proximity which gives to our two countries the same destiny [*un mismo destino*].... No one understands our present and future political situation better than the Japanese.[1]

And as if to stress his imagined identification with the Japanese, Ponce had taken to sending to his fellow nationalists photographs of himself dressed in Japanese clothes standing alongside the Chinese nationalist, Sun Yat Sen, in Western attire (fig. 32). On the wall behind them are photographs of Filipino revolutionary leaders (Emilio Aguinaldo and Antonio Luna) and a Filipina woman (Ponce's wife?). What is startling about this photograph is the manner in which it reproduces the uncanny permeability of emergent nationalist identities at this time. Japanese, Filipino, and Chinese, along with generic European bourgeois signifiers, are mapped together in ways that seem to suggest the circulation and exchangeability of these identities. It was perhaps this photograph's capacity to convey the possibility of recognizing but also assum-

Fig. 32. Don Mariano Ponce and Dr. Sun Yat Sen in the former's residence in Yokohama, Japan (Mariano Ponce, *Cartas Sobre la Revolucion, 1897–1900* [Manila: Bureau of Printing, 1932])

ing other national identities, of marking off yet sliding from one into another culture that fascinated Ponce.

One can find a similar kind of interest sporadically at work in some of the letters of the most renowned Filipino nationalist, Jose Rizal. Ten years prior to Ponce's letter, he writes to his family from Tokyo: "I have stayed here a longer time than I intended, for the country appeared to me very interesting and because in the future we shall have much contact and relations with Japan. I am learning Japanese [and] I can understand it already and can express, although badly, what I want."[2]

In these and other such remarks about Japan, the first generation of Filipino nationalists seemed to be anticipating the more populist aspects of "Pan-Asianism" that the Japanese sought to propagate among the colonized peoples of Southeast Asia four decades later. In fact, throughout the years of U.S. colonial rule, popular resistance movements in the Philippines were often characterized by their perennial invocation of Japanese aid, either in the form of arms or outright military intervention, that would bring independence to the country. "Japan" thus became part of a series of highly charged signs in the history of Philippine anticolonial movements so that the rising sun of its flag was even associated by some Filipinos with the light (*liwanag*) of independence.[3]

Japan could be imagined as a source of help in moments of national distress precisely because it was not seen as a potential overlord. Herein lies a fundamental element in Filipino attitudes toward Japan prior to the Pacific War: Japan was seen as another *nation*, that is, a place free from colonial control and sovereign in its capacity to determine its own history. It symbolized what the Philippines sought to become. It is this aspiration for nationhood that animates, I think, Filipino remarks such as "affinities of race," "common interests," and "same destiny" between Japan and the Philippines. The future ties they envisaged with Japan was not one of subordination to a superior race but one characterized by relations of mutual deference and reciprocal obligations. In other words, it was Japan's ability to re-mark its difference from other countries—an ability that constituted its nationhood—that Filipinos emulated.

One gets a sense of how affinities based on differences were played out among Filipino nationalists by looking at a somewhat minor but no less telling anecdote related by Rizal to his family. While visiting an exhibition of Japanese paintings in Paris in 1883, Rizal, like many other

Filipinos in Europe at this time, was mistaken "as one from Japan." He was then asked by some of the French viewers to provide information regarding the Japanese paintings on display. Rather than rectify this case of mistaken identity, Rizal indulges in the fantasy of being Japanese. He proceeds to "escape into the history of Japan," talking about its constitution and narrating the biographies of some of the Japanese artists he knew about. "They asked about the processes [of the paintings] and they were charmed," he wrote with obvious delight. Nevertheless, he is overcome at one point with considerable embarrassment when a woman asks him to read the Japanese writing on the bottom of the pictures. Afraid of being found out, he produces yet another fictitious explanation: that he could not read Japanese because he was part of a group sent to Europe by the emperor while still quite young in order to learn about the West; and as a result, he's been unable to learn "our native tongue."[4]

This anecdote, like Ponce's photograph, hinges on using a mistake as a point of departure for redrawing the boundaries of a colonized subjectivity. Situated amid a long, rambling account of Rizal's impressions of Paris, this story has the feel of idle talk or gossip. It does not really belong anywhere or lead up to anything; still, it is made to circulate between Rizal and his family in the Philippines, as if to solicit their complicity in the pleasures of misrecognition. Where do such pleasures come from?

Worth noting here is how the imaginative slide from Filipino to Japanese—although precipitated by European assumptions—is nonetheless readily taken by Rizal himself; and how this ontological slippage is held in check by language. It is the unreadableness of Japanese writing that reminds Rizal of the irreducible difference that separates him from the Japanese; but it is also that which allows him to mount yet another fantasy with which to elude the demands of his French interlocutors. Rizal, in this case, seems to regard Japan as a nation whose reality is built on its vernacular specificity rather than the innate moral, much less biological, uniqueness of its people. That Rizal could imagine himself to be Japanese, even if only momentarily, attests to the fictionality and malleability of national identity, one whose limits and coherence is set not by blood but language.[5] Taking an almost perverse delight in being misrecognized, Rizal appears to be saying that he *could have been* Japanese—as in fact most Europeans thought he was—which meant that he need not merely be a colonized subject of Spain. "Japan" affords Rizal the opportunity to realize the arbitrariness of colonial boundaries and the prospect of slipping away from received identities. With "Japan" comes the exhilarating possibility of reimagining a different history, however fanciful, for the indio self. Misrecognition thus provides Rizal with a chance to rehearse various ways of marking himself off from the European other. It is as if the articulation of a national identity is tinged with anticipating—in the double sense of expecting and forestalling— the emergence of other identities elsewhere.

The Contradictions of Official Nationalism   This process of articulation as anticipation would haunt—and to that extent, problematize—the formation of Filipino identity throughout the first half of the twentieth century. Following on the heels of the revolution against Spain, the traumatic war with and subsequent colonization by the United States further fragmented an already hybrid Filipino national identity, caught as it was between the localizing structures of patronage, a Spanish-Christian legacy, and the institutional force of Anglo-American "colonial democracy." Nationalist elites were constrained by having to negotiate in their vernacular languages (Tagalog, Hiligaynon, Cebuano, Ilokano, etc.) and two official languages, Spanish and English. What gradually emerged under U.S. rule was a conservative and counterrevolutionary political order predicated on what Benedict Anderson would call "official nationalism," that is, the "willed merger of nation and empire" carried out by a ruling or emergent elite threatened by populist stirring.[6] Official nationalism works by concentrating the symbolic capital necessary for the projection of nationhood in the hands of those on top while repressing more egalitarian expressions of nationhood from those at the bottom of the social hierarchy. In the Philippines, the chief agent of official nationalism was a cadre of mostly mestizo elites—many of them veterans of the revolution against Spain and war against the United States—who had been rapidly co-opted into the bureaucratic machinery of the U.S. colonial regime. Whereas many found themselves fatally at odds with the retrograde avatars of Spanish colonialism—the friars—the nationalist elite quickly realized that they stood to profit by collaborating with the secularizing, market-oriented regime imposed by the United States.[7]

Unlike Spain, the United States succeeded with a combination of force and suasion in welding the archipelago into a single administrative unit. In so doing, it set the conditions for the creation of a truly national oligarchy made up mostly of scions of the landowning mestizo class that had begun to emerge in the latter half of the eighteenth century.[8] As they acquired a major stake in the machinery of the colonial state through municipal and national offices, inclusion in the civil service, and by the 1930s, control over the entire legislative apparatus and parts of the executive and judicial branches of the government, they also managed to monopolize the symbolic resources for imagining nationhood.[9] Indeed, they came to regard themselves not only as a ruling class with common interests to defend but as the exclusive spokespeople for the rest of the nation, especially in relation to the United States. And since they believed that their class interests were coterminous with the national interest, they thought that their political lives determined the very existence of the Philippines itself.

Through such measures as preferential access for Philippine goods on the U.S. market, the creation of police and constabulary forces to ensure against internal threats to elite rule, and the promise of virtual independence in order to maintain elite legitimacy vis-à-vis the people, the United States proved to be an ideal ally of the emergent Filipino oligarchy. Ironically, then, the national elite prospered as never before under U.S. colonialism, to the point where independence itself became politically and economically problematic for them. On the eve of the Pacific War, while many of them publicly espoused independent status for the country, most privately expressed doubts about the consequences—both for their country and class—of U.S. withdrawal from the Philippines.[10]

When war finally came, it proved disastrous for the ill-prepared country—recently granted Commonwealth status with the promise of independence by the middle of the 1940s—and spelled a profound crisis for elite authority. The Filipino leaders, fleeing to the security of cities, abandoned their traditional basis of wealth—their haciendas—to peasants who lost no time in repudiating rents and replacing cash crops with such staples as rice and corn. Cut off from the lucrative U.S. market by the Japanese, who forbade trade with the enemy, Filipino elites quickly lost their economic preeminence. In addition, they could not rely on the new colonizer to enforce the "law and order" that had protected them from peasant and proletarian challenges in the past.[11] The Japanese, unlike U.S. authorities, could not adequately curtail armed resistance, especially in the countryside, in order to safeguard elite privileges. In substituting one colonial master for another, the Japanese occupation revealed the vulnerability of the Filipino oligarchy, and thus, made painfully obvious the rift between class and national interests, exposing the insoluble contradictions of official nationalism under colonial sponsorship. It is within the context of this contradiction that we might try to understand another set of Filipino responses to the presence of Japan, now incarnate as an occupier rather than an ally.

The Rhetoric of Collaboration   Among the Filipino leaders who stayed in the Philippines (as opposed to those who fled to the United States), the most typical response to the occupation was collaboration with the Japanese Military Administration. With few exceptions, and varying degrees of reluctance or alacrity, the overwhelming majority of the country's ruling class accepted positions in the Japanese-sponsored Executive Council and, by October 1943, the Japanese-sanctioned republic.

The classic apology for elite collaboration can be summed up as follows: It was the only possible alternative in an otherwise impossible situation of military rule. By collaborating with the Japanese, Filipino leaders claimed that they were in fact acting to parry the shock of conquest, using their position to buttress the people from the violent impact of war. As the "most learned, competent and [politically] experienced Filipinos,"[12] they felt duty bound to intercede on behalf of the nation, brokering the demands of the New Regime with the needs of a devastated country.

Even more important, the Filipino leaders after the war insisted on the dissimulated nature of their collaboration, claiming that their actions were merely formulaic gestures and their speeches empty rhetoric designed to fool the Japanese authorities into thinking they were supporting the regime. Indeed, they saw themselves using their positions in the regime in order to supply intelligence to the U.S. Armed Forces in the Far East and surreptitiously convey information regarding allied advances toward the Philippines to the rest of the populace. Several even alleged that they used their privileged positions to work for the release of guerrillas confined by the Japanese.[13]

For the Filipino elites, then, collaboration meant ensuring the survival of the country and preparing it for the return of U.S. forces. Far from being treasonous, collaboration, they argued, should be seen as a heroic act no different from the armed resistance of guerrilla units in the countryside. Elite defense of their actions during the occupation in effect reversed the meaning of signs: "collaboration" was really "resistance" against the Japanese while "resistance," especially on the part of guerrillas in the countryside, was really "collaboration" with the United States. "Everyone was a collaborationist," wrote Jose P. Laurel, president under the Japanese-sponsored republic. "No one was a traitor."[14]

The issue of collaboration-as-resistance (and the reversibility of that equation) revolved around the by-now-familiar questions: Who has the right to speak for whom and under what conditions? Judging from the tone and substance of their apologia, the Filipino oligarchy never doubted their natural right to represent the nation; nor could they conceive of the possibility of a disjunction between their class interests and those of the rest of the nation. Instead, collaboration seemed to them the logical way to salvage their monopoly over the means of representing the Philippines. As Claro M. Recto, one of the chief spokespersons for the collaborationists and a prolific nationalist writer, said, "We are obliged to cooperate with [the Japanese]—and we cannot permit that others be allowed to rule in the interests of Japan or any other person"—where "others" here pertained not only to non-Filipinos but more specifically to those outside the circle of the national oligarchy.[15]

What allowed the Filipino elite to cling to the idea that they continued to speak for the nation by speaking to and for Japan? Before retreating to Bataan, Philippine Commonwealth President Manuel Quezon and General Douglas MacArthur had both instructed the Filipino officials to do whatever was necessary to mitigate the effects of the war on the population, even if this meant limited collaboration. What I am interested in, however, is not an assessment of the truth or falsity of elite statements about their motives for collaborating. Such an approach would have to assume that there existed an objective, transhistorical criteria for distinguishing between collaboration and resistance. Rather, I want to ask about the means with which the Filipino elite were able to dissociate, as they claimed, their actions from their intentions, their words from their meanings.

A cursory glance at the speeches of some of the most prominent collaborators gives one a sense of the inflated nature of collaborationist rhetoric. For example, one of the speeches of Jorge B. Vargas, then head of the Executive Committee, on the first anniversary of the Japanese occupation begins: "We owe the rebirth of the Philippines and the Filipino people to the nobility and vision of the great Japanese empire . . . whose enlightened policies have respected and encouraged our national institutions. We can never make our public avowals of gratitude to Japan commensurate to the vast benefits we have received."[16]

In this and many other speeches, the Japanese armed forces are invariably described by Vargas as "filled with indomitable courage"; the Filipinos are always "filled with admiration and gratitude" for being part of Japan's "holy war" against "Western materialism." By the same token, Japanese judgments of Filipinos are readily accepted—their "addiction to occidental influences" resulting in the "excessive love of pleasure, the shirking of effort and duty, and the desire to comfort ourselves with false hope"—as well as Japanese prescriptions for Filipino salvations—to recover "our lost Oriental values," such as "courage, endurance, honesty, thrift, diligence and industry" (all of which, of course, were already salient characteristics of Japanese culture), and thereby assume "our proper place among the nations of Greater East Asia."[17]

What is striking about collaborationist rhetoric is its mechanical facility for reproducing the main outlines of the East Asian Co-Prosperity ideology—a kind of Orientalism for Orientals. The artificial quality of such speeches makes them seem devoid of human intentionality. Purely formulaic, they appear to come from no one in particular. Part of the emptiness of collaborationist speeches comes, I think, from the fact that they were written and delivered in English. As much as the Japanese sought to rid the Philippines of Western influences by encouraging, among other things, the use of the Tagalog vernacular and the learning of Japanese, English continued to be the language with which the Japanese Military Administration and Filipinos communicated. Indeed, with the exception of the Tagalog literary magazine *Liwayway*, the small number of publications that were officially sanctioned during the occupation, such as the *Tribune*, were all in English.[18]

A curious (and to my knowledge largely unremarked) situation arose whereby occupier and occupied were linked by a language that was foreign to both. Filipino elites until the 1940s spoke with one another mostly in Spanish and with colonial officials and others from the United States in English, using their vernacular languages only when addressing others from their respective hometowns or those lower down the social ladder, such as their servants. Official U.S. policy was to encourage the spread of English primarily through the public school system. The relative success of this project was such that by 1939, only thirty-eight years after the establishment of colonial rule, 26.6 percent of the population could speak English. More significant was the increasing use of English among a new generation of Filipino colonial bureaucrats who needed to know the language in order to pass civil service examinations in light of the rapid "Filipinization" of the colonial government after 1916. English held the attraction that Spanish had in a previous era: that of altering one's place in colonial society by signaling one's ability to speak up to the source of authority.

Yet, where the upper reaches of the colonial state were concerned, Filipino leaders continued to speak Spanish rather than English. This was not surprising inasmuch as the majority of them were educated under the Spanish system of the late nineteenth century. As the linguist Andrew Gonzalez has remarked, "Spanish continued to be used as the language of the educated [class] during the early American period." Spanish also dominated the language of Philippine courts of law until the eve of the Pacific War, so that colonial legislation, as with the proceedings of the Philippine colonial legislature, was primarily in Spanish accompanied by English translations.[19] Hence, for the prewar Filipino elite, English continued to be a new and foreign language. As such, it could not as yet function as the primary idiom for expressing class identity and national consciousness in the way that Spanish and the local languages had been able to.

The relative foreignness of English among the national elite may, in part, help to explain the nature of collaborationist rhetoric and the facility with which Filipino leaders were able to retrospectively separate their intentions from their words. By collaborating with the Japanese in

English, Filipino elites seemed to proffer submission in a language that was not theirs, yet over which they had some command. English allowed them to hold something back—or at least, to appear to do so—in such a way as to enable them in the postwar years to dissociate themselves from their wartime statements. It was as if because they spoke English, they were not culpable.[20] Speaking in English meant they were using someone else's words to express someone else's ideas: here, those of the North Americans and Japanese respectively. In doing so, they kept what was Filipino—in the sense of a hybrid, Spanish-vernacular self, and the imagined community for whom and to whom it spoke—at a remove from the discursive grip of the New Regime. Thus could they regard their task of collaboration a ruse as well as a form of resistance. As Claro M. Recto wrote shortly after the war, collaborationist rhetoric "meant nothing" and was no more than "perfunctory protestations of gratitude" and "ironical paeans of praise." The rhetorical extravagance of such speeches merely signified "noisy collaboration . . . the Filipino leaders played blind, deaf and dumb."[21] By highlighting the artificiality of their rhetoric, the English language allowed the collaborationists to double code, as it were, a discourse on race and empire that, to begin with, was already massively overdetermined.[22]

Collaboration, then, had a linguistic dimension. It worked as a strategy for preserving class prerogatives precisely to the extent that another colonial language—English—could be deployed in obscuring class conflict altogether. Because they spoke in English, the national elites could continue to see themselves as the privileged representatives of the nation. English enabled them to speak to, but also beyond, the Japanese, deferring to their authority even as they parodied their ideology. Similarly, English allowed them to signal to the rest of the Filipinos their continued capacity to exact access to and negotiate with the source of colonial power. What was important about English was less the fact that it could serve as a medium of communication between the Japanese and Filipino leaders (inasmuch as the contents of whatever was conveyed was assumed by the latter to be reversible and retractable); rather, English signified the elite's special purchase over an entire system of signification under colonial rule. Speaking in multiple registers, they could occupy a variety of shifting positions: as "collaborators" seeking to retain their class hegemony; as "nation builders" intent on using the occupation for creating the basis for an independent state; as covert loyalists to the Allied forces; and as "patriots" deflecting the full weight of Japanese demands from the rest of the country. As Jose P. Laurel would write in his memoirs, "There is heroism in collaboration. All depends upon the circumstances, the motives . . . the means and the extent of collaboration."[23] Through English, he and others like him found a means for dissembling their motives, achieving both intimacy with and insulation from the two centers of colonial power. In this way did they retain the basis of their own power, which consisted precisely in their capacity to traverse and colonize, as it were, the boundaries between two empires—the United States and Japan—and two peoples—the Japanese and Filipinos.

It should be noted, however, that the elite interpretation of collaboration was not always readily accepted by all other Filipinos during the occupation. Only after a complex but ultimately feckless series of investigations and litigations by the U.S.-sanctioned People's Court between 1945 and 1946, followed by a general amnesty by Manuel Roxas—the first president of the newly proclaimed Republic of the Philippines and a collaborator himself—in 1947, did the elite version of their actions eventually shape the standard historical explanation of collaboration. The details surrounding the resolution and depoliticization of the collaboration issue in the postwar era need not concern us here. But one might ask how other Filipinos who were neither collaborationists nor resistance fighters responded to the events of the occupation.

Rumor and the Anticipation of Nationhood It is beyond the scope of this chapter to provide a comprehensive survey of the entire spectrum of nonofficial, nonelite responses. Instead, I want to focus on something widely mentioned though never analyzed in various accounts of the occupation period: the circulation of rumors in Manila. Rumors differed in significant ways from the rhetoric of collaboration. Where collaboration sought to totalize its command over the modalities of nationalist representations, rumors tended to suggest other sources and routes for signifying the nation. They worked in ways that were reminiscent of the moments of misrecognition in the photograph of Ponce or the anecdote of Rizal in that they tended to evade received identities and prescribed positions under colonial rule.

Teodoro Agoncillo's two-volume work, *The Fateful Years: Japan's Adventure in the Philippines, 1941–1945* one of the most widely cited and comprehensive accounts of the Philippines under Japan, is illustrative in this regard.[24] In reading this extraordinary text by one whose writings on Philippine history have had an enormous impact on postwar nationalist thinking, I want to draw attention to the ways in which rumors in the context of occupation highlight some of the tensions inherent in conceptualizing nationhood.

Though published in the mid-1960s, much of the material for this book, as Agoncillo writes in the preface, was drawn from the diaries he secretly kept during the war as well as from recollections of conversations he had or overheard. As a young man just out of college when the war broke out, Agoncillo lived in Manila as a kind of participant-observer to the many events he narrates. Indeed, his book is as much a history as it is an ethnography of the Japanese occupation. As such, it mixes narrative genres, moving deftly from anecdote to analysis. Its most arresting moments come when it lingers on the subjective states of people exposed to the hazards of war, crosscutting between public and private memories.

What results is a peculiar sort of nationalist history. In tracking the ever shifting location of nationhood caught in the spaces of inter-imperialist conflict, the author must perforce adopt a variety of subject positions as he translates different languages to get at the various meanings of events. Rather than produce a dialectical narrative of suffering and ultimate triumph, Agoncillo's history lays out the past as a terrain of contested and partial interpretations:

A historian's prejudices and emotions at the moment of involvement in certain events of his time are as much a part of the history of that particular period as the significant and meaningful events in themselves. . . . Thus forewarned, the reader becomes alert and consequently judges the author accordingly. . . . As narrator and interpreter of the events I saw and deeply felt during the three years of the Japanese occupation, I cannot help showing the heart and mind that finally shaped this book. . . . I tried hard . . . to hide behind the lines of my chapters, but my voice is so clear and resonant that it can easily be recognized by perceptive readers. . . . Thus, the use of the first person singular.[25]

This excerpt from Agoncillo's preface displays an acute sense of his personal stakes in the writing of the past. As a second-generation nationalist whose life history is coordinate with a traumatic moment in the formation of his nation, he is compelled to make his voice an element in the events he depicts. The "I" that emerges "can easily be recognized" to the extent that it is split between one that speaks and one that is spoken about. Its borders are in crucial ways coextensive with those of the occupied, archipelagic nation to which it is attached. As a historicized "I," it must, as we have seen in the case of the nationalist elite, pretend to speak for and from a place and people. Indeed, whatever coherence and authority it might have is a function of its ability to be a delegate of, as well as location for, the imagined condition of nationhood. Agoncillo's preface illustrates something of the intractable divisions inherent in the constitution of a nationalist identity within a colonial context. For the "I" that speaks and writes must do so in a mode of constant anticipation, prefiguring the "we" that is about to emerge. It therefore acts both as an agent for and the site of the production of alterity, a self "occupied," as it were, by imagined others who are at once distinguishable from yet linked to a colonial society.

The dynamics of anticipating the constitution of nationhood, however, can take many different forms. Among the Filipino oligarchy, as we saw, prefiguring the nation meant conserving class privileges. Such entailed speaking in a language that could not be privately owned but, by the same token, did not have to be owned up to. The exigencies of official nationalism allowed the elite to legitimize duplicity as state policy in the form of collaboration. In contrast, Agoncillo's account reveals how the emergence of a nation under occupation was anticipated among those who had no access to the symbolic resources of the state. For such Filipinos, there arose a different style of imagining nationhood, which under duress, had to do in some measure with the retailing of rumors.

Rumors are, of course, commonplace in wartime and other moments when authority comes under severe crisis. They substitute for and so displace "truth" in the sense of a consensual, officially sanctioned version of the way things are. Rumors are compelling to the extent that they circulate in ways that can position their hearers and tellers in new and unexpected relation to what lies beyond them. To hear or relate a rumor is to pass on the possibility of something having happened or yet to happen and thereby claim for oneself a place within the circuit on which rumor travels. And by staking for oneself a position from which to imagine the potential occurrence of events (that is, events as they could have been or might be), one begins to share in the circulation of potentiality itself. Put differently, rumors point to the possible unfolding of history and circulation of power elsewhere, at a tangent to the present trajectory of events.

Yet rumors are also impervious to verification, for once verified, rumors cease to be so; they are epistemologically empty. It is for this reason that they tend to be regarded as a kind of subterranean discourse. Like gossip, rumors present one with "the possibility of understanding everything without making the thing one's own."[26] By divorcing understanding from ownership, rumors are ineluctably public, condemned to promiscuous circulation (because, again, a rumor ceases to be a rumor once it drops out of circulation) and a kind of illegitimate historicity. Rumors constitute the "noise" between those events destined for memorialization.[27]

It is nonetheless this other history that Agoncillo's book is particularly keen on relating. In his descriptions of everyday life immediately before and during the occupation, rumors play a prominent part.

During the first months of 1941, when the Commonwealth government was confronted with the mounting tension in the Far East, rumors and prognostications of the war in the Pacific seeped through the mind of the average man. . . . In mid-1941, rumors were rife that there were fifth columns in Manila and the suburbs ready to give the potential enemy important data on military and other objectives.[28]

Here, rumors have a kind of irresistible force that escapes conscious mediation. They "seep through the mind" in ways that seem to overflow the limits of both individual calculation and official channels of information.

We get another look at this excessiveness in a popular rumor regarding the surrender of General Jonathan Wainwright. At the collapse of Corregidor, rumor spread in Manila that it was not General Wainwright who surrendered to the Japanese but somebody who looked like him. How, people asked, could *that* man be Wainwright when the photographs of the surrender and the one in which the supposed Wainwright was shown before a microphone of the station KZRH had a rumpled and dirty uniform?

And so many Filipinos kept wondering whether Wainwright did surrender or went to the mountains to wait for the ten-mile long American convoy bringing planes, tanks, guns, bombs and food.[29]

Rumors in this case work by separating seeing from believing. The image of the defeated Wainwright in the official media only provokes stories of another Wainwright eluding his Japanese captors. Through rumors, he is displaced elsewhere, becoming a node in the current of popular wishfulness waiting in anticipation for "bombs and food." For Filipinos, "Wainwright" becomes both person and possibility, a synecdoche, like "MacArthur," for another history parallel to the present moment of occupation.

In his preface, Agoncillo writes of the avidity with which he noted down rumors during the war. He had originally wanted to devote an entire chapter to rumors but "on second thought . . . I gave up the idea and instead chose some spicy rumors and dispersed them in several chapters."[30] The significance Agoncillo places on rumors lies in the fact that they comprised part of "what I saw and felt during those fateful years and for me to depend almost entirely on lifeless documents would be to rob history of its color, nay, of its very life."[31] By calling attention to rumors in his history, Agoncillo seems to be blurring the line that separates actual events from their fictional anticipation and recollection. Rumors, by adding "spice" to "lifeless documents," come across as highly charged moments of public interest. In the context of occupation, they had an inordinate ability to shape the texture of everyday life.

The protracted battle of Bataan, for example, spawned rumors of imminent Japanese defeat before the Christmas of 1942. Such rumors quickly served as the basis for a kind of conspiratorial understanding among Filipinos in Manila. A heightened sense of community emerged:

In crowded streets like Rizal Avenue and Azcarraga, men and women could be seen whispering to one another and smiling meaningfully. There was a strange sparkle in their eyes that meant so much to their harassed lives, that meant, in brief, liberation from the enemy. . . . As they parted with warm handshakes, they would walk on and then pause before another group of men and women. There for several minutes they seemed to be filled with an eternity of unspeakable happiness, they would again exchange news from the front and again bring out the fact that the Japanese were . . . losing in Bataan.[32]

It was as if rumors had the effect of remapping the boundaries between the known and unknown that had been disrupted by the war. As such, they reset the terms for fantasizing about the future. People took delight in such imaginings because they produced feelings of empowerment, though not necessarily of domination, as the following rumor shows:

One fine morning in February 1942, a man spread the rumor that the USAFFE [had] installed electric wires in rivers and ponds [in Bataan] in order to electrocute the thirsty Japanese who would be careless enough to drink from these sources of water. "*Tubig kuru-kuru*"—"Water *boiring*" . . . were the words allegedly said by the Japanese soldiers who were lucky enough to get through such an ordeal.[33]

Here, rumor shades into humor, when the Japanese are duped. The laughter occurs not at the prospect of Japanese submission but at the point of Japanese mispronunciation. The grim relations of power between occupier and occupied are suddenly punctured by a pun rather than a racist retaliation, as the life-and-death quality of war is flattened out momentarily by a phonetic slippage.

In another rumor, hearers and tellers are placed in the position of voyeurs, taking in the spectacle of Japanese desire and disgust:

Rumor flew thick and fast in the middle of 1944 that the Japanese commander in the Philippines . . . had in his private suite shapely Filipina girls doing the striptease for his delectation. His suite always had the air of a Roman Holiday, so it was alleged, so that even the Japanese themselves, including the members of the highest commanders' Staff, were scandalized and eventually protested to the Imperial General Headquarters the behavior of the fun-loving general. It was this, so rumor ran, that was responsible for the general's relief.[34]

Through such stories, one could imaginatively penetrate the circles of power of the New Regime. The lurid detailing of the Japanese general's private suite allows one to take on multiple positions, identifying alternately with the spectating general, his Japanese superiors disturbed by such spectacles, and the Filipina stripteasers, compelled to perform and thus watch themselves being watched by the Japanese. That the story trails off with the dismissal of the general signals a momentary victory of sorts without, as in the "Water *boiring*" incident, the subordination of the Japanese to the Filipinos. By imaging an end to the command of the "fun-loving general," the rumor displaces rather than reverses the hierarchy between colonizer and colonized.

Rumors about empowerment, however, circulated alongside their opposites: rumors about death and disaster. "People whispered about executions by the Japanese kempetais," about decapitations and "Japanese bestiality," especially with regard to the raping of women.[35] Stories about violence and death were ways of anticipating the sudden appearance of the Japanese soldiers who seemed so irrevocably alien. Whereas Filipinos in earlier periods had read into Japan the translatability of nationhood, and therefore the possibilities of the same destiny of sovereignty, Filipinos during the occupation tended to regard the Japanese as sources of random and undecipherable violence.

The most common and oft-remarked exemplification of this violence was the Japanese practice of slapping people in public. Filipinos resented being slapped, for they saw in it a kind of unwarranted "speech" to which they could not respond but only suffer in shame (*hiya*). It is not surprising, then, that rumors about the meaning of slapping arose; and even more widespread were rumors about other responses to slapping. For instance, there existed rumors that President Jose P. Laurel had been slapped by a Japanese officer during a state banquet and that Laurel retaliated by throwing a dish of ice cream in the officer's face.[36] In this story, slapping is repulsed by slapstick, as the rumor makes hearers and tellers party to a scene of resistance.

Other rumors tended to displace anxieties about Japanese violence and the possibility of death onto stories about the disruption of the most mundane occurrences. Agoncillo relates a popular rumor that due to war shortages, Chinese restaurants had taken to routinely serving dog and cat meat. Even more bizarre and horrifying were rumors that they had also started using dead babies in their food and that the sign of this was the recent absence of burials of babies. Stories abounded of people finding baby parts, especially fingers, mixed in with their noodles.[37]

In the rumors above, an entire chain of substitutions is effected: in place of the Japanese, the Chinese—a foreign yet far more familiar group in Philippine society—become the source of inexplicable deaths; dead babies serve as a metaphor for Filipino victims rendered speechless by the violence of the New Regime; and food furnishes a context for discovering the proliferation of death instead of nourishment. Such stories image the radically unsettling effects of the Japanese occupation, rehearsing in muted and dispersed form the shocks of quotidian conquests and common brutalities. Rumors provided the means for representing— and thereby managing, in however attenuated a fashion—the anxieties attendant on occupation. They became ways for dislocating the dislocations of war.

Unlike collaborationist rhetoric, rumors were not predicated on dissimulation and duplicity. Stories about escaped generals and dead babies did not proceed through the calculated reversal of signs or mechanical reproduction of one set of official discourse by way of another imperial language. Rather, the capacity of rumors to circulate and generate intense interest had to do with their vernacular quality. Not only were they prone to be told in the local language; more important, they assumed a public space of discourse tangential to the ideological mandate of the New Regime as well as the limits of official nationalism.

Such is not to say that rumors furnished the basis for a more radical anticolonial nationalism; only that they suggested different routes toward its potential imaging in some other place at some other time. This is why Agoncillo sought to "enliven" the history of the occupation with rumors of the period. As with photographs and anecdotes of "being Japanese" among nationalists of an earlier era, rumors from the Japanese occupation are the residues of larger historical narratives. Hence, rather than dominating the interpretation of the past, rumors recall what eludes monumentalization: the shared sense of ambiguity and uncertainty that, under colonial rule, reiterated the contingent borders and possible futures of Filipino nationhood.

5 Patronage, Pornography, and Youth
Ideology and Spectatorship during the Early Marcos Years

In the aftermath of the February 1986 revolt that forced Ferdinand and Imelda Marcos out of the Philippines, the government of Corazon Aquino turned the presidential palace, Malacañang, into a museum meant to put the Marcos's legacy of excess on display. A guidebook on the palace describes one instance of that extravagance, in which the doors leading to the grand staircase "depict the Philippine legend of 'Malakas' [Strong] and 'Maganda' [Beautiful], the first Filipino man and woman who emerged from a large bamboo stalk. Mrs. Marcos liked to think of President Marcos and herself in terms of these legendary Primordial Filipinos." Thus did they have portraits hung of themselves as Malakas and Maganda in the palace—seminude and emerging from a forest of bamboo stalks (fig. 33). In 1985, they even went so far as to commission a group of Filipino academics to rewrite the legend in terms that would culminate in the celebration of the Marcos regime.[1]

As Malakas and Maganda, Ferdinand and Imelda imaged themselves not only as the father and mother of an extended Filipino family. They also conceived of their privileged position as allowing them to cross and redraw all boundaries: social, political, and cultural. To the extent that they were able to mythologize the progress of history, the First Couple could posit themselves not simply as an instance, albeit a privileged one, in the circulation of political and economic power; they could also conceive of themselves at the origin of circulation itself in the country.

In this chapter, I trace the genesis of this authoritarian wishfulness as

Fig. 33. Ferdinand Marcos as Malakas

it first emerged during the early period of the Marcos presidency. I am particularly concerned with asking how the Marcoses and their supporters produced and disseminated the couple's tendentious reconstruction of history—both in the sense of what happened and what was "new" and yet to happen—in relation to prevalent ideas about the circulation and display of power in postcolonial Philippine society. Such ideas, I argue, grew out of a crisis in existing notions of patronage within the logic of an expanding capitalist economy. At the same time, new images of female ambition and subjugation emerged in film and politics that would furnish a context for reworking the positions of leader and followers in terms of the relationship between spectacle and spectators, seers and seen. Finally, I ask about the limits and challenges to the Marcos's style of rule, focusing on the rise of the youth movement in the mid-1960s and the ways it momentarily disrupted the reigning logic and logistics of power.

A Man of Destiny, a Woman of Charm   Appropriating the legend of Malakas and Maganda was but one way that the Marcos regime sought to set itself apart from its predecessors. The juxtaposition of images of primordial strength and eternal beauty was symptomatic of a dominant obsession of the Marcoses: the conversion of politics into spectacle. We can begin to see this at work by looking at the ways in which Ferdinand and Imelda's private and public careers were represented prior to 1970 in their respective biographies and the Philippine press.

In the presidential campaigns of 1965 and 1969, Ferdinand Marcos often referred to his wife as his "secret weapon." Imelda's presence was considered important at political rallies all over the country in attracting and holding onto the crowd, who waited for her to sing, which she did after routinely appearing to be coy. Her husband would invariably join her in a duet, much to the delight of the audience.[2]

Both were adept at working their audiences. Ferdinand's rhetorical style distinguished him from other politicians. The mere sound of his voice seemed to command attention. One account describes it as a "rich masculine boom . . . that invests him with power and authority. . . . The deep-toned voice, solemnly and slowly articulating words, where the other [speakers] choose to be just loud and strident, is the voice of authority, no doubt." Because of the immediate distinctiveness of his voice, rather than the specific content of his speech or elements of his oratory, Ferdinand was widely regarded as "one of the best performers among present-day politicos."[3]

For her part, Imelda forged a new style of political campaigning in a largely male-dominated field. She came across as a striking presence: tall and youthful in her formal gowns, generously granting requests for songs. According to writer Carmen Navarro-Pedrosa, "It did not matter whether her audience were urbanites or poor barrio folk: she was an actress putting on a stage appearance. She wore ternos [formal gowns with butterfly sleeves] even for appearance on small, rickety makeshift stages of rough wooden planks covered with nipa palms."[4] Imelda made herself accessible to an audience, but this meant that the crowd at political rallies was placed in the position of spectators waiting to see and hear her. As spectators, they did not have to articulate their interests but only had to be alert for the appearance of something that would show and tell them what they wanted yet till then had not thought of. Like voyeurs, they could thrill to the thought of seeing without having to be seen.

Because Ferdinand and Imelda worked so closely together in getting him elected to office, they could conceive of the public sphere of politics as coextensive with their private lives. Singing together at political rallies, they turned their private lives into public spectacles, staging a stylized version of their intimacy.[5] That intimacy was formalized to a remarkable degree and made over into a staple element of the Marcos myth, particularly in their respective biographies, whether officially commissioned or not. Indeed, the interviews granted by them after their overthrow and exile invariably dwell on the events pertaining to the beginning of their romance with a kind of formulaic wistfulness.[6]

Prior to meeting Imelda in 1954, Ferdinand, then a congressman, is described in his biography as a sexually active bachelor: "The young Representative was immensely popular, especially with the ladies. . . . There were whispers that men introduced their sisters and daughters to him at their own risk, a reputation which caused him trouble." Society pages in Manila daily newspapers referred to him as the "Number One Bachelor."[7] Ferdinand was often romantically linked to women from prominent families, including the daughter of former President Manuel Quezon. However potentially upsetting, Ferdinand's libidinal energy was nonetheless regarded as an indubitable sign of his virility. But this also meant that a woman of special qualities, one specifically destined for him, was needed in order to sublimate his sexuality. "You remember how we used to tell you that the girls you went with were not right for you?" Ferdinand, then thirty-one years old and preparing to run for Congress, is asked by his neighbor, Mrs. Severa Verano. "You remember how we used to ask, 'How would she be as First Lady?' You must be even more careful now when you choose a bride, because a man's wife is very important in politics; she can ruin him. You have a special mark. . . . Don't scar yourself with the wrong woman."[8]

Ferdinand seemed never to have entertained any doubts about Imelda. She had first come to his attention through newspaper photographs in connection with her involvement in a Manila beauty contest. Later, seeing her eating watermelon seeds at the cafeteria of the former Congress building, Ferdinand was seized by desire: "He stood motionless for a moment, an action which did not go unnoticed by canny politicians present, whose eyes miss nothing unusual. Other members of the House drifted in. Marcos asked to be introduced to the fair stranger."[9] He was convinced that she was the "archetypal woman," the "wife that he had been waiting for all his life . . . who in this case appeared to have all in a woman to make [a] matrimonial alliance . . . simply ideal."[10] As Ferdinand would recall, meeting Imelda for the first time "made me feel as I never felt before. [It was as if] I had her in mind many times before, but who she was and where she was, I [didn't] know—now, here she is."[11]

What is striking about the various narratives of the Marcos romance is the way in which they all indicate the presence of others watching the process of the "matrimonial alliance" develop. This includes Ferdinand himself, who initially sees Imelda's photograph in the papers and then is stirred by her unexpected appearance in his midst. It is as if her appearance confirmed what he had in mind all along but could not quite articulate. Similarly, the "canny politicians" present in the cafeteria recognized the scene as "unusual"—something set apart from casual meetings. Throughout Ferdinand's pursuit of Imelda, a third party invariably was present to witness the courtship. The position of this third party, however, was not occupied by the couple's parents, as might be expected in lowland courtship rituals, but rather by other politicians, journalists, or the public. For example, the couple was introduced by another congressman, Jacobo Gonzalez, while Ferdinand's journalist friend, Joe Guevarra, was seemingly at every single moment of the fabled elevenday courtship in Bagiou that led to the couple's marriage. Indeed, Ferdinand's mother never figured in the romance, and Imelda's father was informed of the couple's marriage only after the civil ceremony was performed by a local judge in Trinidad Valley. Just as Ferdinand had first discovered Imelda in the newspapers, Imelda's father, Vicente Orestes Romualdez, first learned of Ferdinand from articles in old magazines that featured him as one of the outstanding congressional members of the year. Parental authority is thus marginalized, or more precisely, subsumed into a larger category that includes the public as it is constituted by newspaper readers. The relationship between Ferdinand and Imelda seemed from its inception to have been a part of their official history. Rather than held back from view, it is exposed for all to see, an integral moment in the unfolding of his future as president and hers as First Lady.

The chronicling of the Marcos romance, like the identification with Malakas and Maganda, was a piece of their larger attempt to manufacture their pasts. The biographies of Imelda and Ferdinand rework their respective pasts to make it appear as if they were always meant to be the First Couple. Ferdinand's commissioned biography, for instance, opens with the sentence, "Ferdinand Edralin Marcos was in such a hurry to be born that his father, who was only eighteen years old himself, had to act as his mid-wife."[12] Having dispensed with the burden of paternal influence altogether, the narrative quickly focuses on the son's life. Its portrayal of Ferdinand's past is relentlessly and monotonously one-dimensional. His destiny is never in doubt. Every detail of his life—from schoolboy to law student, from guerrilla fighter to congressman, from lover to father—is seen from a single vantage point: his future as president of the Philippines. It is as if everything in his life was meant to happen. Accused of murdering his father's political rival in 1939, Marcos turns the trial into an opportunity to gain national attention. He defends himself while studying for the bar exam—which he inevitably passes with honors.[13] "Ever since his escape from the youthful murder conviction, the Ilokanos had said . . . that this favorite son would one day be president," his biography claims.[14] Even minor incidents are seen as auguries of greatness. As a young boy, Marcos, punished by his father for some mischief, is made to work in the mines. There, he learns how to use dynamite, a knowledge that becomes useful years later when Ferdinand battles the Japanese during the war.[15]

One gets the sense from reading about Ferdinand's life that biography merely confirms destiny. All outcomes are foretold from the start. Personal and public history converge predictably so that events occur in ways that could not have happened otherwise. The point here is not the accuracy of events or objectivity of the biography. Indeed, many details in the official accounts have been shown to be spurious, particularly the stories of Marcos's war record.[16] Marcos's biography is yet another instance of his characteristic tendency to revise the past in the interest of projecting a spectacle of personal prowess. His notion of destiny, which

I take to mean a kind of transhistorical and thus natural right to rule, is made to function as the unassailable context determining not only his past but that of other Filipinos as well.

In contrast to accounts of Ferdinand's life, Imelda's biographies stress the element of luck and uncertainty in her climb to power. While his past is always and everywhere made to bear the marks of an inescapable future, hers seems to have left the future to chance. It is well known that Imelda's family, the Romualdezes of Leyte, was part of a class of landed elite whose privileges were largely sustained by the U.S. colonial machinery. Imelda's uncles rose to prominence in local and national politics after World War II. Her father, however, was weak and feckless in the care of his family, and for this reason, Imelda's childhood was spent in relative poverty. Educated in Leyte, she moved in with her rich uncle in Manila, working first as a music store clerk and later in the public relations department of the Central Bank of the Philippines. She initially came to the public's attention after being chosen Miss Manila in 1953 and appearing on the cover of a weekly newsmagazine. Her life was marked by a series of such transitions: from relative wealth to relative poverty, from countryside to city, from clerical obscurity to cover-girl prominence. Until she met Ferdinand, her involvements with other men seemed to have had no certain trajectory, least of all toward marriage. One reads of Imelda's past and gets a sense of how things could have been different.

The possibility of that difference is nevertheless figured by her biographers as the operation of fate. Carmen Navarro-Pedrosa is explicit: "Imelda Romualdez Marcos more than anything else is a child of fate. Her life... is a Cinderella story... for her fairy godmother visited her on the evening of April 6, 1954, and with the magic wand, brought her into the life of Ferdinand E. Marcos."[17] She then quickly comes under his tutelage and works as his "secret weapon" to deliver the votes. Imelda becomes "The Other Marcos, [sic] beautiful, tender and appealing."[18] "It was she who filled that gap—the need to make her husband more popular—because she was not just a woman but a special kind of woman whose natural charms were lethal," contends Navarro-Pedrosa.[19]

Imelda's potency is linked to her difference from Ferdinand. Whereas his claims are couched in the idiom of an irresistible destiny, her power consists of projecting certain kinds of "natural charms." What did these charms consist of? As the "Other" Marcos, Imelda is also the other of Ferdinand. He takes over the direction of her life in the same way that she is said to "fill a gap" in his. Thus, Imelda provides Ferdinand with an occasion to display his mastery. He turns her into an avid campaigner and a good student of politics by teaching her to defer to his authority. "She adopted his ways.... She also took care not to make her husband's mind up for him. 'Even if he asked me,' she once said, 'I would never dare make a decision for him.'"[20] Through Ferdinand, Imelda discovers politics as a way of articulating her ambitions in ways that would not have been otherwise possible. In doing so, she came to see her power as the result of submitting to the destiny of her husband.

Still, mere submission to male ambition does not account for the potency of her charms. Charm suggests the ability to fascinate and compel the attention of others as if by magic. Its Latin root, *carm* (song or magical formula), points to the necessarily performative, even theatrical nature of that which is charming. Because of its association with ritual magic, the power to charm can be understood as the ability to present oneself as both the source and object of desire. As various accounts indicate, Imelda's body and voice were compelling. They forced people to watch and listen to her in rapt expectation. A woman journalist and admirer of the Marcoses describes the workings of Imelda's "lethal charms" during a political rally in 1965:

Led to the microphone, she touches it, and prepares to sing her winning repertoire: *Dahil sa Iyo, Waray, Dungdunguen can to la unay*. She has lost weight considerably, her bones show through her torso. It is a slight and vulnerable back that rises above the scoop of her neckline. But this is not the girl from Olot anymore, not this woman tonight; her face is drawn, fatigue sits on those shoulders, but she looks triumphantly at the scene. From the convention floor at the Manila Hotel nine months ago, to this stage tonight, stretch innumerable miles and countless lessons, and she has learned each one very well.... She knows the excitement of power. The crowd waits, like a trapped and unresisting prey, for Imelda to begin using that power; this is the secret they share, the crowd and Imelda, Imelda and the crowd. She will smile and flick those wrists and sing her little songs.... She bends and barely sways, beating time glancing at the guitar and then lifts her face to point with her chin at the night bright with neon lights and a moon—the old charisma, with its look of suffering, potent tonight as never before, the brilliance of beauty commingling with the brilliance of pain, the haunted, agonized, tragic look encircling the plaza and holding her audience in thrall.[21]

This passage recalls the difference between Imelda and Ferdinand of which I spoke earlier. The juxtaposition of contrasting qualities—"fatigue" and "triumph," naivete and cunning—in the person of Imelda evokes the transitions she has had to negotiate. Power excites her precisely because she did not always expect to possess it. In this case, her power comes less from her husband's destiny than from her ability to turn herself into an image recalling a sense of shared "suffering" among those who watch her. The crowd willingly submits itself to her charms like an "unresisting prey." Thus do audience members eagerly assume the position of spectators, sharing in the fantasy of loss that Imelda plays out. The secret she shares with them resides in her ability to stir a desire to see without being seen, to hear without being heard.

Imelda's charms were lethal to the extent that they were provoked by and fed the wish for a kind of depoliticized community, one that would make the hierarchy between the leaders and followers seem thoroughly benign. Through a series of stylized gestures and a standard repertoire of love songs in the vernacular, she created an atmosphere of generalized melancholia. Yet, this aura of longing was but one of the effects that her charms were calculated to generate. Other sensations doubtlessly grew out of seeing her, for her charms compelled others to stop thinking and start looking. Ferdinand himself is said to have fallen prey to her allure. When he saw her for the first time in the flesh, he stood "motionless." A journalist wrote that "Imelda was such a simple girl then and she had a way of making even the eloquent Congressman tongue-tied."[22] During the early stages of Marcos's first run for the presidency in 1965, "the oft-heard remark about the prospect of a Marcos victory was 'Well, whatever kind of president he will make it is certain that if he wins, we will have the most beautiful and the youngest First Lady.' "[23] During the first inauguration of Marcos, journalists reiterated this sentiment. The crowd, they wrote, seemed less concerned with the message of the speeches than the appearance of Imelda,

as if to say, "If there is anything the incoming administration can boast of it is having the fairest and youngest First Lady." "Just to see, just to see!" they screamed in mob fashion. It was very little they asked. . . . Most people who had gone to the Luneta grandstand that morning were merely there to see the celebrated beauty of the new First Lady of the land. . . . Even as they heard the President declare "This nation can be great again," a marvelous slogan calculated to impress the public mind, they preferred the soft smile of the Lady by his side.[24]

News reports made it seem as if the people viewed political gatherings as no more than an occasion for them to constitute themselves as an audience in a spectacle whose central figure was the First Lady.

It is, however, important to note that her visibility was thought to stand in relation to his destiny. The mythology of the Marcos romance underlined not only the lethal charms of Imelda but also Ferdinand's conquest of those charms. He married her, taught her, drew her into his future, and in doing so, turned her into his secret weapon. Rather than disrupt his ambition, her charms worked as an instrument for its realization. Imelda's difference became useful in depoliticizing the encounter between the candidate and crowd. Converted into voyeurs, the people took in her feminine charms, but at the price of acknowledging its masculine owner.

On one level, then, narratives of the Marcos romance are about the domestication and deployment of sexual and historical differences in the realization of one man's ambition. Stories of Ferdinand's eleven-day "coup-courtship" of Imelda reformulated her difference as an asset that redounded to his credit. Her charms made up the feminine surplus that she brought into their marriage alliance and that was put into circulation during political campaigns and throughout Marcos's tenure as president. This surplus was constituted, as we have seen, by the power to elicit interest, setting the stage for the exchange between her husband and the public. Imelda's striking presence thus allowed power to circulate between Ferdinand and the crowd. While she reduced the people to spectators, he overwhelmed them with slogans and speeches with his booming voice. They looked at her while he spoke to them. To employ Imelda, the "archetypal woman," is to control the conditions of possibility for the circulation of authority, just as in the courtship stories such employment also requires a representation of the past from the perspective of a single, totalizing male ego. Imelda makes visible the link between history and contingency. By domesticating her, Ferdinand could claim to establish symbolic dominance over both.

Film and Female Ambition Imelda Marcos's deference to her husband's ambitions was, in some ways, entirely traditional and expected. Previous First Ladies had done no less. Beginning with Aurora Quezon, First Ladies involved themselves in such ostensibly apolitical activities as the Red Cross, the Catholic Women's League, and various charities and civic projects. Others, like Esperanza Osmeña and Evangelina Macapagal, played active roles in redecorating the palace and beautifying national parks. Living largely in the shadows of their husbands, they seemed to have accepted their place without any qualms. As one writer put it, "All were out to be real helpmates to their husbands and each did it loyally and in the context of what their husbands set out to accomplish."[25]

Imelda's spectacular difference lay in the degree of attention that she attracted and cultivated. Her cultural projects, such as they were, refashioned the landscape of metropolitan Manila. Her active participation in her husband's campaigns, her role in projecting an international image for the Philippines, the innumerable rumors of her extravagance, and her own political ambitions: all these placed her constantly in the public eye. Yet, by the late 1960s and early 1970s, that public eye had become accustomed to the spectacle of women acting out their ambitions. The rise of a new kind of First Lady coincided with the emergence of a new image of woman: the *bomba* star. Bomba, literally meaning bomb, was a popular way throughout the 1960s of characterizing impassioned political rhetoric. It was also a synecdoche for scandalous charges and countercharges of graft and corruption made by politicians in Congress or during political campaigns. As Philippine newspapers and magazines of this period make clear, for a politician to "hurl" or "explode" a bomba was to reveal something to the public about another politician that the latter would have preferred to keep secret. By exploding a bomba, one exposed what was once inaccessible to the public eye, thereby gaining for oneself a new visibility. The *bombero* or *bombera* is he or she who is able to stir public interest at the expense of his or her rival. That interest was directed as much to the nature of the other's crime as it was to the fact that it had come to light. What was once hidden is now exposed for everyone to see and hear.

Bomba thus referred to the sudden yet motivated emergence of scandal, that is, of that which is new by virtue of being out of place. In this way, it allowed for the imaging of scandal as spectacle not only in the domain of national politics but in other contexts as well. For example, bomba also came to refer to the wave of soft- and hard-core pornography in print media and movies that swept the Philippines during this period. The latter came with provocative titles such as *Uhaw (Thirsty)*, *Hayok (Hungry)*, *Saging ni Pacing (Pacing's Banana)*, and the like. In addition, bomba referred to the specific scenes in movies when women exposed their bodies to the camera for the audience to see as well as to lurid scenes of simulated or actual sexual intercourse. Such scenes were often tenuously related to the narrative of the film, and at times, were arbitrarily inserted (*singit*) or added on (as a bonus) in the middle or at the end of the movie.

Women who appeared in these movies achieved a degree of notoriety, guaranteeing further exposure on magazine covers, television talk shows, and in gossip columns. Indeed, most magazines in the Philippines, from the gossip sheets to the respectable weeklies, such as the *Philippine Free Press* and *Weekly Graphic*, often featured bomba stars on their covers to increase sales. Their photographs provoked others to look in expectation. One magazine that featured a bomba star on its cover printed the following caption under her photograph: "Besides the ability to peel off her clothes in a provocative manner, what other attributes should a bomba star possess? Annabelle Rama, our cover girl for this issue, and the rest of her kind come up with very startling and exciting revelations."[26]

These "revelations" consisted of a kind of double exposure: that of the woman revealing her body to the camera and that of a largely male audience viewing scenes removed from everyday life. We can think of the audience in a bomba movie, in fact in any film, as being drawn to identify in the first place with the camera. As Walter Benjamin has remarked, part of the fascination of watching films involves having one's gaze joined to the mechanical facility of the cinematic apparatus. The camera provides us with a prosthesis for seeing, extending, and mobilizing our eyes. In this way, we come to see things that would otherwise be unobserved or inaccessible in various places and times where our bodies need not be present. Abstracting our sight from our physical circumstances, the camera comes to supplement our eyes in the double sense of standing in for and replacing them.[27] Herein lies one of the peculiar pleasures of watching movies: we seem capable of seeing everything on the screen without those on the screen seeing us.

Some of the pleasures of identifying with the camera, for example, come across in the following remarks of a movie reporter describing the bomba sequence in the film *Igorota:* "In the opening scene, a group of Ifugao [sic] maidens are shown bathing *au naturel* in a stream and every now and then, the camera zooms in on bosoms and behinds for intimate close-ups."[28] Watching this scene, audiences are able to see what is usually hidden in ways both unexpected and, as the writer's insertion of a foreign term for nudity implies, natural in an unnatural sort of way. Zooming in and out, the camera fragments and recomposes the images of women's bodies on the screen even as it extends and expands the viewer's capacities to apprehend them. Hence do bomba movies sustain the interests of a predominantly male audience by mechanically reproducing the "explosion" of female bodies on the screen.

Bomba movies were tremendous commercial successes. They often played to capacity crowds in Manila and the provincial cities. The Board of Censors occasionally banned such movies or cut some of their more lurid scenes. The effect of such government action, however, was to further incite people to see these movies, and the excised versions were either amended with bonus scenes or restored in prints that circulated in the provinces. As one movie producer put it, "Bomba is bombshell at the box office. Working on the proposition that sex almost always sells, local movies have more and more caught on to all the world's sin-erama."[29]

But bomba movies sold images of women, not the women themselves. What viewers saw on the screen and read about in magazines were understood to be the simulation, not the actual occurrence, of violence and sex. For instance, it was common for bomba films to feature the rape of a woman. "The rape scene . . . became more and more realistic with the entry of such cuddly pussycats as Bessie Barredo, Gina Laforteza, and Menchu Morelli."[30] The men who portrayed the rapists were usually typecast as *kontrabidas* (villains) or "bomba specialists" who were expected to give in to their urges. Here, the realism of rape had to do with the way in which it led to the fulfillment of an expectation. Indeed, audiences were prone to yell *harang* (foul, cheat) at the screen when bomba scenes that were promised never emerged. Hence, the scandal surrounding the exposure of women was neutralized. More precisely, bomba movies generated both scandal and its containment insofar as what appeared on the screen were mechanically reproducible images existing in a space and time irreducibly separate from that of the viewers. Equally significant was the fact that they also seemed to be the product of the intentions of others. We get a sense of this in other more benign but no less tendentious versions of the "revelations" of women in bomba movies. "The sexpots in local movies showed appetizing glimpses of their superstructures in swimming pool scenes where they donned itsy-bitsy, teeny-weeny bikinis which often—oops—got detached in the water, or in the bathroom scenes where their only covering was a curtain of water."[31]

Movies were invested here with the capacity to motivate accident and intend surprise. Shock was aestheticized as the product of a prior set of calculations. Perhaps this was the reason bomba movies could engage in the most graphic violence against women and yet project them as "reasonable" people seeking to realize their ambitions apart from their roles as victims. For example, the trajectory of one bomba star's career was described as follows:

"It was only of late that I've consented to appear in bomba scenes," Mila del Rosario, 23, admits. "In my first twelve pictures, I never thought I could be so daring."

Mila started exploding in *Pussycat Strikes Again* when Bino Garcia, one of moviedom's most hated villains, undressed and attacked her in one scene, kissing her torridly and pawing her. In *The Gunman*, she had a torrid love scene in bed with Van de Leon. In *Ligaw na Sawimpalad* [Wayward Unfortunate], she was one of several girls victimized in a brothel. She had another love scene with Henry Duval in *Vice Squad*. "I only consent to appear in a bomba scene if such a scene is extremely necessary to the plot and story. After all, European and Hollywood pictures have infinitely more salacious scenes."

Before she entered the movies, Mila was an art model. She insists that all the bombas she explodes are done in good taste and with finesse.[32]

Here, the bomba star is given a voice with which to speak rather than simply a body with which to act. She is depicted not as a passive victim of male intentions but as one who consents to and actively participates in the making of bomba scenes. She comes across as reasonable: open to negotiation and able to express her opinions. It is as if her complicity in the explosion of her own body makes those scenes the product of a prior contract between the star, director, producer, and consumers of the films, a contract that also implicates the writers and readers of magazine articles about them. Framed in this way, the explosiveness and exploitativeness of bomba movies could be legitimized as part of a network of market transactions that include Europe and America. As such, viewing bombas in cinemas or reading about them in magazines was conventionalized and made part of a larger ethic of consumption correlated with female ambition. The scandal of male violence against women is reformulated in terms of the "bold" and "courageous" yet "tasteful" acts of women in exposing their bodies. In bomba movies, women acted out their ambitions within sight of the public gaze. Such movies, then, established a new context for articulating female desire as a function not only of male desire but also of the interests of an anonymous audience of movie viewers and magazine readers.[33]

Imelda Marcos, in some ways, personified the notion of female ambition that the bomba movies seemed to project. She saw her own desire not simply as a function of her husband's but also a matter for public display. As one biography observes, "She dressed to please Ferdinand . . . she lived she said to see him look at her. 'I want to stand out in his eyes.'"[34] Just as his destiny validated her fate, it is through her husband's eyes that her existence takes on a form for everyone to see. "Politics was his life and Marcos was hers—since she lived for Marcos, she would live for what Marcos lived. . . . Her days rose and fell by the Marcos sun," this same biography continues. Driven by his destiny, she finds a way of expressing her ambition by responding to his desire "to revive national pride and curb national weakness." So while he governed, "she would inspire" and "sow beauty where she could. . . . 'Culture and art and a taste for the beautiful must lead to goodness,' she said."[35]

This peculiar mix of ambition and deference on Imelda's part recalls the coupling of boldness and vulnerability among bomba stars. The notion of bomba could furnish a means of conceptualizing what was new and potentially unsettling about the First Lady. It could do so, to some degree, because of the workings of mass circulation media, which brought together into sharp juxtaposition formerly disparate objects, people, and events. For example, it was not uncommon for magazines to feature bomba stars on their cover with stories and photographs of Imelda Marcos on the inside one week, then to reverse this order of appearance the next. Since the problematic position of the First Lady could thereby be imagined in conjunction with the "explosive" appearance of women in the movies, the ambivalent representations of Imelda came to share in the conditions of reception of bomba films. Visualized beyond the public stage of electoral politics, her images, like those of bomba stars, created an audience that came to expect the political style of Ferdinand. For just as she appeared to move back and forth between traditional roles and unexpected prominence and accessibility, her husband sought to project a modern, postcolonial nationalist appeal that at the same time capitalized on an older ethos of clientage and factionalism.

What had allowed for this reconfiguration of sexual with political imagery in ways that anticipated and so constructed the terms of the Marcos's popular reception in the 1960s? To answer this question, it is necessary to consider the larger historical context within which power was spectacularized: the breakdown of traditional patron-client ties in the face of an expanding capitalist market that characterized the dynamics of power in colonial and post–World War II Philippine politics.

The Simulation of Patronage Imelda's numerous attempts to spread beauty and culture were of a piece with Ferdinand's nationalist pretensions of "making this nation great again." As recent studies have shown, Marcos succeeded in monopolizing the resources of the country by joining a modernizing nationalist pose to a parochial, factionalist-oriented politics. As with previous presidents, Marcos turned the state into an instrument for asserting his factional hegemony over the country's competing elites. Yet he also scrupulously translated factionalist practices into the modernizing vocabulary of nation building. This language left its most visible marks on the country's landscape by way of new schoolhouses, extensive roads, and expansive bridges, more of which were built under Marcos than any other previous president thanks largely to his ability to secure foreign loans.[36]

Imelda's cultural projects were logical extensions of Ferdinand's attempts to leave traces of his power everywhere. He sought to instrumentalize nationalism by embarking on development projects that also served as occasions for the expansion of patronage and pork barrel. He appointed technocrats to his cabinet, thereby gaining control of a new elite with no prior base of influence. She sought to complement these moves by turning state power into a series of spectacles, such as cultural centers, film festivals, historically themed parks, five-star hotels, and glitzy international conferences. Mounted with great fanfare and publicity, these spectacles seemed to be everywhere even as their source was infinitely distant from those who viewed them. These spectacles cohered less around egalitarian notions of nationhood than the fact that they all originated from her and reflected her initiatives, which in turn had been sanctioned explicitly by the president. Whether on the campaign trail for Ferdinand or in her capacity as First Lady, Imelda was in a unique position to rework Philippine culture into the sum of the traces left by the regime's patronage. National culture was construed as so many gifts from above bestowed on those below.[37]

Imelda's role in imaging culture as state munificence cannot be understood apart from the vicissitudes of a notion of patronage that pervades the history of Philippine political practice, a notion that assumes that power is synonymous with the ability to provide for all the discrete and multifaceted needs of *specific* others. Patronage implies not simply the possession of resources but, more significantly, the means with which to stimulate the desire for and circulation of such resources. In a political context ruled by a factional rather than class-based opposition, patronage becomes the most important means for projecting power. Resting on the assumption that the conservation of a benign hierarchy (usually measured along generational lines) guarantees the flow of benefits from above to those below, it also naturalizes the claims of those above over the labor and resources of those below. Patronage mystifies inequality to the point of making it seem both inescapable and morally desirable. In this way, it recasts power in familiar and familial terms: one is fated to be caught in a web of inequalities the way one is fated to be part of a family. The display of patronage, as such, is meant to drain the social hierarchy of its potential for conflict. Despite the fact that historically conflicts have erupted between patrons and clients, the ideology of patronage regards conflict ideally as that which occurs only among factions (rival patrons and their respective clients, as in elections when only those with sufficient means may aspire to have purchase over others), and not between patrons and clients.[38]

Given the neocolonial character of the state and society, the ideology of patronage (with its roots in the Spanish and U.S. colonial regimes) determined to a large extent the shape of postwar political discourse in the Philippines. The economic and social bases for realizing traditional patron-client ties as they had been conceived in the prewar era, however, had been eroding steadily since the 1930s. As Benedict Kerkvliet has so brilliantly shown, the intensified penetration of capitalist modes of production into the countryside around Manila, a long process that had its roots in the late eighteenth century, resulted in intensifying the trends toward wage labor, mechanization, and absentee landlordism on the eve of World War II. Such developments led to the subversion of the economic and social bases of patronage, while at the same time encouraging peasants to frame their demands ever more forcefully in terms of traditional reciprocal indebtedness. In the face of a shifting political economy, they demanded a return to the moral economy of patronage.

As we saw in chapter 4, the Japanese occupation had the effect of momentarily dislodging Filipino elites from their agricultural base of power, creating an opening for more militant resistance from peasant armies. The return of elite collaborators to political and economic power at the end of the war, coupled with the harassment and repression of peasant and workers' groups, pushed the newly independent nation to the edge of civil war in the form of the Huk Rebellion from the late 1940s through the mid-1950s. Though mostly concentrated in Central Luzon, the Huk rebellion was a flashpoint both in the geopolitics of the cold war and the reconstruction of the Filipino oligarchy's hold on power. With massive U.S. aid, and under the leadership of CIA-supported President Magsaysay, the rebellion was brutally quashed. As Kerkvliet argues, the rebellion and its suppression did nothing to restore real or imagined notions of a precapitalist mode of personal relationships. Rather, the very same impersonal contracts and money-based relations among peasants, landlords, and their local agents that had fueled unrest in the first place were further institutionalized. Under the sponsorship of the Philippine state, which in turn was heavily dependent on the military and financial support of the United States, the material and moral matrices of traditional notions of patronage rapidly unraveled.[39]

These developments in the Philippines, of which Central Luzon and the Manila areas are the most notable examples, led to the consolidation of a capitalist economy by the mid-1960s. Nonetheless, there persisted a lag between a capitalist economy and national political culture. For the spread of the former did not, as one might expect, lead to the establishment of ideas and practices of class-based politics. With the defeat of the Huk rebellion, the specter of class conflict seemed to have been exorcised, at least for the time being. Instead, a generalized longing for traditional practices of patronage, never far from the surface even in the most militarized phases of the Huk rebellion, resurged. Such sentiments, however, were remarkably contradictory. The longing for hierarchy simultaneously relied on the circulation of money to forge and sustain what we might think of as instant patron-client ties. National and local elections under the newly independent republic became the privileged venues for playing out this desire for patronage, as vertical alliances reminiscent of traditional patron-client ties were contracted, consolidated, and redrawn.[40]

Yet such ties were deeply problematic insofar as they tended to be determined less by the exchange of moral obligations than the circulation of money. Money had the effect of turning patronage into a commodity. Investing the ideal of patronage with money made it possible for a candidate running for national office to accumulate a clientage beyond any specific locality over a drastically shortened period of time. Moreover, these clients remained largely anonymous to the candidate. The exchange of money for votes, a practice almost universally commented on by those who have written about postwar Philippine politics, turned elections into markets.[41] Elections were seen neither in the liberal-democratic sense of expressing one's will on matters of political representation nor as rituals for the reiteration of reciprocal indebtedness between leaders and led. Instead, in a society increasingly governed by commodity exchange, elections became moments for the simulation of patronage. The extremely common practice of buying votes recreated the sense and sensation of patronage as wealthy men (and a few women) distributed money through their agents, thereby giving the impression of being in control of circulation. Yet the treatment of votes, like patronage, as commodities undercut the moral and ethical bases of traditional patron-client ties as well. While money made it possible to have instant access to a mass of anonymous clients, it also enabled such clients to switch patrons readily in order to evade their influence. In short, money attenuated the moral force of reciprocity by trading the desire for patronage with its calculated retailing.

Philippine politics in the 1960s was caught up in the profound contradictions between the ideology of patronage and the material and social conditions set forth by capitalism, between an apparently generalized wish for authority and hierarchy stabilized by traditional idioms of reciprocity, and a national state whose links with various localities were mediated by money. It was precisely at this historical juncture that the Marcoses emerged onto the national scene. Their success was a function of their ability to seize on, rather than resolve, the central contradictions of postwar Philippine politics. Ferdinand and Imelda played on them, seeking to utilize money and what it could buy in order to simulate patronage and the imaging of benevolent power (inexhaustible strength and eternal beauty) at the top of the national hierarchy. Herein lay one source of their early popularity: they seemed to be able to furnish a way of conceiving the "new" and alienating changes these contradictions implied in the familiar and familial terms of patronage.

The Marcoses deployed a varied repertoire ranging from the narrative of virility and romance to spectacles of nationalist vigor and feminine allure, appearing to evoke change while simultaneously eschewing the imperatives of social reform. They seized on the crisis of authority generated by the traumatic changes in colonial regimes and postcolonial upheavals; yet, they sought to project the aura of patronage precisely by resorting to the very means that guaranteed its disintegration, thereby calling forth its repeated simulation. Converted into grand public gestures and discrete forms of commodities, patronage could in this way blur the difference between popular and mass culture, between the ambitions of one couple and the history of the entire nation. Thus did the projection of state power in the early Marcos years also seek to dictate the ideological conditions under which the Marcoses were to be received.

Imelda's biographies give an idea of how the couple simulated patronage. They depict her as the consummate patroness of the Philippines. As she tells one of her biographers, "People come to you for help. They want jobs . . . or roads or bridges. They think you're some kind of miracle worker and because of their faith, you try to do your best." In this regard, she also saw herself as a privileged mediator between the rich and poor. Rather than reverse or abolish the difference between the two, she sought to drain it of its tension, "officiating at the marriage of public welfare and private wealth." Her generosity is characterized as excessive. Constantly besieged by callers of all sorts, from mayors to fashion models, ambassadors to barrio folks, she comes across as a dynamo on the move:

Day after day, at the stroke of 9 a.m., undeterred by lack of sleep, fainting spells, miscarriages, low blood pressure, kidney trouble, bad teeth, the brutal barrage of newspapers, and the ire of Benigno Aquino, she sits upright in a French sofa, receiving callers. Forty callers on lean days; fifty on the average; a hundred when they come in delegations. . . .

She eats a late lunch. "I take no siesta," she says. In the afternoons, before she goes out to "cut a ribbon, maybe," inaugurating a hospital pavilion, attend the opening of a hotel, or launch a tanker, a book, or a painter, she has two or three free hours. "I sit down and am quiet." No one disturbs her while she runs mentally through a list, checking and cross-checking what she could have done and failed to do.[42]

Virtually impervious to adversity, Imelda is seen as the symbolic origin of all activity, from ribbon cuttings to book launchings. Nothing escapes her, for she keeps a running account of things that had been and are yet to be accomplished. We get the fantasy of a panoptic consciousness wedded to a body that, like money, is in constant circulation. This image of inexhaustible patronage stirred a great deal of interest.

Then before I go to sleep, I have to go through the correspondence I received during the day . . . usually 2,000 letters a day. This one asking for a job, that one telling about a child that had to be hospitalized, this one asking for a picture, that one for an autograph. It takes me one or two hours just signing letters: they all want your real signature.[43]

Which is to say: "They all want a part of me. They cannot help but think of me." They ask not only for favors but the marks of her person as well: her photograph and signature. The circulation of her patronage and, by extension, that of her husband was conjoined to the dissemination of their images.

Imelda was acutely conscious of the link between patronage and its imaging. For instance, it was common for palace visitors to be presented with souvenirs, including "pictures, small bottles of perfume, bound copies of a favorite Marcos speech. Who before her ever took the trouble and the thought to make each palace visit [into] An Occasion? [sic]"[44] In a country that has no precolonial tradition of royalty, the Marcoses were noted for giving guests the royal treatment. By converting such moments into occasions for the display of patronage, the giving of souvenirs was not only meant to commemorate the mere fact of having been in the presence of the Marcoses but also provided the means for memorializing the distance separating the benefactor from his or her client long after the visit had occurred. The status of such objects as souvenirs lay precisely in their ability to convey the aura of their source to the extent that they forged a relationship of indebtedness between the giver and receiver. In doing so, such objects ensured that the latter continued to keep the former in mind. Souvenirs as tokens of patronage prompted reciprocation and acknowledgment of the power of their source.

As fetish objects, however, images of patronage also invoked their character as commodities, especially when they appeared in mass-circulation newspapers and magazines. Mechanically reproduced images of patronage simultaneously denied and confirmed the workings of money at the basis of national politics. A focal point of this tension was the figure of Imelda herself. As suggested earlier, she shared a kind of spectacular visibility with bomba stars, whose public display was thought to be desirable as much as it was disempowering. The following example might illustrate Imelda's "explosiveness"—in a sense, the real meaning of her lethal charms—which recalls patronage by evoking its breakdown *and* restoration. Shortly after the reelection of Marcos in late 1969, the *Philippine Free Press* published photographs of three oil portraits of Imelda.[45] These paintings were given to Imelda by the artists themselves and hung in the palace along with her other portraits, "above stairwells and along corridor walls where they startled."[46] An anonymously written commentary in English accompanies the photographic reproductions and helps us anchor our reading of these portraits. Done by academically trained painters, the portraits were reproduced in an influential weekly usually purchased by educated readers inside and outside of Manila. Hence, both the paintings and the com-

Fig. 34. Imelda Marcos by Claudio Bravo

mentary on them are not necessarily representative of the mass response to the Marcoses. Notwithstanding, it is possible to see them as symptomatic of precisely the kind of reception that the Marcoses would have wanted to generate across class divides. They provide us, then, with a small but no less instructive moment in the history of the Marcoses' attempt to encourage and contain the complicity of those whose cultural and social influence was considerable.

The commentary explains that the artists were trying to express the "real" Imelda in a way that would adequately sum up her many roles as a "figure of state, a politician, a housewife, and mother, a fashion pacesetter, a civic worker, a connoisseur of good living, a patroness of the arts."[47] Both the artists and commentator were seeking to come to terms with what seemed to be a new dimension of Imelda: she exceeded the traditional categories associated with being a woman and First Lady. Imelda provoked attention because, as with bomba stars, she exposed herself in novel situations and made her body available for all to see. But while the bodies of bomba stars bore the signs of the marketplace, Imelda's served both to focus and mystify the history of patronage in the midst of the marketplace.

The first portrait, by Claudio Bravo (fig. 34), shows Imelda gliding past some mysterious landscape. The accompanying commentary is worth quoting at length for its attempt to match the allusiveness of the painting:

The figure moves in a light that never was on sea or land. The details are precise: the parasol tugs at the hand and is tugged by the wind blowing a skirt into rich folds. Yet the landscape is not so much seen as felt: a seaside, early in the morning, on a cool day. And the figure seems not to walk but to float on the stirred air. The expression on the face is remote; this is a woman beyond politics and palaces, a figure from dream or myth. It's the pale ivory color that makes the scene unearthly, as though this were a frieze from some classic ruin. Just beyond the frame will be sirens choiring, the swell of a striped sail, and across the perfumed seas, Troy's burning roof and tower. ("Three Images," 93–94)

The remoteness of the figure, combined with its "pale ivory color," gives this portrait an uncertain quality. One looks at it, feeling that although one can recognize Imelda's features, one cannot quite establish a context

Fig. 35. Imelda by Federico Aguilar Alcuaz

for them. Indeed, just as the figure seems "to float on the stirred air," so the mind that contemplates this painting drifts outside the frame toward thoughts of a distant Greek epic. Because this portrait seems so removed from the world of politics and exists as if in a dream, its precise details cannot but take on a hallucinatory quality: they set the mind in motion, inducing it to think of that which is not there. This painting leads one to perceive not simply the likeness of Imelda but, as with bomba films, the possibility of seeing something that is out of place transformed into an object to be seen. At stake here is the imaging of patronage as something to which one can lay a claim, because it is shaped by one's own gaze. The figure is compelling not only because one feels one can see through and past it but also because one is reminded of the unbridgeable distance that separates one from the source of power that the portrait represents. The viewer is haunted by the absence that the figure makes present.

This sense of being haunted is even more apparent in the second portrait, by Federico Aguilar Alcuaz (fig. 35), where

> the scene is definite enough. Malacañang is in the background; so this must be the park across the river. . . . Nevertheless, it's not the Palace or park, certainly not the city that we feel here. This is provincial verdure, pastoral ground. And the figure in old rose is a Country girl . . . of whom kundiman and balitaw sing. Indeed the melancholy tone of our folk music is in her wistful face. She has been sniffing at the white flower in her hand and it has stirred a memory. She herself stirs memories in us. . . . Her quiet dignity evokes a nostalgia for childhood's vanished countryside and its lovely simple girl. ("Three Images," 94)

Again, the painting evokes the sense of the familiar sliding into something strange. What looks like the presidential palace and its immediate surroundings is conflated with memories of pastoral grounds, folk music, and childhood's "vanished" places. It thus summons the imaginary scene of patronage untainted by the complexities of the marketplace. Symbolic of this is the figure of the woman in deep reverie. What is curious is that although we are never told about the contents of her thoughts, we are nonetheless invited to reminisce with her. Recalling her childhood, the viewer may also be drawn to look back on another time and place in which women were simple and presumably knew their

Fig. 36. Imelda by Antonio Garcia Llamas

place. In this way, the figure calls forth something no longer present. The nostalgia-inducing effect of this second painting is not very different from the hallucinatory quality of the first: both lead the viewer to think of something absent and to expect its appearance.

A notable contrast with these two portraits of Imelda is the third painting, by Antonio Garcia Llamas (fig. 36). Here, the figure of Imelda is backlighted in such a way as to completely obscure any sense of place. The background exists as mere shadings, serving to highlight the foreground. The figure is erect and so made to seem wholly autonomous, its sovereign presence underlined by the absence of details on the dress and the centering instead of distinctive features on the face. The effect of this composition is to lead one to focus on the figure's gaze:

> A poised modern woman looks us over. It's not we who eye her, we can only respond to her glance. She is definitely of the city and of our day, as lustrous with nervous energy as the powerful cars she rides or the go-go committees she chairs.... The glance we respond to flashes across the muddled cityscape we must unravel to get to where the white-on blue decorum is, the promise of a civilized society. ("Three Images," 94)

In this portrait, we are confronted with a somewhat jarring reversal of the relationship between the subject and object of spectatorship. Unlike the other two, which exist as objects for our gaze, this figure "looks us over," causing us to take notice of her and reflect on the fact that we are doing so. Her glance "flashes across the muddled cityscape," opening up a path toward the "promise of a civilized society." What we see in her seeing is a kind of future to which we feel compelled to respond. It is that future that makes up the condition of possibility of our sight. We experience the painting as the presence of a powerful eye that sees all and, for that reason, can be apprehended only in flashes. Such is the experience of modernity—of a "now" that stretches indefinitely into the future and thus always feels like a promise—that this glance conveys.

Additionally, the power of Imelda's gaze grows out of an association with the nervous energy of cars and "go-go committees" that can operate at all times of the day and night. This is how we can account for what initially seems like a discrepancy between what we see of this gaze and what the commentator is led to see. Although Imelda does not, in fact, look directly at the viewer but off to the side, the commentator claims that she looks at us. It is as if our position as viewers has been split into two: we are at once in front of the portrait, yet also at the margins of the frame—spectators to the extent that we have been incorporated into a prior and largely invisible spectacle. Just as the audience in bomba movies comes to sense its subjection to the staging of revelations intended by others, the viewer of the painting is made to realize his or her identity as one who sees to be the result of having been seen by someone else.

When taken together with the couple's biographies, these paintings suggest some of the ways in which assumptions about patronage can work to aestheticize and so dehistoricize politics. Since the relationship between ruler and ruled is converted into fantasies about seeing and being seen, the viewer then imagines him or herself as alternately the subject and object of the intentions of others. Imelda's privileged visibility resulted from her use of Ferdinand's name in carrying out projects meant to enhance their positions as national patrons concerned with the needs of the country. Her visibility, however, corresponded to a pervasive invisibility, as indicated by the third portrait. Constructing her role as patroness meant that she, like money, had to be in constant circulation. Her photographs in newspapers confirmed her ability to appear to be everywhere. Thus were they constructed as traces of a presence whose gaze, except for flashes, remained essentially hidden from our sight. This is perhaps why Ferdinand referred to Imelda over and over again as his secret weapon. Given the foregoing discussion, we might take this to mean that she served as his favored bomba, exploding her lethal charms for an audience grown habituated as much to the staging of scandal as the commodification of politics. In both politics and the movies, women were made to represent instances of larger intentions at work, galvanizing the interests of people while demarcating their position as mere viewers of spectacles.[48]

Youth and the Destruction of Spectacle   The politics of bomba and the aestheticization of patronage that it implied did not, however, remain unchallenged. Indeed, shortly after Marcos's reelection in 1969 in what was then considered by most Filipinos as the most corrupt and violent election of the postwar period, Marcos's rule came under increasing criticism. As one might expect, Imelda became a ready target. Rival elite factions such as the Liberal Party accused her of undue political involvement and feared that she was using her position as First Lady to campaign for office.

As early as 1968 and throughout 1969–1972, rumors were rife that Imelda was being groomed to run for president and that her victory would amount to giving Ferdinand the third and possibly even fourth term barred to him by the current constitution. Such would set the stage for a Marcos dynasty and virtual dictatorship. At no point, then, did elite critics see an Imelda presidency as something that might be distinct from Ferdinand's. In a sense, their fears confirmed popular assumptions about her status as his secret weapon. Their criticisms unfolded along the same logic of patronage and spectatorship on which the Marcoses based their rule.

Several mass-circulation magazines ran highly critical articles about the possibility of Imelda running for president. The *Philippine Free Press*, for example, published retouched photographs of Imelda taking her oath of office with Ferdinand and her family blankly looking on.[49] What we see in these photographic fantasies is the visual equivalent of rumor. The self-generating persistence of Imelda-for-president rumors gave them a certain hallucinatory force. It is as if in hearing rumors of Imelda's designs, which were thought to originate from Ferdinand, we can see her actually realizing them. That is, we are led to anticipate the possibility of rumor coming to pass, and through these photographs, we assume the position of spectators to our worst fears. The criticism of the Marcoses' ambitions ends up retailing the very possibility of their actualization.

One of the most vigorous critics of the Marcoses was then Senator Benigno "Ninoy" Aquino. His attacks on Imelda tended to spring from the belief that she was exceeding her place as Ferdinand's wife. Like the photographic fantasies above, such attacks were complicitous with the very terms with which the Marcoses put forth the nature of their relationship. "I am not maligning her," Aquino says in a 1969 interview.

I think she is a thing of beauty, a joy forever. . . . No amount of effort could deglamorize [*sic*] Imelda. I consider her the prettiest Filipina of our generation. . . . But a president should not use his wife for politics. The moment she comes down from the pedestal to the gutter she is bound to get mud. Ferdie uses Imelda as a shield. She is a lovely woman but I think politics should not be for women. But if a woman indulges in politics, then she should share in the brickbats.[50]

Aquino claims that Imelda does not act the way a woman, much less a First Lady, should. She allows herself to be used for political ends. The current of misogyny that runs through these comments is borne by a notion that politics ought to consist of strong men facing off against one another. Men should do their own fighting and leave women out of their contests. Imelda's move from "the pedestal to the gutter" adds to Ferdinand's influence and poses an impediment to Aquino's own ambitions. Aquino himself is taken in by her glamour. But because of his own desire for the presidency, he seeks to resist the depoliticizing hold of her charms. In this way, Aquino acknowledges, albeit in a negative mode, the novelty that Imelda had introduced into national politics. His criticisms of the Marcoses in effect reiterate the belief that Imelda's difference mattered to Ferdinand's plans.

Opposition to the Marcoses, however, came from quarters other than contending elite factions in the senate or press. One other significant source was the youth movement of the mid-1960s to early 1970s, which had a considerable impact on altering the terms of political discourse in the Philippines. A definitive account of the youth movement in postwar Philippine history has yet to be written. Complicating any such attempt would be the intractable difficulties involved in defining and historicizing the social type *youth*. As a sociologically ambiguous category in Philippine—and perhaps any modern—society, it tends to be negatively defined. That is, a youth is one who is not yet an adult but at the same time is no longer a child. Youth might also encompass both secondary and university students as well as nonstudents, male and female, middle class and working class. Indeed, it cuts across regional, gender, and class distinctions, supplementing though never wholly defining the qualities of certain groups. Hence its perpetual liminality. On the social map, *youth* can only exist as a highly unstable and transitory location: the embodiment of a history that is always yet to arrive from the future.[51] Yet, it is the very elusiveness of *youth* in both the historical and sociological sense that allows us to understand the peculiarities of its political style as it emerged in the period leading up to martial law in 1972.

Most accounts trace the emergence of postwar youth activism to the early 1960s, focusing mostly on its institutional manifestations among small groups of university students on various Manila campuses such as the state-run University of the Philippines and the Lyceum as well as the Catholic, privately run Ateneo de Manila University and De La Salle College. For example, in 1961, students at the University of the Philippines formed the Student Cultural Association of the University of the Philippines (SCAUP), which called for greater academic freedom on campus in response to the anticommunist investigations that were then being held by the Committee on Anti-Filipino Activities. Under the leadership of Jose Maria Sison, SCAUP led the first in a series of small demonstrations in front of Congress, at one point barging into the halls and disrupting committee hearings. In 1964, the group held a larger demonstration in front of the presidential palace protesting the unequal trade treaties between the United States and the Philippines contained in the Laurel-Langley Agreement. The police forcibly broke up the protest, making this the first violent clash between youth and police in this era. Shortly after this incident, Sison, who had been recruited into the old Partido Komunista ng Pilipinas (PKP), formed a new organization designed to be the youth arm of the party open to students and nonstudents alike, the Kabataang Makabayan (KM) or Nationalist Youth. But ideological differences between Sison and the old party leaders eventually led to a split in 1967. Influenced by Maoism, Sison, along with some of his KM followers, then formed a new Communist Party of the Philippines in 1968.[52]

The KM was far from the only youth organization of this time. Several other more "moderate" groups emerged, mostly in private Catholic schools, that called for reforms rather than revolution. With ties to an older generation of middle-class nationalists, they identified themselves as Christian humanists and social democrats—the National Union of Students of the Philippines (NUSP) led by Edgar Jopson, for example, or the Lakasdiwa—as against the more radical national democrats. Indeed, by the end of the 1960s, relations between these groups had become sharply antagonistic. Moderates hoped to alleviate social inequalities through legislation and by redrawing the constitution. Many of them were also anticommunists, fearing that revolution would bring about a state of Stalinist terror. Radicals, for their part, regarded moderates as counterrevolutionary and, because of the latter's association with religious groups, "clerico-fascists." They adopted a political view that yoked nationalism with Marxist-Leninist-Maoist categories. Briefly, this consisted of seeing the Philippine state as a captive of elite interests in servile collusion with U.S. imperialism. Such resulted in the perpetuation of semifeudal conditions that condemned the country to supplying cash crops and cheaper labor to markets abroad and the intensification of social inequalities at home. What was needed was a social revolution with the Communist Party as its vanguard that would overthrow the sources of oppression, namely imperialism, feudalism, and bureaucrat capitalism. Its strategy would consist of a protracted armed struggle emanating from the countryside and a sustained propaganda campaign to enlighten people of all classes and bring about a national democracy.[53]

This is not the appropriate place to assess the cogency of the political lines pursued by these different groups. Here, I simply want to indicate some of the complex institutional and ideological contexts that accompanied and shaped the rise of youth politics up to the point of the Marcos presidency. The emergence of the radical and reformist youth organizations historically paralleled the rise of the Marcoses. It is difficult to determine, however, the extent to which many of those who joined demonstrations or attended teach-ins and discussion groups held views that were consistent with those of the leadership in these organizations. Indeed, the views of leaders themselves were in flux and not yet rigidly codified, as they would be in the years after martial law. What mattered at this juncture was the fact that youth from all classes and genders were drawn to this movement; that their very identity as youth was, in large part, determined by their participation in it.[54] With teach-ins and demonstrations, they found new idioms for addressing the world. Whether keyed to revolution or reform, this movement spoke of change and thereby evoked a world separate from those above, whether parents, the church hierarchy, or the state. Its language, ripe with foreign borrowings and urgent appeals, seemed new. And in its newness, it impelled movement outside of institutional confines and into an uncertain arena of historical possibility that linked youth at home with other youths abroad. Despite, or perhaps because of, its fractious and contradictory tendencies, the youth politics of this time was the shifting boundary against which dominant political conventions, particularly those pertaining to patronage, were constrained to reassert if not reconfigure themselves.

During this period, youth politics had a specific style. Consigned outside the structures of political institutions, youths took to the streets, articulating with their massed bodies, slogans, banners, and placards their marginalization and discontent. They presented to those in power the sight and sound of something different and out of place. Rather than stay in school or at home, where they traditionally belonged, youths moved out and occupied public spaces. Their presence was provocative, especially to the most visible representatives of state power, the police. At times, provocation spilled into violence as the police and military stepped in and forcibly dispersed demonstrators.[55]

It was the demonstrations of January 26 and 30, 1970, however, that precipitated what were till then the most violent clashes between youth and police. What set these confrontations apart was the extraordinary rage with which the police set on the demonstrators, moderates and radicals alike, resulting in the injury of at least a couple hundred and the death of four students. So significant were these events that they have come to be known in Philippine historiography as the First Quarter Storm. The storm set in motion a wave of marches and rallies protesting the "fascist" behavior of the state, many of which resulted in further violent clashes. The First Quarter Storm was thus a kind of bomba that set off other bombas, but one whose explosion differed from those in the movies and conventional political practices. It is instructive to look more closely at these events and to ask about the difference they made to those who saw and became a part of them.

The January 26 rally was held in front of the congressional building in Manila primarily to call for a nonpartisan Constitutional Convention the following year. Organized by moderate student groups led by NUSP, the demonstration was swelled by the ranks of more radical youths such as the KM and Samahang Demokratiko ng Kabataan (SDK) along with allied labor groups and peasant unions. Inside the halls of Congress, President Marcos delivered his State of the Nation Address as other politicians, their spouses, and journalists listened. Outside, students held their own assembly, listening to a series of speakers. Toward the end of the rally, tensions arose between moderate and radical students over who would be allowed to use the microphone to address the crowd. Leaders of the former were fearful of having the demonstration they had organized overtaken by the latter. But these differences would vanish once violence broke out and all the youths were indiscriminately targeted for attack by the police. Such violence began with a series of linguistic assaults. Radical groups chanted revolutionary slogans while baiting police and military security forces. In what is perhaps the most vivid account of the rally, journalist Jose Lacaba writes:

> Their slogan (in Tagalog) was "Fight! Don't be afraid!" and they made a powerful incantation of it: "Ma-ki-BAKA! H'wag ma-TAKOT!" They marched with arms linked together and faced the cops without flinching, baiting them, taunting them. "Pulis, pulis, titi mong matulis!" (Pigs, pigs, uncircumcised dicks!),[56] "Pulis, mukhang kwarta!" (Pigs, you're only about money!), "Umuwi na kayo, walang maglalagay sa inyo dito!" (Go home, no bribes to be had here!), "Takbo kayo ng takbo, baka lumiit ang tiyan niyo!" (You keep running, your pot bellies might shrink!), "Baka mag-rape pa kayo, lima-lima na ang asawa niyo!" (You might be thinking of raping someone, you already have so many wives!), "Mano-mano lang, o!" (Let's have it out, one on one!). . . . The very sight of a uniformed policeman was enough to drive demonstrators into a frenzy.[57]

Youth, particularly males, were angered by the mere presence of the police. They responded with obscenities, parodies, and dares, openly mocking the police's claims to respect and deference. Refusing the logic of patronage, which entails regarding inequality as a guarantee of security, the demonstrators placed themselves at a remove from hierarchy. This began with the use of the vernacular, Tagalog, as a way of distinguishing themselves from the proceedings in Congress carried out in English. But the Tagalog they used drew its political charge precisely from its impolitic nature. Cusswords and obscenities were at once infuriating to the cops that they were directed to as much as they were a source of pleasure and solidarity among the youth. Rather than acknowledge authority as the giver of gifts, the language of the demonstrators negated the conventions of regulated exchange across social boundaries. Taunts replaced respect, opening a gap between the language of the state and that of the students. Concomitant with this negative moment of disruption was the affirmation of an alternative basis of identification. Again, this move had a linguistic aspect. Chanted slogans like "Makibaka! H'wag matakot!" ("Struggle! Fear not!") figured prominently in all demonstrations. As with the sounding of other slogans, its collective voicing felt like it originated from one's own body yet was drawn from outside of oneself. The rally itself created a context that made language seem coterminous with community. The power of slogans came from the sense that they gave adequate expression to individual impulses, indeed gave those impulses a form that one did not realize they had. Finding oneself possessed of and by the language of slogans—a language that given its formulaic nature could not have originated from oneself—one found a way of stepping out of a prior identity and assuming another in common with those who chanted the same words. Thus did slogans furnish the basis for collective action.

By contrast, the police stood by and looked on in silent rage. As Lacaba points out, most of them removed their nameplates, concealing their identity, during a riot so as to avoid detection and disavow blame. In this sense, they sought to become anonymous and invisible. Their truncheons and guns spoke for them, manifesting the content of state power to the youths. Standing at the outermost perimeter of the congressional building, the men in uniform formed a line separating the demonstrators from the politicians. That line, however, quickly collapsed at the appearance of President and Mrs. Marcos. Emerging from Congress, the First Couple was roundly booed. A papier-mâché coffin with the word *demokrasya* was hurled their way, then tossed back to the crowd by the president's security guards, only to be tossed back again. Then another papier-mâché figure, a crocodile clutching fake dollar bills with Marcos's initials and "$$" painted on its body, was also thrown toward the First Couple. Rocks, sticks, bottles, and placards followed. One of these barely missed the president and instead hit one of his body guards. Ferdinand and Imelda were quickly pushed into their car and spirited back to the presidential palace. With the First Couple gone, the police swiftly moved in. What ensued over the next few hours was a pitched battle between demonstrators and police.

Youth demonstrations clearly differed from the conventional political rallies of the elite-dominated Nacionalista and Liberal Parties. The latter were organized, as we have seen, as spectacles that staged bombas and displayed patronage. In so doing, they secured the boundary between viewer and viewed, client and patron. The former, however, literalized their nature as a movement, provoking others into action, spreading out and engulfing all those who looked on, including the watchful agents of the state. Exploding taunts and slogans, the demonstrators disrupted the link between patronage and spectatorship. The result was a contagious confusion. As one reporter remarks:

> One emerged [from Congress] to find confusion outside. The President and his wife had sped away—"Binato si Marcos!" ["Marcos was stoned!"]— and the crowd milled in the lobby. A congress employee manfully paged cars through the loudspeaker, but the system was not working and no cars came.... Who was the enemy and who the friend was not clear at all.... Come and go, duck and dart.[58]

The breakdown of the paging system for cars became a synecdoche for evoking the more generalized failure of conventions of communication precipitated by the clash of youths and cops. By the same token, friends and foes were difficult to distinguish as one lost a stable vantage point from which to tell things and persons apart.

As Lacaba strikingly notes, the loss of this stable perspective was reinforced by the radical detachment of images from their sources unleashed by the clash:

> Thunder of feet, tumult of images and sounds. White smooth round crash helmets advancing like a fleet of flying saucers in the growing darkness. The tread of marching feet, the rat-tat-tat of fearful feet on the run, the shuffle of hesitant feet unable to decide whether to stand fast or flee.... And everywhere, a confusion of shouts: "Walang tatakbo!" "Walang uurong!" "Balik!" "Balik!" "Walang mambabato!" "Link arms! Link arms!" [sic], "Maki-Baka! H'wag Mata-KOT!" (Nobody run! Nobody retreat! Come back! Come back! Fight, Don't be afraid!). (45–46)

Caught in the middle of the clash, the writer finds himself confronted not with cops and youths but with the fleeting advance and retreat of images and sounds that are wholly removed from their putative origins. He thus finds himself in extreme intimacy with opposing forces at the very moment that he is unable to personalize those forces. His position, therefore, differs considerably from that of the viewer of Imelda's portraits. While the latter is the subject that receives and reciprocates a pervasive and ever distant gaze, the former is one who loses himself in the swirl of disembodied voices that he is unable to respond to and the rush of sights that he can barely recognize. He is shocked out of his position as a spectator and finds himself contaminated by the confusion that he witnesses. As a result, he is cut off from his identity as a reporter. "It was impossible to remain detached and uninvolved now, to be a spectator forever," Lacaba writes. "It was no longer safe to remain motionless. I had completely forgotten the press badge in my pocket" (46–47).

Hearing cries of pain, Lacaba recounts how he tried to help some students only to find himself being attacked by "crash helmet, khaki uniform and rattan stick." He manages to grab the middle of the police officer's stick with his hands as it is about to come down on him and screams at the cop, "Putanginamo!" (47). Putanginamo literally means "son of a bitch." It is a common but no less highly charged cussword in the vernacular made up of the Spanish *puta* (bitch) and the Tagalog *ina mo* (your mother). Responding to the force of authority, the writer begins to assume a position allied with that of the students. He takes up the language of youth.

The violent encounters between youths and police on the night of January 26 were repeated during the rally of January 30 protesting police brutality in front of the presidential palace. In this latter rally, four students were killed. On both occasions, the clashes followed a similar pattern. The police would advance on the youth, swinging their clubs and firing their weapons. The demonstrators would then retreat into the darkness of the streets. A lull would follow as students regrouped. They would then proceed to advance on the police, hurling stones, placards, ripped bits of metal, and whatever else they could pick up off the streets. Molotov cocktails were also hurled during the January 30 demonstration. Caught by surprise, the cops would retreat. Another pause would follow while the police regrouped and the youths waited in expectation of another charge. This would come, and the cycle of retreat, regroup, and advance would begin all over again. The demonstrators seemed to have no set strategy other than evading and then challenging the police. They had no desire to win territory, occupy buildings, hold hostages, or engage in any other such action that might have improved their position relative to the police.

In the January 30 demonstration, fire trucks were called out to repel the students with water cannons. Youths responded by stoning the truck and forcing it to back away as some yelled, " 'Mahal ang tubig! Isauli n'yo na 'yan sa NAWASA!' (Water is expensive! You should return that to NAWASA [the National Water System Administration])" (Lacaba, 46). Some managed to take over a fire truck, which they then rammed against one of Malacañang's gates. This act was done on the spur of the moment, however. As one student put it, "There was no plan at all to sack Malacañang."[59] Again, it was as if the demonstrators were not interested in gaining strategic advantage over the forces of the state. They challenged state authority but did not see themselves taking the place of those on top of the hierarchy. They did not identify themselves with those in power in the way that Senator Ninoy Aquino, for example, had identified himself with Ferdinand Marcos as the latter's potential successor. Neither were the students concerned with holding onto whatever property was seized in the course of the demonstrations. Stores were not looted. The cars of government officials were smashed and burned as with the lights and windows of palace offices. Rather than appropriate property, youths spurned it, pulling it out of circulation. They sought to evade the pull of power as patronage altogether, exposing the violence that sustained its operation.

Marcos responded by claiming that the demonstrators' ranks were infiltrated by communist agents. He blamed these agents for inciting students to violence in order to set the stage for a coup.[60] Such would become the typical Marcos move to any and all challenges to his regime. He sought to tame the unsettling force of youth by ascribing to it the workings of hidden intentions. For him, the demonstrators were mere dupes of a powerful patron and so he read their actions in traditional political terms. In the wake of the First Quarter Storm, rumors floated that Marcos would declare martial law. Students storming the palace gates gave rise to specters of dictatorship. The president repeatedly denied such rumors even as he spread others regarding communist conspiracies that might make the imposition of martial law necessary. Provoked by the disconcerting politics of youth, Marcos sought to retake the political initiative by conditioning people to expect what he simultaneously told them would be unlikely to happen. In so doing, he clung to the prerogative of manufacturing alarm and its domestication.

The trajectory of Marcos's rule was thus determined, in part, by something that he could not wholly control much less comprehend: the politics of youth. During his first term, Marcos claimed to be different from past presidents. His own youthfulness and that of his wife seemed to confirm this assertion. Yet his claim of embodying the new hinged on his capacity to display his dominance over the appearance of differences. In this regard, as I have tried to argue, Imelda played a crucial role. She made her sexuality and concern with beauty a matter of public interest that invariably worked to her husband's advantage. The emergence of a youth movement and the radical politics it engendered pushed the protocols of domination into crisis. As the events of January 26 and 30 showed, the politics of youth, at least during its wild but short-lived moments, offered an alternative to existing conceptions of authority and submission. Rather than accede to the state's attempt to reify power, they sought to literalize politics, converting mass spectacles into a mass movement. By disordering the calculated disorder launched by the Marcos regime, they furnished a counterlegacy to the years of dictatorship that were to follow.

6 Taglish, or the Phantom Power of the Lingua Franca

In her celebrated novel, *Dogeaters*, the Filipina-American mestiza writer Jessica Hagedorn begins with a memory of watching a Hollywood movie in a Manila theater in the 1950s. She evokes the pleasures of anonymous looking amid the intimate presence of foreign images and unknown bodies:

1956. The air-conditioned darkness of the Avenue Theater smells of flowery pomade, sugary chocolates, cigarette smoke and sweat. "All That Heaven Allows" is playing in Cinemascope and Technicolor. Starring Jane Wyman as the rich widow, Rock Hudson as the handsome young gardener, and Agnes Moorehead as Jane's faithful friend, the movie also features the unsung starlet Gloria Talbott as Jane's spoiled teenage daughter, a feisty brunette with catlike features and an innocent ponytail.... Huddled with our chaperone Lorenza, my cousin Pucha Gonzaga and I sit enthralled in the upper section of the balcony in Manila's "Finest! First Run! English Movies Only!" theater, ignoring the furtive lovers stealing noisy kisses in the pitch-black darkness all around us.

Jane Wyman's soft putty face. Rock Hudson's singular, pitying expression. Flared skirts, wide cinch belts, prim white blouses, a single strand of delicate blue-white pearls. Thick penciled eyebrows and blood red vampire lips; the virgin pastel-pink cashmere cardigan draped over Gloria Talbott's shoulders. Cousin Pucha and I are impressed by her brash style; we gasp at Gloria's cool indifference, the offhand way she treats her grieving mother. Her casual arrogance seems inherently American, modern and enviable.[1]

Before the brilliantly colored images and magnified sounds of this Douglas Sirk film, the narrator, Rio, and her cousin Pucha—mestiza girls of privileged means in neo-colonial Philippine society—initially acknowledge the strangeness of the theater. Plunged in darkness, they are surrounded by odors from unknown sources and the obscured figures of lovers. But as consumers of the film, they take delight in the novelty of their surroundings, avidly attending to the cinematic images, especially the movie stars. Absorbed in the intimate details of the stars' appearance, they recount the colors and textures of the objects on the screen. Thus are they filled with a sense of something missing in their lives. Rio and Pucha regard the stars with envy, seeing in them clues to what might lend form to their own sense of lack.

Here, looking takes on the quality of a residual religiosity. The Filipina viewers approach images from the United States as if they were devotees facing saintly icons. Seeing leads to a desire to fuse with the objects of vision, as images take on the feel of objects available for touching. By lingering over specific scenes and details, the viewers disengage themselves from the sheer narrative trajectory of the love story. As such, Rio, Pucha, and presumably their servant Lorenza are joined momentarily in their common absorption into the cinematic images.

Yet that absorption, like the sense of identification with the stars, is precisely that: momentary. Emerging from the movie, the three also emerge into the light of social differences signaled by the workings of a vernacular sensibility:

We compare notes after the movie, sipping TruColas under the watchful gaze of the taciturn Lorenza. "I don't like her face," Pucha complains about Jane Wyman, "I hate when Rock starts kissing her." "What's wrong with it?" I want to know, irritated by my blond cousin's constant criticism. She wrinkles her mestiza nose, the nose she is so proud of because it's pointy and straight. "Ay! Que corny! I dunno what Rock sees in her"—she wails. "It's a love story," I say in my driest tone of voice.... "It's a *corny* love story, when you think about it," Pucha snorts. Being corny is the worst sin you can commit in her eyes. "What about Gloria Talbott? You liked her didn't you? She's so...."—I search frantically through my limited vocabulary for just the right adjective to describe my feline heroine—"interesting." Pucha rolls her eyes. "Ay! *Puede ba*, you have weird taste! She's really *cara de achay* if you ask me." She purses her lips to emphasize her distaste, comparing the starlet to an ugly servant without, as usual giving a thought to Lorenza's presence. I avoid Lorenza's eyes. "She looks like a cat—that's why she's so strange and interesting," I go on, hating my cousin for being four years older than me, for being so blond, fair-skinned and cruel. Pucha laughs in disdain. "She looks like a *cat* aw-right," she says with her thick, singsong accent. "But if you ask me *prima*, Gloria Talbott looks like a *trapo*. And what's more, Kim Novak should've been in this movie instead of Jane Wyman. Jane's too old," Pucha sighs. "Pobre Rock! Every time he has to kiss her"—Pucha shudders at the thought. Her breasts, which are already an overdeveloped 36B and still growing, jiggle under her ruffled blouse. (Hagedorn, 4)

Inside the theater, the three women find themselves addressed as anonymous viewers. They experience the movie as part of a mass audience whose prior identities count for nothing in front of the screen. Indeed, they assume the place marked out for them by the film: viewers whose looks cannot be reciprocated by the actors and objects on the screen.[2] They see but cannot be seen. Outside the theater, however, a different economy of looking takes place. Lorenza as the parental surrogate who is also the girls' class inferior serves as a foil for the cousins' conversation. While acknowledging her presence, they dismiss Lorenza's authority insofar as it derives from a kind of watching that sees nothing. Her silence is read as a form of deference to social hierarchy rather than a sign of potency held in reserve.

The two cousins, by contrast, voice their disagreements not so much about the meaning of the story but rather the appearance of the stars. Once again, their exchange hinges on envy as a mode of identification. Rio's fascination with the "interesting" and catlike Gloria Talbott is ridiculed by Pucha, who disdains the actress's "*cara de achay*" (servant-like face) and "*trapo*" (dish rag)-like appearance. Pucha regards the female stars as if they were part of a chain of substitutions that extends from Rock Hudson to herself. Rio's envy of Pucha further extends that chain, so that the former's fantasy about the actress is mediated, because constantly interrupted, by her cousin's remarks. Hence, both see themselves in relation to the stars though they may differ on the specific points of their identification. Worth noting, nevertheless, is the manner by which these differences are somatically marked. As the servant Lorenza's own cara increasingly recedes from sight, Pucha's mestiza features come into focus as the objects of envy. From the narrator's point of view, it is as if her mestiza body could retrace and thereby *almost* substitute for the images of the American stars themselves.

Mestiza Envy   To understand the logic of this envy of and for mestizaness, it is useful to recall that in the Filipino historical imagination, the mestizo/a has enjoyed a privileged position associated with economic wealth, political influence, and cultural hegemony.[3] Unlike the United States, but more like Latin America, mestizoness in the Philippines has implied, at least since the nineteenth century, a certain proximity to the sources of colonial power. To occupy the position of mestizo/a is to invoke the legacy of the ilustrados, the generation of mostly mixed-race, Spanish-speaking, university-educated nationalists from the Chinese mestizo Jose Rizal to the Spanish mestizo Manuel Quezon—both credited with founding the dominant fictions of Filipino nationhood. Betwixt and between languages and historical sensibilities, mestizoness thus connotes a surplus of meanings as that which conjures the transition from the colonial to the national—indeed, as the recurring embodiment of that transition.

For Rio, then, to envy Pucha's fair skin, blond hair, straight nose, and "overdeveloped 36B" breasts is equivalent to Pucha's envying of Jane Wyman and Gloria Talbott's access to Rock Hudson (and quite conceivably, Rock's to them). To be mestizo/a is to imagine one's inclusion in a circuit of substitutions. It is to cultivate a relationship of proximity to the outside sources of power without, however, being totally absorbed by them. In the context of neo-colonial Philippine society, such requires a heightened sense of alertness to what comes before and outside of oneself. As such, mestizoness comes to imply a perpetual and, as we shall see, privileged liminality: the occupation of the crossroads between Spain and the Philippines, Hollywood and Manila. This is clearly at work in the movie theatre. Rio and Pucha seem adept at consuming cinematic images, discriminating and delineating differences among these without being wholly consumed by them. They fasten onto movie stars while dismissing the narrative, or play one star off against another like so many disposable idols. Thus is looking tinged with envy: of Pucha imagining herself in the place of Jane Wyman, Gloria Talbott, Kim Novak, or perhaps Rock Hudson; of Rio envying Pucha's capacity to be so brazenly envious of what she is not; and of Lorenza's silent presence overhearing and tacitly participating in the circulation of envy.

Here, it is as if envy drives the formulation of a certain kind of agency, one that arises from the sense of being excluded coupled with the desire to be included. The force of envy sharpens one's capacity to imagine being other than oneself, to think that one's "I" could also be other "I's" elsewhere beyond one's immediate setting. Predicated on envy (or what, in more politically charged moments of colonial history, would manifest itself as *ressentiment* escalating into the desire for revenge and revolt), mestizo/a identity is perforce split along shifting lines of identification. Such lines (like those of a train or telegraph) allow mestizos/as to travel in and out of particular social locations, linking them to those below as well as those above and outside.[4] Their position is analogous to and often coterminous with that of the Filipino elites that we saw in chapters 3 and 4. For this reason, mestizos/as (and those who come to identify with them) have historically had an ambivalent relationship with sources of power, whether the masses below or colonial rulers above. They have collaborated with one against the other at different moments, or with both at the same time. They can thus claim the privilege to solicit as well as contain the workings of power, whatever its source. And because of their dual association with the history of revolutionary nationalism and counterrevolutionary colonial regimes since the late nineteenth century, mestizos/as—whether Chinese, Spanish, or North American—have been regarded as the chief architects of the nation-state.[5]

We can think, then, of mestizos/as as the traces of the hybrid origins of the nation-state. But we should also recall that this hybridity seems always already organized, at least within Philippine neo-colonial society, along a social hierarchy. What pervades the scene above from Hagedorn's novel is the sense of the mestizo/a as a position from which to address the relationship between the colonial and national, the elite and popular, the outside and inside as if they were potentially substitutable yet never commensurate with one another. In the darkened theater, the mestiza girls literally look up to watch the American stars on screen. The latter are objects of envy in that they seem so romantic in their modernity and so modern in their romance. Looking at them, the mestiza girls feel themselves to be simultaneously excluded from yet entitled to inclusion in this fantasy world. As spectators, they submit to the dominating images of the stars; yet they also show themselves capable at the end of the movie of evaluating or dismissing their appearances. The envy of and for mestizoness, therefore, has to do with its capacity to allow one to move in and out of the social hierarchy: to appear to be part of yet apart from it.

The doubleness of mestizo/a identity, however, has a linguistic dimension. In the scene above, the girls speak a mixed language popularly known in the Philippines as Taglish. Pucha, for example, talks in a combination of at least three languages: English, Spanish, and Tagalog. It is as if she moves between colonial and vernacular languages, simultaneously evoking and collapsing the hierarchical relationship between them. Her English is keyed to that of the film and so has the narrative function of ordering sense and sensation. Nonetheless, bits of Spanish and Tagalog constantly break into the stream of her English, abruptly punctuating its flow and obstructing its ability to set the terms for the production of meaning. To Rio's remarks on Gloria Talbott's "interesting" character, Pucha exclaims, "Ay! *Puede ba*, you have weird taste! She's really *cara de achay* if you ask me" ["Oh! Spare me. She's got the face of a maid!"]. In so doing, she ironizes the hierarchy between star and viewer by breaching the divisions among English, Spanish, and Tagalog. Indeed, the ejaculatory intrusions of the latter two languages have the effect of inflecting English into a language other than itself, just as the singsong delivery of English anticipates the bursts of Spanish and Tagalog fragments in her speech. Mestizoness is the capacity, among other things, to speak in different registers, as if one's identity were overlaid and occupied by other possible ones.[6]

Bakya and the Prospects of Overhearing The link between mestizoness and Taglish might be better understood with reference to the historical workings of a hierarchy of languages in the Philippines. English as the legacy of U.S. colonialism as well as postwar neo-colonial relations has functioned as the language of higher education and, until the mid-1970s, the dominant medium of instruction in public and private schools. Its use is associated with the elite circles of multinational corporations, the diplomatic corps, the tourist industry, overseas labor recruitment, metropolitan newspapers of record, and the medical and legal professions; it is the chief official language of the legislative, judicial, and other policy-making bodies of the state. And English is, of course, the language of foreign movies, mostly from the United States, which continue to dominate the country's film market.

Spanish, on the other hand, has never been widely spoken or understood in the Philippines. Less than 1 percent of the population has ever been fluent in Spanish at any given moment in Spain's 350 years of colonial rule. Owing to the Spanish practice of converting the native populace in their local vernaculars and given the absence of a comprehensive, secular public school system throughout the Spanish regime, the learning of Spanish was limited to an elite, mostly mestizo (Chinese and Spanish) minority with access to a university education in Manila and Europe.[7] By the later U.S. colonial period, and more so throughout the postwar republic, Spanish became largely supplementary, a way of signaling class attachments to an ersatz, aristocratic lineage that predated U.S. rule or reclaiming the legacy of late-nineteenth-century nationalist figures.

The history of Tagalog is no less complex. As I have detailed elsewhere, Tagalog was grammatically codified and phonetically reduced to Roman characters by Spanish missionaries for purposes of translating prayers and Christian texts as early as the late sixteenth century.[8] Hence, Tagalog as a print language has long been infused with foreign borrowings. Latin and Spanish terms for Christian concepts with no direct equivalents in Tagalog were left untranslated, lodged as the traces of an alien presence periodically erupting into the fabric of the vernacular texts. But as the medium of conversion, Tagalog also tended to dislocate Christian-colonial meanings by supplying native hearers with an array of associations that exceeded missionary control. Tagalog betrayed, in both senses of the word, Spanish Christianity and colonialism.

To the extent that Tagalog has been used as a language for addressing a mass audience—that is, an audience required to give up its local identity in order to assume a more global one, as in the case of Christian conversion—it has always been entangled in the grammar of colonial discourse and subjected to colonial control over the means of mechanical reproduction. Tagalog lent itself to the solicitation and expression of deference with its honorifics, such as *ho* and *po* to signal social and generational distance between speakers, whether these be God, government bureaucrats, Spanish friars, landlords, and so forth. But it is also important to point out that since the 1890s, Tagalog has been the focus of various nationalist concerns. Projected as the potential language of cultural authenticity with which to articulate a precolonial past with a decolonized future, Tagalog has been regarded as one site for translating the colonial order into a national one. Insofar as Tagalog could furnish the means with which to elicit the attention of a mass audience, nationalist elites, like their Spanish colonial predecessors, could imagine it as a language that might fuse the interests of those above with those below the social hierarchy across a variety of vernacular, non-Tagalog-speaking communities.

Accordingly, Tagalog was designated as the basis of the yet-to-be instituted national language (*wikang pambansa*) by the Commonwealth government in 1938 and again by the Japanese occupation regime in 1943. But objections by non-Tagalog speakers in the national legislature during the postwar period resulted in a series of name changes. The Philippine legislature renamed the putative national language "Pilipino" to stress the national vocation of Tagalog. In 1973, however, the constitutional convention held under the martial law regime of Ferdinand Marcos changed this name yet again, to "Filipino," while admitting that it was merely designating a Manila-based lingua franca that was still far from having a truly national currency. The constitution of 1986 has upheld this term to designate not so much the national language as what the national language might be called should it ever emerge. Filipino continues to be based on Tagalog with greater infusions of English and bits of Spanish rather than, as nationalist linguists had proposed as early as 1915, a fusion of all the different Philippine vernaculars. As the linguist Andrew Gonzalez has noted, "One must class the Philippines as among those nations thus far without a national language although with a non-local common language as an official code with which to conduct [official] transactions."[9] In effect, there continues to be a lack of fit between the officially designated national language and officially conceived borders of the nation-state.

At the bottom of the linguistic hierarchy, Tagalog is the most unstable and elusive as well. Its history—from its reformalization by Spanish missionaries and its reification by the Institute of National Language into an "archaic" and therefore "classical" language of the country to its mutations in popular and official discourses—suggests something of its thoroughly impure origins and highly malleable and contingent workings. Seized on by the new social movements of the 1960s—consisting of left-wing student, worker, and women's organizations—Tagalog as Pilipino or Filipino has been a popular medium for mass mobilization at political rallies in and around Manila. Outside the Tagalog-speaking regions in such cities as Cebu or Iloilo, however, English and the local vernacular continued to be the languages of political movements. Similarly, while the teaching of Tagalog grammar and literature in secondary schools has been mandated by the state since 1946, and while the Bilingual Education Policy of 1974 has provided for the use of Filipino as a medium of instruction alongside English, Tagalog has yet to replace English as the sole language of official transactions and higher education. In this sense, Tagalog cannot be thought of as a language of national identity that subsumes all other local identifications.

Yet even if Tagalog does not represent the nation, it does serve as the language of commercially driven mass media, specifically radio, television, and film. As the lingua franca of the mass media, Tagalog manages in fact to have a translocal reach. It does so, however, only and always in conjunction with other translocal languages: English and Spanish. Thus, it is as another kind of language, Taglish, that Tagalog comes across as a lingua franca, providing the conditions for the emergence of a mass audience in the contemporary Philippines.

In the 1960s, the nationalist historian and Tagalog writer Teodoro Agoncillo wrote scornfully about Taglish, then perceived as a corruption of Tagalog. For Agoncillo, Taglish represented the dilution of Tagalog with English phrases and Spanish malapropisms. It reflected the ignorance of its speakers—in this case, largely middle-class, university-educated, English-speaking, Manila-based, postwar youth along with radio announcers and movie personalities. Comprising what we might think of as the vanguard of an emergent consumerist culture, their sensibilities were at variance with those of old guard nationalists like Agoncillo. To him, their Taglish came across as a "bastard language" designed for the marketplace rather than the task of national unification. Taglish could only defer, according to Agoncillo, the emergence of a truly national language, one that in "fusing" different Philippine vernaculars, would merge the interests of the masses with those of the nationalist elite.[10]

For Agoncillo and other nationalists who would follow in his wake, Taglish was insufficiently "intellectualized" and therefore illegitimate. The seemingly arbitrary conjunction of languages in Taglish meant that it defied official codification, eluding nationalist authorship and the regulatory force of state institutions such as the Institute of National Language or Bureau of Education. Since the 1940s, both had sought to standardize and administer Tagalog from above and beyond the diverse Philippine vernaculars. By contrast, Taglish seemed like the result of the promiscuous commerce of languages. It placed English, Spanish, and Tagalog as equally substitutable rather than hierarchically related.[11]

Taglish thus appeared to be less a single language than the constant possibility of fragmenting and recombining languages. For this reason, Taglish lent itself, indeed was made possible by, the formation of a commercially driven popular culture. It furnished another kind of lingua franca, one that seemed to originate from no one in particular and so could address anyone in general. Like money, the currency of Taglish as a lingua franca depended on its capacity to provide a kind of anonymous speech with which to address a new, postwar, mass audience, one responsive to the call of market consumption.

Agoncillo's worry about Taglish is symptomatic of larger nationalist anxieties about the ability to shape the terrain of a national-popular culture and the language appropriate to it. In the late 1960s and early 1970s, nationalist attempts to contain the effects of Taglish were reflected in the urban, middle-class discourse regarding the lower classes. A new term emerged to designate this heterogenous population: the *bakya* crowd. Coined in the early 1960s by Filipino film director and national artist Lamberto Avellana to describe the types of audiences his serious films were explicitly *not* meant for, the bakya crowd (bakya being a reference to cheap wooden clogs) was a way for the urban intelligentsia to conceptualize its other. Jose F. Lacaba has written most instructively about the bakya as "anything that is cheap, gauche, naive, provincial and terribly popular; and in this sense it is used more as an adjective than as a noun."[12]

Within the nationalist framework, the bakya appears as one version of the crowd: the depoliticized and indiscriminate mass of consumers. It is not surprising that for Lacaba, the bakya sensibility should be borne by what seemed like a perverse linguistic economy in addition to a kind of kitsch aesthetic. More specifically, it was characterized by an English full of humorous malapropisms. To recognize such bakya speech is precisely to see it as funny; but it also requires that one reproduce such speech, setting oneself apart from its ostensive speakers.[13] Lacaba does precisely this, retelling apocryphal stories about a movie star:

Movie idol on seeing the chandeliers at the Cultural Center: "Wow, what beautiful chamberlains!" To a fan: "Would you like my mimeograph?" To a waitress in a crowded, smoke-filled room: "Please open the door. I'm getting sophisticated." On being offered a glass of wine after a companion has replied, "I'm afraid not": "Me, I'm not afraid." At the dinner table: "Please pass the salt. My hands cannot arrive." On seeing a black cat pass by: "That's a bad oinment" [i.e., omen]. After singing a song that has met with appreciative applause: "Thanks for the clap."[14]

Here, the fictitious movie idol displays what seems from the writer's perspective like a failed relationship to the linguistic order. In the mythical world of the bakya, every attempt to speak English is marked by mistakes. Even more significant is the idol's failure to mark her/his mistakes. It is not only the case that the bakya speaker misuses English, but that s/he is unable to recognize that fact. Misrecognition is the source of humor for Lacaba and its recognition as such the basis of his identity as a non-bakya. He sees what the bakya speaker cannot: that the latter's English isn't really English at all (because if it were, then s/he would be able to correct her/himself). Rather, it comes across as another language, one that is meant to be overheard and passed on like gossip. In repeating these stories, Lacaba positions himself as someone who has overheard something that the speaker did not intend and was not aware of. He serves as a medium for relating the fragmentation and disruption of English. Through him, readers are positioned to share in the joke: that English, like Tagalog and Spanish, is a language that can come across otherwise. Through the bakya use of English, Lacaba thus discovers the workings of Taglish.[15]

The delight in telling and hearing these stories that, to this day, continue to be well known among the urban elite are twofold. On the one hand, Lacaba and those who share his position set themselves apart from the bakya crowd by signaling their knowledge of English and its difference from other languages. In so doing, they delineate their own place on the social map. Retelling these stories and so keeping them in circulation, on the other hand, provides their speakers and hearers with the opportunity to share in the pleasures of anonymous hearing. It is to imagine being in another place, hearing what was not originally meant for one and witnessing scenes of mistranslation that one can repeat but also ironically disclaim. In short, the pleasures of overhearing reproduce the effects of Taglish: moving between languages and identities without fully surrendering to any one of them.

By contrast, one who is supposedly bakya is out of place without realizing this fact. From the point of view of the urban intelligentsia, their attempts to speak English betray their superficial command of the language of authority. Instead, they are an embarrassment in that they unselfconsciously dislocate English. That is to say, they suffer from being non-ironic, failing to assume another position from which to see their disposition. To be bakya is to be stranded between aesthetic sensibilities and geographies, and by extension linguistic registers, without the means with which to represent that predicament. One indication of the negative inbetween quality attributed to *kabakyaan* (i.e., the appearance of being bakya) is its synonym in Taglish, *promdi;* a shortened version of *promdi probinsya*, from the provinces. One who is bakya or promdi comes across, then, as a failed version of the urban elite. As one who is unconsciously transitional, the bakya speaker is one who speaks Taglish but thinks s/he is speaking English.

Delineating the qualities of bakya, Lacaba echoes Agoncillo's anxiety about regulating the borders of a national culture, which entails demarcating the divisions between languages. But because he comes from a younger generation of nationalist writers educated amid the confluence of mass culture and marxist politics, Lacaba is far more alert to the possibilities for recuperating kabakyaan and mobilizing the bakya crowd for other purposes. Indeed, in a later essay, written in 1979 during the martial law period, Lacaba links the category of bakya with the more politicized one of *masa*, or masses.[16] Through a consideration of the notion of the bakya, he consequently saw in Taglish and the conventions of anonymous hearing and looking it enjoins possibilities other than those presented by the marketplace.

Ikabod *and the Politics of Taglish* That Taglish could be used for political purposes apart from those of reproducing social hierarchy proved to be the case by the mid-1980s. In the context of the Marcos dictatorship where the publishing and broadcasting industries had come under either direct control or close scrutiny of the state, the ironizing effects of Taglish proved to be a rich and popular resource for marking oneself off from the regime. Because it is a kind of speech that can signal one's ability to overhear and see anonymously, Taglish became the preferred idiom of popular dissent. Especially in the period following the assassination of Benigno "Ninoy" Aquino in 1983 and culminating in the People Power Revolt of 1986, urban discourse critical of the Marcoses took the form of puns, jokes, and assorted wordplay on the regime's pronouncements and the names of its leaders. Elsewhere, I have discussed the explosion of political humor during this period.[17] What is worth noting here is the role of Taglish in furnishing the means for evading the pressures of the linguistic hierarchy that, at certain points, broached the possibility of reconfiguring the social order.

One way of getting a sense of the political uses to which Taglish was put during this period is to take a look at the work of the most popular Filipino cartoonist of this time, Nonoy Marcelo. Already well known for his comic strip *Tisoy* (the Taglish term for mestizo), which dealt with the lives of urban youth in the mid- to late 1960s, Marcelo created a new series beginning in the early 1980s entitled *Ikabod*. As political allegory, the strip was set in a country called Dagalandia (literally Ratland) with its capital at Keso City (Cheese City, a play on Quezon City), where the currency was called kesos (pesos). Populated by characters drawn as rats, ants, cats, pigs, frogs, and bats, Dagalandia became a site for parodying the claims of the Marcos regime. Marcelo's use of Taglish permitted him to double code the dialogue of the characters in ways that deflected even as it acknowledged the regime's power to regulate discourse.

For example, in a cartoon drawn at the end of 1983, two male rats greet each other with "Merry Crises-mas!" Overhearing this allusion to

Fig. 37. "Merry Crises-mas!" (Nonoy Marcelo, *Ikabod* [Manila: Solar Publishing House, 1987])

the regime's problems, the officious cat, Bos Myawok, orders them to stop dwelling on the "crisis-crisis" and instead exchange greetings like "Happy New Year or something like dat?!?" To which the rats reply, "Nineteen eighty poor 'pre!" (fig. 37).[18] Through Taglish, one becomes party to a scene of hearing someone who has arrogated to himself the sole right to overhear, thereby seeing what was not meant to be seen. The Marcos regime's attempt to hide its economic profligacy and contain rumors about its ill-gotten wealth is exposed with a remarkable economy of words: "Merry Crises-mas!" and "Nineteen eighty poor."

In another similarly subtle attempt to reverse and displace the regime's control over the dissemination of news, Lolo Umboy, the grand-

175   *Taglish*

father rat, tells Bos Peter, the local ruler of Keso City, about the "good news and the bad news" for the coming year. Lolo Umboy: "First da good news—lahat halos ng ibabalita ng mga jaryo ay good news!!!" ("the newspapers will report nothing but good news!!!"). Bos Peter: "Yhehay!!!" Lolo: "Ang [the] bad news—lalong walang maniniwala sa mga jaryo!!!" ("the newspapers will become even less believable!!!"). Shifting between English, Tagalog, and Tagalized Spanish, Lolo Umboy disrupts the flow of official speech and drives Bos Peter into a glum silence. Taglish has the effect of exposing the disparity between *jaryo* and news, between what is said and what is believed. *Ikabod,* then, suggests that the really good news may be the bad news: that we know that we don't know and so can begin to see what has been kept from us.

The art historian Alice G. Guillermo writes in her introduction to Marcelo's collected cartoons that their

comic appeal lies in Nonoy Marcelo's play with words. His wordplay centers primarily on the Filipino use of English, which in his characters reveal a cultural alienation. It is in his spelling of Pilipino-English that the cartoonist also conveys cultural incongruity stemming from the use of a language basically unfamiliar to the masses: *bes preng* [best friend], *wa-es* [wise], *donkworry* [don't worry], *wassamata?* [what's the matter?], *wajawang?* [what do you want?], *dasbitor!* [that's better!]. He has coined words which have become integrated into the vocabulary such as *jeprox* [hippie]. He has used swardspeak (gay lingo): "Say mo?" ["What do you say to that?"]. He has put words together: "Weno?!" for "O . . . e ano?!" ["Well, so what?"] the better to catch authentic intonation. Or he has jumbled his terms: the serious "colonial mentality" becomes the comic "mental colony." (Marcelo, 3–4)

That comic effect should be linked to "cultural alienation" has to do precisely with the capacity of Taglish to reproduce a scene of translation that involves distancing oneself from a hierarchy of signification. As with Lacaba's attempt to reproduce and ironize bakya English, Marcelo's strips defamiliarize English, Tagalog, and Spanish. Marcelo highlights the ability of Taglish to peel away from the grammatical and social contexts of English, Spanish, and Tagalog, juxtaposing them instead in a relation of constant interruption.[19] As such, the speaker and reader of Taglish participates in a surprising conjunction of languages in ways that produce new constellations of meaning. In this way, s/he begins to disengage her/himself from the discursive grip of the state and approximates the mestizo/a's ability to peel away from what comes from the outside. But whereas the mestiza cousins in Hagedorn's novel avail of Taglish in order to distance themselves both from the totalizing grip of a Hollywood cinematic narrative and the undifferentiated masses in the theater in the late 1950s, the mestizo/as in Marcelo's comic strips of the 1980s speak in Taglish as a way of announcing their alliance, however tentatively broached, with a new mass politics. We can see this in the following cartoon, where two presumably working-class male rats demonstrate behind the ranks of mestiza rats:

> KADO: Let's make baka, don't be takot!!! [Let us struggle, don't be afraid!!!]
> FRIEND: 'Tong si Kado, oo! Magdedemo lang namimili pa ng mga kasama—ang type pa . . . byutyus colegialas! [Can you believe this, Kado! He's going to demonstrate but he needs to have companions that are his type . . . beautiful convent schoolgirls!]
> SCHOOLGIRLS' PLACARD: Na itsahan ka! [They put one over on you; this is a play on the pro-Aquino slogan, "Hindi ka nag-iisa!" ("You are not alone")] (fig. 38)

In this cartoon, a radical cry from the 1960s, "Makibaka, Huwag Matakot!" ("Fight! Don't be afraid!") is transposed into Taglish and linked to the rise of a middle-class feminist movement alongside the complex coalitions of cause-oriented groups mobilizing against the Marcoses. The conditions of anonymous looking and hearing characteristic of the marketplace are here transposed to the streets as the two male rats find themselves addressed by the marching mestizas, following their lead and taking on their speech. "Their" speech, however, is already the result of a prior translation that in turn recalls another historical moment: the student movement of the 1960s and the women's organization from that same period called the Malayang Kilusan Ng Bagong Kababaihan (Independent Movement of New Women) or MAKIBAKA. Marcelo's strip becomes a social hieroglyph where the conjunction and reinscription of languages constitute dense layers of historical associations articulated in novel public settings. In this context, Taglish opens a route to recuperating a past as much as it seeks to unsettle the circulation of signs and division of classes in the present.

Taglish as a lingua franca of dissent multiplies sense as much as it

Fig. 38. "Let's make baka, don't be takot!!!" (Nonoy Marcelo, *Ikabod* [Manila: Solar Publishing House, 1987])

calls attention to the sensuousness of translation, here understood as the reciprocal interruption of languages. One speaks and hears not just a surplus of referents; one also senses the audible, material workings of translation as one shuttles between languages spoken in a mode of exclamatory urgency. The multiple exclamation marks that punctuate *Ikabod's* dialogues suggest a kind of frenzy, even delirium, as the tone most appropriate to Taglish. Such urgency was partially a response to the Marcoses' attempts at co-opting Taglish through their monopoly of the mass media. Hence, Marcelo's linguistic inventiveness, such as the contraction of words, reversal of phrases, and coining of new expressions—skills associated with the rhetoric of advertising—becomes a tactic for maneuvering around the regime's attempts at dominating the lingua franca.

In reading these strips, one senses how Taglish between 1983 and 1986 had been politicized by being made to stand outside the hierarchy of languages. Taglish took on a radically public character and was reworked into an arena of uneven and ongoing translations. Owned by no one, yet potentially accessible to everyone, Taglish seemed capable of appearing anywhere: in the marketplace, on the streets, in comic strips, and among Filipino overseas communities. *Ikabod* was but one example among many of the deployment of Taglish in the mobilization of a mass audience for mass action. By February 25, 1986, masses of people would take to the streets, congregating on Epifanio de los Santos Avenue (EDSA) in front of the military camps Crame and Aguinaldo, driven there in part by the disembodied voices of the Chinese mestizo Cardinal Sin broadcasting from Radio Veritas and the mestiza American actress June Keithley on the underground station Radio Bandido. That Sin and Keithley spoke in English mattered less than the fact that their voices were overheard, intercepted by an audience that had become steeped in the techniques of interrupting the circulation of signs from above. By responding to these voices, they showed themselves alert to the workings of Taglish.

Movies and the Lingua Franca In the aftermath of the EDSA revolt and initial euphoria surrounding the Cory Aquino presidency, the forces of a pre–martial law oligarchy eventually reasserted themselves. After half-hearted negotiations, Aquino moved swiftly to brutally repress the Left, especially through the use of vigilante death squads, while repulsing and finally containing the right-wing forces of the military by putting down several coup attempts. Subsequent national and local elections have resulted in the restoration of what Benedict Anderson has referred to as "cacique democracy" in the Philippines.[20] Concurrently, there has emerged a climate of cultural conservatism most evident in the reassertion of Catholic moralism under Sin and Aquino, the spread of Protestant fundamentalism, particularly among younger members of the middle class, and the rehabilitation of the Marcoses, both the living and dead, culminating in their return to the fold of Manila's elite circles within the first year of Fidel Ramos's term. A flurry of natural disasters from floods to the eruption of Mt. Pinatubo, coinciding with the dismantling of the Clark and Subic military bases, the breakdown of energy-generating infrastructures leading to frequent and massive brownouts, and the mounting indebtedness to the World Bank and IMF, have all led to further shrinking of economic prospects for many Filipinos, driving hundreds of thousands to seek overseas employment so that the export of labor, mostly female, now constitutes the largest source of dollar revenues for the country.

By the 1990s, whatever democratizing promise the EDSA revolt held out has long been extinguished. The return of cacique democracy has also meant the containment of mass politics away from the scenes of its emergence and in the direction of the new sites of popular gatherings: the new and enormous shopping malls of metro Manila. Perhaps it is not too far-fetched to suggest that the latter period of Aquino's regime will be remembered as the era of the mega-malls, when a consumerist ethos managed to substitute the privatized, tightly policed, air-conditioned, and brownout resistant spaces of Robinson's and Shoemart for the communal exhilaration and confrontational politics of EDSA and Mendiola, the street that led to Malacañang.

In these malls, people find themselves joined by the common activity of looking at commodities. Their identity as consumers, like their identity as citizens, is premised on their ability to overhear and so translate the call of that which lies beyond and before them. Yet, in responding to the allure of consumption, they defer to a lingua franca now rendered inseparable from the commodity context of its appearance. Not surprisingly, then, the political energy unleashed by the lingua franca has been contained and redeployed in order to project the realm of commodities as the matrix of public culture. Put another way, Taglish has lately become the means for depoliticizing social relations, conflating the allure of mestizoness with the voice of the commodity. To get a sense of the changing role of Taglish in the post-EDSA period, we might turn to one of the most widely consumed commodities in the country, a commodity that is also one of the most powerful sites for the reproduction of mestizoness: Filipino movies.

From their inception in the first decade of the U.S. colonial period, Filipino movies have always been market driven. State subsidies were by and large nonexistent so that there is, in fact, hardly any tradition of independent filmmaking in the Philippines. The rare exceptions, such as the works of Kidlat Tahimik or Nick de Ocampo, have been made with outside, usually European funding. Instead, a handful of family-owned companies have historically dominated the production and distribution of films. At the same time, the market for Filipino films has tended to be constricted. The industry has been forced to compete with foreign, principally Hollywood movies on a limited number of screens. It is also taxed heavily by the government and compelled to pay steep tariffs on imported film stock, placing severe restrictions on the amount of film that can be exposed per movie. And because it is dependent on outmoded equipment, from cameras to processing facilities, Filipino movies often fail to meet the technical standards required for international, non-Filipino circuits of distribution. To maintain a level of profitability, local films tend to bank on formulaic plots: melodramas, action and comedy genres, or what middle-class urban critics derisively call *iyakan, bakbakan, tawanan* (all crying, all fighting, all laughing). And most important of all, Filipino films rely on a stable of movie stars instantly recognizable by a mass public.[21]

The material and commercial conditions of filmmaking thus tend to give Filipino movies a certain insularity. While a handful of films are regularly shown at international venues (while doing poorly at the local box office), the overwhelming number of movies made are explicitly for a Filipino mass audience, which since the late 1970s, has also come to include a sizable migrant and immigrant viewership abroad.[22]

Within the Philippines itself, the practices of film going have long been class rather than gender specific. In the current marketing idiom, audiences are thought to be divided into categories. At the top are the "As" and "Bs": discerning, educated, urban, and economically well-off audiences fluent in English who watch mostly Hollywood movies and the occasional "quality" Filipino film that may have garnered some kind of international reputation. Below this are the "C" and "D" audiences or what in the 1970s would have been called the bakya crowd: less-educated viewers with lower incomes and of humbler, perhaps provincial origins. While attracted to Hollywood blockbusters, these audiences tend to prefer Filipino films.

The hierarchy of viewership is aligned with a linguistic hierarchy as well. "A" and "B" audiences watch movies in English, thereby signifying their proximity to outside sources of knowledge and the larger networks of power to which they are attached. As with the mestiza cousins in Hagedorn's novel, such viewers constitute their identity at the interstices of the "foreign" film and "local" context of their exhibition. As such, they locate themselves as privileged receivers of signs and meanings that come from elsewhere while remaining distanced from the full weight of their demands. Their access to English is an indication of their place on the social map as part of, yet apart from, a hierarchy of languages.

By contrast, "C" and "D" audiences gravitate toward movies in Taglish, the lingua franca of Filipino movies. In the theater, they, too, place themselves in a position to overhear and observe fragments of languages and scenes that lie beyond and above their immediate situation without themselves being seen or wholly implicated. At the same time, they are reminded of the limits of such imaginings. It is not only the visual quality of local films—the flat lighting, dullness of color, and outlines of images that lend a two-dimensional, surface-like quality to most local movies—that make them identifiable as Filipino. More important in setting Filipino movies apart from other films is the use of Taglish. In its particular articulation of languages as both hierarchically ordered *and* arbitrarily configured, Taglish has the effect of maintaining viewers within the borders of the existing social imaginary.

Two films from 1993 serve to illustrate the simultaneously disruptive and constraining workings of Taglish. These are *Makati Avenue Office Girls* and *Maricris Sioson: Japayuki,* both produced by one of the largest production companies in the Philippines and featuring well-known movie stars.[23] In the first film, Taglish serves to organize the signifying economy of the workplace and home. Set in metro Manila's financial district and the well-tended houses of mestizo elites, the film's appeal lies in its invitation to witness scenes of the lifestyles of the rich yet miserable. It is also typical in its use of Taglish for demarcating lines of authority that separate managers from workers and parents from children. Two scenes exemplify such operations. First, a fragment of a scene at an office, where a rich manager, Corrine, played by Maricel Laxa, speaks with her secretary, Edith, as a male co-manager looks on:

EDITH: Ma'am?
CORRINE: Edith, ano ba ang manga appointments ko for today? [Edith, what are my appointments for today?]
EDITH: Mamayang five ho, kay Mr. Santos. Yung dinner n'yo ho at seven sa bahay ng brother ninyo. At saka tumawag nga pala si Mr. Mayoralgo. Inireremind ho kayo sa dinner party mamaya. Huwag ho daw kayo malelate at para daw sa inyo 'yon. [Later, at five, you have an appointment with Mr. Santos. Then dinner at your brother's house at seven. And Mr. Mayoralgo called. He's reminding you of the dinner party. He says you shouldn't be late since it is for you.]
CORRINE: Okay. Icancel mo na lang yung kay Mr. Santos. [Just cancel the appointment with Mr. Santos.]
MALE CO-MANAGER: Ano? Kinancel mo na naman? [What? Cancel again?]
CORRINE: Huwag kang mag-aalala. May crush sa akin 'yun. Hindi tayo titigilan no'on. [Don't worry. He's got a crush on me. He won't let go of us.]

While Edith the secretary speaks Taglish, she does so as someone who acknowledges her place relative to Corrine with the Tagalog honorifics "ho" and "po" that intersperse her speech (and that elude translation into English). In addition, she qualifies her assertions and reminders with the particle "daw," signifying that what she says are not her words but something she has overheard and is now compelled to pass on. Hence, while the conjunction of Tagalog and English allows Edith to communicate with Corrine, it also signals the social distance between them.

Edith's position is one who speaks only to the extent that she acknowledges her words to have a prior origin and destination other than herself. Corrine, by contrast, dispenses with Tagalog honorifics altogether so that her speech seems bereft of deference. It is as if she could speak to and for anyone. We can see this sense of a self-directed speech not only at the office but at home, when Corrine talks with her parents. In this scene, they argue over her parents' wish to require her fiancé, Philip, to sign a prenuptial agreement:

CORRINE: I can't give this to him.
DAD: Bakit hindi? Wala namang masamang nakasulat diyan. [Why not? There's nothing wrong with it.]
MOM: At saka pumirma din sa ganyang arrangement si Stella bago sila kinasal ni Robbie. [And besides, Stella signed a similar agreement before she was married to your brother Robbie.]
CORRINE: Ma, pero babae si Stella. At saka she wouldn't care less kung hindi siya makakuha ng kayamanan kay Robbie because her family is richer than our family. [But Ma, Stella is a woman. And she wouldn't care less if she doesn't get any of Robbie's money.]
DAD: This is for your own protection, Corrine.
CORRINE: Maiinsulto si Philip, Papa. [Philip will feel insulted, Papa.]
DAD: Bakit nagiging masyado kang emotional pagdating sa dokumentong ito? [Why do you get so emotional when it comes to this document?]
MOM: Bert, let me handle this. Hija, we're not questioning the love you have for each other. I think Philip is a wonderful guy. He's intelligent, he's sensitive...
CORRINE: Then why do we have to sign a prenuptial agreement?
MOM: Dahil wala tayong masisiguro sa buhay natin.... We're only after your protection. [Because we cannot be sure of anything in our lives.]
DAD: Look what happened to your Tita Lydia.
CORRINE: Okay, I'll think about it.
MOM: Next week na ang kasal mo. [Your wedding is already next week.]
CORRINE: Then I have a week to think about it.
DAD: I'll make it easier for you. If Philip doesn't sign this agreement, at magpakasal pa rin kayo, kami na ang gagalitin mo. [... and you still decide to get married, then it is us who you will anger.]

Taglish as a means for dramatizing Corrine's predicament raises the specter of an agonistic relationship with the figures of authority. Yet that possibility is domesticated along the axis of generation (will she defy her parents and so displace their will?). While Corrine speaks to her parents as if she could speak for them and thereby take their place, she does so only in the privacy of their home. For audiences, to overhear this exchange is to understand that it was not meant to be overheard. Such is what makes the scene compelling: it shows what otherwise would remain hidden. But to watch this scene is also to assume the position of Edith, the secretary, whose inclusion in the lingua franca is premised on her deference to the sites of its production. Taglish as a lingua franca of dissent becomes the monopoly of a certain class. And while their words may be overheard and intercepted by an anonymous audience, it is also an audience whose presence need not be recognized or deferred to.

The possibility, of course, existed that at certain points such an audience may want to be recognized. Like the cousins in *Dogeaters*, or Corrine in the movie, they, or at least some of them, may want to approximate if not substitute for what they see. As such, and under certain conditions, they might take the linguistic mobility and conjunctural identity afforded by Taglish somewhere else, outside the movie theater and shopping mall.

The post-EDSA possibility of disrupting the regulated disruption encoded in Taglish is frequently raised in a number of contemporary movies, only to be contained. The dialectics of overhearing comes across, for example, in the figure of the *bakla*, the petit bourgeois male homosexual who frequently appears in small roles in many Filipino films. The Filipino film critic Emmanuel Reyes has noted that the bakla in Philippine cinema is often the source of comedy, usually articulated in terms of homophobic rage. Typically, baklas are portrayed as those "unable to control their sexual urges; they cannot be disciplined which makes them a threat; . . . and since they defy social conventions, [baklas] are in a position to blurt out the most outrageous remarks in a movie."[24]

Baklas are, as such, expected to be the source of shock effects inasmuch as they embody the novel conjunctions of signs. In their capacity to disrupt and so reveal the arbitrariness of linguistic and gender hierarchies, they seem to project the permanent possibility of Taglish emerging anywhere and suddenly. In this sense, the bakla would also approach the position of the mestizo/a whose identity is poised between languages. As we have seen, mestizoness, whether male or female, rests on this capacity to invoke the phantasm of translation—the sense of moving between languages—and therefore induce the desire for alterity: to be someone and someplace else. To be mestizo is, for this reason, to be an object and carrier of envy.

The bakla, however, is stereotypically cast in movies as one who has a hysterical rather than historical relationship with the lingua franca. As the site of linguistic slippage that is also immediately the confusion of sexual difference, the bakla images the unregulated disruption of hierarchy. Whereas the mestizo/a derives his/her privileged position from his/her ability to speak in the place of what comes from outside, the bakla is made to figure the consequences of indiscriminately speaking out of place. In this sense, the bakla is a kind of mestizo parody.

We can see this attempt to situate the bakla as the source of negative alterity in a scene from *Maricris Sioson: Japayuki*, a film that tells the story of a Filipina entertainer brutally murdered in Tokyo by her Japanese employers. In one scene, Maricris is rehearsing a dance number with other Filipina recruits prior to their departure for Japan. The instructor is bakla. He interrupts the rehearsal and addresses the women in a state of considerable agitation:

BAKLA: Gretchen, patayin mo muna. Mga loka kayo. Ilang lingo na nating ginagawa ito? Ano ba naman yan? Kaunti namang lambot ng inyong katawan. Kaunti lang, parang awa niyo na. Pupunta kayo sa Japan para maging dancers, para magsayaw, hindi para maging executives. Kaya dapat bawat kilos ng inyong katawan at bawat lantik ng inyong mga daliri at bawat pungay ng inyong mga mata ay importante. The end all and be all ng lahat ng mga dinadakdak ko dito ay entertainment na ibinibigay ninyo sa mga lalaki doon sa audience. Saka ito, ha, tandaan ninyo ito. Itanim niyo sa kokote niyo: Magsasayaw kayo sa Japan hindi para ipromote ang cultural heritage ng Pilipinas. Hayaan niyong iba na ang gumawa noon.

Magpupunta kayo sa Japan para ipromote ang commercial and entertainment value of Filipina women! Kayo 'yon, gaga, kayo 'yon, naintindihan ninyo? Kaya naman, kaunti namang landi! Kaunting projection! Kaunting giling! O, ano, naintindihan niyo? Janette, from the top!

[Gretchen, turn that off for a second. You idiots! How many weeks have we been doing this? What's with you? Just a little more suppleness. Just a little more, I beg of you. You're going to Japan to be dancers, to dance, not to be executives. That's why each movement of your body, of your fingers, of your eyes is important. The end all and be all of everything I've been yammering about here is entertainment that you're going to be giving to the men in the audience. And this, ha, remember this. Plant this in your heads: you're going to be dancing in Japan not in order to promote the cultural heritage of the Philippines. Let others do that.

You're going to Japan in order to promote the commercial and entertainment value of Filipina women! That's you, you idiots, that's you! Do you understand? That's why you've gotta be more flirtatious! A bit more projection! And more sexy movements! Do you understand? Janette, from the top!]

The blatantly misogynist drift of this passage, in particular the characterization of the women as commodities rather than icons of "cultural heritage," places the bakla in the position of a *bugaw*, or pimp. Yet the frenzied delivery of his words is met with silence. The camera pans the women's faces as they teeter between amusement and mild discomfort. As such, they appear to defer to the bakla instructor even as they dismiss the meaning of his words. Thus do they implicitly disentangle themselves from their ascribed "commercial and entertainment value." That they do not protest and instead return to rehearse suggests that what they heard in the bakla's speech was something else. We might think of it as the sound of envy, the sense in the bakla of wanting to become other than what he is. In this way, they hear by overhearing, attending to him as if he were a mestizo with access to other circuits of exchange.

But this is, in fact, the last that we see of the bakla instructor. As with most other Filipino movies, baklas are not the stars of the story but serve as ephemeral players. The rest of the film focuses on the travails of Maricris and the attempts of Filipina feminists to investigate the circumstances of her death. The movie ends with her performance of a "sexy dance," presumably learned from the bakla instructor, as the film's credits roll. Whatever she heard from the bakla in, and despite, his misogynist rantings she seems to have taken on. While she heard the bakla, however, she does not identify with him. Instead, Maricris, as played by the popular star Ruffa Gutierrez, fashions herself into an object of desire rather than one of ridicule. She becomes a locus of envy (though for different reasons) for both men and women, even as her story is meant to have a cautionary effect. Such is because Ruffa the movie star exceeds the character Maricris. Her identity as a star lies precisely in the ways in which no single appearance can ever exhaust her appeal but can only lead audiences to want to see more of her.

The bakla, by contrast, is only and always a bakla. His class position coupled with his sexual ambiguity places him on the margins of mestizoness as its perverse double. The bakla, in this sense, recalls the bakya speaker of English as one whose desire is out of place as evidenced by the inability to speak correctly. But where the bakya suffered from a lack of irony, the bakla is excessively ironic. As one who cannot be spoken of as a "he" or "she," the figure of the bakla is a way of recalling what must be repressed en route to speaking the lingua franca. Just as the bakya speaker's English had to be retailed in order to be set off from the speech of an urban intelligentsia, the bakla version of Taglish, called swardspeak, periodically recurs in movies (and other mass media) so as to be cast apart from mestizo discourse. In this way, the recurrence of the bakla, especially in the form of swardspeak, is one way of intimating the limits of Taglish in the post-EDSA era: the point where its interruptive spread needs to be represented in order to be suppressed.[25] And the special medium for carrying out this double movement is the movie star. For it is the star who embodies the site for the merging of Taglish with mestizoness as a set of images, the consumption of which serves to distance the viewer from the specter of the uncontrollable speech of the bakla, even as the bakla figures the desire to be like a movie star.

Taglish in contemporary movies, then, functions to domesticate the crowd into consumers receptive to the alternating invocation and revocation of linguistic hierarchy. Movies routinize the shock of hearing and speaking otherwise. In consuming such films, audiences buy into the pleasures of anonymous hearing and seeing. But in doing so, they give in to the reified version of anonymity. That is, they experience it in the mode of envy for those who appear most fluent in Taglish yet, unlike the baklas or bakyas, are capable of ordering its circulation: the movie star. Indeed, Filipino films would never survive financially without well-known names. The sight of stars is avidly awaited in networks of publicity such as gossip sheets, personal appearances, talk shows, and even the occasional political scandal. It is the stars who become the focus of audience interests, and movies are vehicles for anticipating their recurring appearances.

Movie stars in the Philippines are almost always mestizo/as, and even those who may not have started out as such, as for example famed singer/actress Nora Aunor, take on the aura of mestizoness once they achieve mass recognition.[26] Their glamour[27] has both a historical resonance, as we have seen, as well as linguistic component. As stars, actors and actresses come to typify the very elite audiences that are least inclined to watch Filipino movies, the "A" and "B" crowd. Hence, within the logic of the market, the identity of the "C" and "D" viewers can only derive from their envy of "A" and "B" audiences. Such envy is sublimated by their consuming interests in movie stars. Through stars, audiences are invited to share in the phantasm of translation that entails the nimble negotiation of linguistic registers and the social domains they imply. Constructed as privileged sites for the intersection of mestizoness with Taglish, movie stars conjure the phantom power of the lingua franca. In consuming images of movie stars, audiences submit to that power and so participate, if not actively desire, the reproduction of a mestizo/a social order.[28]

7 Writing History after EDSA

From the mid-1980s until his untimely death in September 1996, my father was in the habit of sending me thick envelopes containing rich samplings of articles from Manila's newspapers that he himself had clipped. As I moved from New York to Hawaii, and then to California, my father's letters followed me; he took delight in conveying the everyday quality of Philippine society as reflected in these newspaper clippings. Among the newspaper columns that he religiously sent me were those of Ambeth Ocampo. Though he never explicitly commented on Ocampo's columns, I took his interest in them as a sign of their value. The installments of *Looking Back* were tokens with which he and I exchanged one another's tacit concerns about the state of the nation and the understanding of its history across the physical and generational distances that separated us over the greater part of this last decade and a half. It is difficult for me to consider Ocampo's essays without at the same time thinking of the links it helped forge between my father and me, and the historical setting within which such a relationship took place.

I suspect that I am not alone in feeling this affinity with Ocampo's writings. It is not for nothing that he has become the most popular historian of the Philippines in the post-EDSA period, suggesting his ability to bridge the differences separating older from younger generations, academic from general readers, and Filipinos in the Philippines from Filipinos overseas. What is it exactly that is so particular to his writing that allows it to speak to and for such a wide variety of

Filipinos—at least among those who can read English and afford to buy newspapers and books? And what sets his work apart as a national phenomenon specific to late-twentieth-century Philippine society?

We can begin with some dates. Born on August 31, 1961, some 100 years after the birth of his beloved Jose Rizal, Ocampo is part of the generation known as the martial law babies who grew up knowing no one else except Ferdinand and Imelda Marcos as rulers of the country. Too young to have experienced the militant youth movement that unreeled with the First Quarter Storm and its aftermath in the late 1960s and early 1970s, his generation was raised in the latter part of the martial law era and came into adulthood during the turbulent years of 1983–1986. In the wake of Ninoy Aquino's assassination and the People Power Revolt at EDSA, Ocampo's generation tends to be weary if not disdainful of the nostrums of the National Democratic Front (NDF) while more receptive to the rhetoric of nongovernmental organizations (NGOS). Suspicious of authoritarian politics on both the Left and Right, it is nonetheless drawn to the neoliberal discourse of civil society. It is also a generation that may have ambivalent feelings about the Catholic Church and its entrenched hierarchy but seems no less enthusiastic about eclectic forms of religion and religiosity from born-again to new age, from beliefs in reincarnation to gleeful fantasies about aliens from outer space. While it is leery of economistic approaches to society and social analysis whereby everything tends to be reduced to the clichés of "investment strategies" or "imperialism-feudalism-bureaucrat capitalism," it is no stranger to the lures of consumer culture and shopping malls. Finally, while it is generally skeptical of the traditional authority of the state, schools, and church, it is nevertheless enthralled by the dominating sway of media images, multinational culture industries, and telecommunication technologies.

Of course, martial law babies are far from being a homogeneous group. But those who tend to define themselves as such are likely to be part of a relatively small but massively influential class educated in private schools such as Assumption, Ateneo, De La Salle, St. Theresa's, and St. Scholastica's, as well as some from the Diliman campus of the state-run University of the Philippines. Moreover, they are distinguishable from their public school–educated and poorer urban and rural compatriots by their air-conditioned cars and the walled, heavily policed "villages" and subdivisions in which they live. Inheritors of the Philippines after EDSA, martial law babies constitute the new generation of a ruling class anxious about the basis of its legitimacy and uncertain about the sources of its privilege. Skeptical of the totalitarian tendencies of the Left and Right, and utterly bored with dogmatic and largely unimaginative academic approaches to Philippine history, it is no surprise that such a group has sought other ways to reshape its national identity and that it should turn to historical sources for such a project.

Since its inception in 1987, Ocampo's newspaper column, *Looking Back*, has been a major touchstone of this post-EDSA project. Beginning as a regular feature in the Lifestyle section of the *Daily Globe*, then eventually migrating to the editorial pages of the *Philippine Daily Inquirer* (which with its circulation of about a quarter of a million is as close as one gets to a newspaper of record in the Philippines), Ocampo's column has been staple reading not only among his peers but also among older generations of English-reading Filipinos in the last decade.

Ocampo's style and popularity are rooted in the evolving conventions of mass-circulation newspapers in the Philippines. Journalism in the 1980s was very much a contested terrain. It is well known that Marcos's ability to manipulate information and administer the truth lay at the foundation of his power from 1972 to 1983. Such media monopoly was fed by and fed into the political economy of crony capitalism, the result of which was to foster in the reading public a deep cynicism toward anything they saw in the papers or on television networks controlled by Marcos cronies.

But all throughout the dictatorship, subterranean sources of information countering the claims of the regime appeared in many places and many forms: from mimeographed sheets to overseas Filipino newspapers, from protest songs and the theatrical productions of the Philippine Educational Theater Association to everyday gossip and jokes about the Marcoses. By the early 1980s, Filipino publishers and writers had become further emboldened to launch more frontal attacks. Oppositional views grew more insistent, with the women columnists of *Mr. & Ms.* and the *Daily Globe* among its leading voices. It was especially after the assassination of Ninoy Aquino and the explosion of People Power at EDSA that opposition newspapers began to gain a much wider readership. Along with the Catholic Church, newspapers became the locus of new ways of speaking and critically engaging social relations amid the military disarray and internal dissension within the NDF forces, humiliation of the traditional politicians, and widespread nervousness surrounding the newly politicized military. Among the new crop of journalists that emerged in the postassassination period, none were more widely read than the daily columnists.[1]

Given the relative lack of influence and prestige among Filipino academics in the public sphere, newspaper columnists stepped in as mediators between a society undergoing unpredictable transitions and their individual members restless for change and flushed from political revolt. A newly politicized middle class turned regularly to the columnists as indispensable guides to complex events. Readers relied on columnists not just for coherent renderings of such events as coup attempts, election campaigns and boycotts, economic reforms, controversies over U.S. bases or Marcos's hidden wealth, and the crimes both common and grand that unfolded everyday. More important, readers derived a measure of reassurance in the appearance of differences of opinions and interpretations of these events among columnists. Despite, or perhaps because of, the shrillness and at times pettiness of their tone and content, such arguments were taken as signs that some sort of democracy existed, at least where the circulation of information was concerned. In addition, the very form of the column—its conciseness and portability designed for quick perusal and daily disposal—meant that writers were in a position to communicate to a wider audience grown habituated to the sharp turns of phrases and shocking revelations nurtured by the anti-Marcos media.[2] Such a charged environment proved to be hospitable to the emergence of different voices, including those purporting to take an idiosyncratic, even iconoclastic, approach to Philippine history such as that of Ocampo.

Ocampo, of course, is not the first historian-journalist. Journalism as a genre for historical reflection can be traced as far back as the late nineteenth and early twentieth centuries in nationalist newspapers from *La Solidaridad* to *Renacimiento Filipino*. The generation before Ocampo included well-known writers (and mentors) such as E. Aguilar Cruz, Carmen Guerrero-Nakpil, Miguel Bernad, Doreen Fernandez, and the great Nick Joaquin. Yet today, Ocampo is unmatched in popularity among journalist-historians as gleaned from the sheer number of books he has sold and the startling amount of affection as well as envy that his columns attract. His book sales can, in part, be attributed to the marketing muscle of Anvil Publishing, an arm of the largest bookseller in the country, National Bookstore, while the daily mass attention he has garnered can be chalked up to the wide circulation of the *Philippine Daily Inquirer*. The scope and significance of his impact, however, cannot be fully understood without taking stock of the style and substance of the writings themselves. There are many qualities that set Ocampo's work apart from other journalist-historians and academics working in the Philippines today, but let me just mention the three that I take to be crucial.

First, there is Ocampo's irony. Eschewing the friarlike pedantry of a lot of nationalist rhetoric and whiny sententiousness of other columnists, Ocampo approaches heroes and events with a shrewd eye for their odd features and contradictory appearances. Rizal's frugality and uprightness is countered by his romantic obsessions and baroquely erotic dreams. The revolutionary hero, Antonio Luna, is shown to be a hostage to his swollen masculine ego. His brother, Juan, comes across not simply as a great artist but also a brutish man who murders his wife, Paz Pardo de Tavera, and mother-in-law. Aguinaldo's leadership is undercut by his immoral complicity in the assassination of Bonifacio and Luna. And Bonifacio's heroic reputation is deflated by evidence not only of his military incompetence but also of the jejune quality of his literary productions.[3] While Ocampo celebrates the very fact of an anticolonial revolution in 1896, he is relentlessly critical of its farcical aftermath in the form of the Malolos republic under the leadership of self-serving ilustrados.[4]

Indeed, little escapes Ocampo's ironizing regard, as he scopes less for evidence of Filipino greatness than for signs of its human limitations. He handles—actually holds in his hands—Jose Rizal's underwear, Apolinario Mabini's bones, and Antonio Luna's student notebooks with the unconstrained amusement of one discovering telltale secrets hidden in his grandfather's *aparador*. In fact, the word *amuse* and its variants frequently recur in his texts as if to underscore the "fun" (another favorite word) one can have looking at the all-too-human remains of figures who are all-too-frequently regarded as gods.

This ironizing sensibility opens up to a second characteristic of

Ocampo's essays: the willingness with which they explore the permeable divide between fact and fiction. In this, Ocampo unwittingly rediscovers the deep etymological kinship between the two terms, thereby reminding us of the imaginative wellspring of historical thinking. History, he tells us again and again, is not a mere collection of dates and names. Rather, it speaks and listens, so forming the very language by which the living and dead attend to one another. History is then a lot of other things: signifying systems, interpretive schemes, contending narratives, and expressive energies that subtend the very possibility of social life.

It is in this light that his writings entertain subjects that might seem trivial and marginal to most historians but in fact constitute the substance of other, often forgotten but no less important stories the way dreams constitute the residues of repressed elements in one's waking life. It is not strange, then, that Ocampo should repeatedly dwell on the subject of Rizal or the ilustrado writer Marcelo del Pilar's dreams, or that he retails gossip about the possible poisoning of Juan Luna by agents of an aggrieved Trinidad Pardo de Tavera seeking to avenge his sister's murder, or tells the story of the probable rape of Gregoria de Jesus, Bonifacio's wife, by soldiers loyal to Aguinaldo. In a similar vein, Ocampo takes great interest in the pseudonyms of Filipino heroes, their tales of mistaken identity while traveling abroad, and their penchant for cross-dressing in order to escape colonial surveillance by projecting alternative identities. In so doing, he stresses the variety of linguistic disguises, fictional persona, and calculated lies that such figures were drawn to assume. These are facts of a sort that imply other events yet to be accounted for and open up avenues of interpretation yet to be taken. Insisting on the facticity of fictions, rumors, jokes, and dreams, while at the same time fictionalizing facts by shaping them into palimpsests of what-could've-beens and roads-not-taken, Ocampo links the past to the currents of contemporary wishfulness.

The task of awakening the past to the concerns of the present is, of course, the avowed concern of every historian. But with Ocampo, this act of communing with the deadweight of the past tends to focus on an obsessive, one might even say fetishistic, delight in the details of everyday life. This brings us to the third quality of his essays: the careful attention they devote to the common, the overlooked, the ordinary, what we might think of as the splendid *basura* (trash) of the archives—

the *sari-sari*, the *tira-tira*, the *anu-ano*, as well as the *diumano* of the past. One minute he's noting down the contents of the youthful revolutionary General Gregorio del Pilar's pockets as he lay dying in Tirad Pass; the next, enumerating the dishes, dances, and decorations for Aguinaldo's birthday celebrations as he was escaping U.S. forces. He ponders the arrangement of Mabini's bones in his tiny coffin, examines the curling irons for Luna's moustache, tracks down the exact Tagalog expletive used by General Mascardo to goad General Luna to fight him, gawks at the vaginal clamps used by the ilustrado doctor Galiciano Apacible and the "pickled appendix" of Aguinaldo. He pores over the financial accounts of the revolutionary forces and wonders about the nature of their purchases—from guns and bullets to beaded slippers and silk undershorts—as if these were items that we ourselves might have purchased in a surge of consumerist desire to relieve the inevitable moments of tedium in waging an anticolonial war. He not only gives us the genealogy of the national anthem but actually tells us how it was played in a different key and time signature from what we are used to hearing, allowing us to imagine how it must have sounded to its original auditors.

In other words, Ocampo sees history not only as a set of documents to be decoded but as an entire array of objects to be fondled and felt. Yet rather than order these objects into a static, museumlike classificatory system, he lets them simply hang, suspended between speculation and spectacle. In this way, his concern with the everyday and ordinary yields a veritable historical sensorium that restores to the past its haunting, not-quite-dead-nor-alive quality.[5]

These features of Ocampo's writings—an ironizing sensibility, an alertness to the crossings of fiction and fact, and a materialist fondness for the everyday—when taken alongside the political economy and cultural history of book publishing and newspaper writing since 1983, help to partially explain his considerable readership. The popularity of his columns and books become even more noteworthy when one considers the language in which they are written: English.

What is the place of English in Ocampo's work? What does its use signify in the understanding of history after EDSA and the shadow of "Philippines 2000"?[6] We can begin to approach these questions by inquiring into the remarkable resilience of linguistic hierarchy in post-

EDSA society. For as we enter the twenty-first century, what we see in the Philippines is the persistence of a regime of linguistic difference—principally involving English, Filipino/Tagalog, and Taglish—that reflects even as it refracts social differences.[7]

Since the 1970s, there has been a steady growth in the publication of fiction and poetry in Filipino/Tagalog. Such a development was spurred by the strange confluence of opposing forces: on the one hand, the Marcos regime's sponsorship of new journals for the publication of writings in the vernacular (thanks, in part, to the collaboration of various academics at the University of the Philippines); on the other hand, the active promotion by the Left, principally the NDF, of protest literature in this language. Marcos and the NDF thus sought to use Filipino/Tagalog as a way of projecting their different ideas about the future of the nation in and through the demarcation of its linguistic borders. In this sense, Filipino/Tagalog was a crucial element in each side's strategy to incite mass participation and secure political legitimacy. Despite their ideological differences, each mirrored the other in terms of their investment in the representational capacities of Filipino/Tagalog.

Meanwhile, English continued to be used by the Marcos state for its official pronouncements and newspapers. Marcos (who, despite being Ilocano, was actually the first president to deliver his inaugural address in Filipino/Tagalog) gave speeches, issued numerous presidential decrees, and held press conferences in English. He was playing not only to a first world foreign audience on whose dollar loans, political legitimacy, and military support he depended but also to the rest of the Filipino elite, whose consent he had to coerce and silence he had to secure. Like Manuel Quezon and other presidents after him, Marcos could switch between languages as conditions required, occupying the position of the preeminent translator between the putative interests of the masses and the demands emanating from the imperialist order of things. English was used to speak up to authority and across to the Filipino middle classes (for what would a Filipino bourgeoisie be that was not literate in English?), while Filipino/Tagalog was used to speak down to the "masses" as if to establish cross-class solidarity.

The People Power Revolt at EDSA had the effect of reconfiguring, momentarily at least, the social hierarchy, and with it, the hierarchy of languages. EDSA was a revolt conducted in Taglish, the hybrid, unofficial language of popular culture emanating from the marketplace, movies, radio, television, and tabloids. During EDSA, both English and Filipino/Tagalog ceded their representational purchase to the worlds, respectively, of the high and low. As I suggested in chapter 6, the uprising at EDSA conjugated linguistic levels into a relation of interruption and complementarity in the same way that the rich and poor, religious and lay, civilian and military found themselves placed side by side by the force of historical events. Prior notions of rank and social distinction momentarily vanished in the face of a common foe and amid the sharing of common fears and hopes. And the language that seemed most appropriate for this social alchemy was the democratizing speech of Taglish. With Taglish at EDSA, English and Filipino/Tagalog came to revel in their promiscuous mixing, providing a new language for the articulation of new, potentially more egalitarian social relations.

The aftermath of EDSA, however, brought about the reaffirmation of social hierarchy, and with it, the reinstitution of linguistic levels. Filipino/Tagalog has continued to grow as a print language mainly for fiction, poetry, and theater, but it has yet to gain dominance as the language of the state and a medium of instruction in schools, despite its increasing usage in arts education and some of the sciences at state universities (along with the writing of academic dissertations in this language). The fact remains that it has yet to gain a clear hegemony in the production of knowledge in the Philippines. Taglish continues to be the lingua franca for such commercial media as movies, radio, television, tabloids, and advertising as well as classroom lectures and more informal forms of political discourse (see, for example, President Joseph Estrada's press conferences). But it continues to be discounted as far too "corrupt" and far too difficult to codify because of the rapid changes of its lexicon and its numerous subcultural variations (such as swardspeak). It cannot thus serve as an effective substitute for either English or Filipino/Tagalog. English, for its part, has reasserted itself as the official language of the state, the courts, and transnational business and diplomatic communities as well as the idiom of newspapers of record and most of academe. Post-EDSA middle-class society nationwide continues to invest in the prestige of English, seeing it as a source of political and cultural capital (which explains the periodic panic among elites regarding the deteriorating ability of Filipino students to speak English and thus compete in the global marketplace).

At the same time, English has undergone an important transformation. Unlike generations past, the post-EDSA middle classes no longer seek to affect the sound and sensibility of American English. In an era that has seen the closure of two large U.S. military bases, Clark and Subic, English has been reclaimed not as a sign of colonial dependency but as part of the national culture. In this sense, the Filipino bourgeoisie has sought to vernacularize English in the same way that the ilustrado generations of the late nineteenth and early twentieth centuries attempted to nationalize Spanish.[8]

Ocampo's use of English is thus linked to a linguistic practice that has its roots in the Spanish colonial era, conceivably stretching as far back as the seventeenth century in the works of ladino poets like Fernando Bagongbanta and Tomas Pinpin. Just as Rizal and company reworked Spanish into an idiom of anticolonial dissent, so Ocampo and other Filipino writers and intellectuals use English as a medium of nationalist identification.

Yet as with Spanish, so with English: their use has fostered historically intractable contradictions in that they provide their speakers with a way of marking themselves off from the masses, yet positioning themselves as their "enlightened" representatives. In this way, Ocampo participates in the predicament of Filipino intellectuals everywhere, past and present. In seeking to speak for and of the nation, they find it necessary to occupy a different position by speaking on a different register: the language of an other, dominant power. In doing so, they simultaneously identify with *and* dis-identify from those at the lower, non-English-speaking rungs of the social hierarchy. Similarly they are critical of, yet at some level complicitous with, those on top of that hierarchy. It is this political ambivalence that Ocampo and his generation share with the ilustrados of a century ago, as with many other Filipino intellectuals of the twentieth century. For it is precisely this ambivalent positioning that has made them essential mediators and necessary brokers of power in the history of the Philippines. Such ambivalence has historically proven to be both a privilege and curse. For that structural uncertainty of being simultaneously part of yet apart from the "people" is precisely the condition that constitutes not only the class identity of the Filipino middle classes; it also delineates the national basis of its power. English today, like Spanish in the past, is one of the most pervasive ways of registering and reasserting the powerful effects of this legacy of political hybridity.

It is arguable, then, that the appeal of Ocampo's texts is indissociable from the continuing authority that English exercises over other languages in the Philippines. It is because he writes in English that Ocampo can signal to his readers his access to vast archival resources, especially those in Spanish. English mediates the recovery of Spanish, which increasingly seems so distant and foreign to present-day readers. With this recuperation of the archives in Spanish, Ocampo accomplishes two things. First, he is able to circumvent the authority of Filipino academics, reaching beyond their professional prose and giving a larger nonacademic public a sense of the actual words of those in the past—words that are now readable in English.[9] Second, by making this archive available in English, Ocampo at once draws the past nearer while keeping it at a distance, alerting us to its enduring difference. His use of English highlights rather than conceals the artifactual and therefore constructed nature of these records, reminding readers that what they are reading are translations that are subject to differing interpretations.[10] In this sense, Ocampo's use of colloquial English to relay records largely in Spanish or official American English is analogous to the ilustrados' use of Spanish. His writings convey his ability to take on and translate the rhetorical authority associated with past colonial masters. It is as if by reading Ocampo's English, one is able to hear Spanish yet bypass, and so replace, its authority. (And for the generation that grew up after World War II, the memory of that authority is invariably linked to having to endure the tedium of state-mandated Spanish language classes where teachers presided over students like the Damasos and Victorinas of the *Noli* and where many things were learned except, of course, Spanish.) Thus, Ocampo's use of English not only co-opts the power of past colonial rulers; it also displaces and deflates their influence. One result of that displacement is that English comes across as if it were a new language. How so?

The novelty—that is to say, the colloquial character—of Ocampo's English, like that of his fellow newspaper columnists, has to do with its locus of address. This post-EDSA English is not directed to a larger audience abroad but solely and specifically to a national audience at home. As such, it readily incorporates Taglish inflections even as it no longer bothers to spell out various local usages and references, taking these for granted. Hence, it is written with the sense that it is meant for no one else—least of all for North Americans—other than those who identify themselves as Filipinos—middle class, to be sure, but also others from lower down the social ladder who aspire to such status. As with the overwhelming number of writings in English published in the Philippines since EDSA, Ocampo's essays neither solicit nor engage an international readership except in the most adventitious sense. English as it has been written in the Philippines over the last decade or so does not seek to reach beyond the borders of a national imaginary but functions precisely to redraw and firm up such borders. It is for this reason that the political ambivalence that is signaled, if not produced, by English does not appear—at least not for the moment—as a problem and is not worked into a set of propositions understandable in other, non-Filipino contexts.

Such a situation has the effect of consolidating the cultural authority of Filipino writers in English. Rightly or wrongly, they regard themselves to have been liberated from the pressures outside and below. They feel that they do not need to submit to the judgment of others, least of all non-Filipinos associated with a colonial past, and certainly can dispense with the opinions of those who cannot write or speak English below them. And given the fact that the number of writers of English in the Philippines is relatively small to begin with, there is little compunction nor a public forum to engage in systematic critical evaluation of each other's works. (Indeed, what often takes the place of criticism in the Philippines today is either gossip or the ritual of book launchings and awards.)

Thus the paradox of writing in English after EDSA: on the one hand, English has become decolonized and domesticated into part of a national hierarchy of languages; on the other hand, it has resulted in further consolidating social divisions, whereby its privileged speakers and writers need no longer feel accountable to anyone else except themselves and the demands of the marketplace.

The following questions then arise: Has the nationalization of writing in English come at the expense of parochializing its contents and conserving its social context? Is the popularity of Ocampo's work propelled by even as it contributes to this paradox? Or can the ilustrado ethos embodied in Ocampo and others' writings also be read as a kind of defensive, even subtly militant response to the encroachments of new, as well as some old, colonizing presences: Taiwanese investors, Japanese businesspeople, European and North American multinationals, the IMF, the World Bank, and the economic and cultural pressures they are increasingly bringing to bear on the country? At a time when shopping malls and El Shaddai[11] offer the splendors of submission to the alienating effects of products and prophets, Filipino writing in English such as Ocampo's provides, at the very least, a lifeline to worldly skepticism and the armor of a relativizing irony through the mediation of a Philippine history rife with conflict and hence possibilities.

Popularity has its hazards. The work of historical writing like that of journalism in the Philippines cannot but tack with the shifting winds of change. Coming in the wake of People Power, such changes include the seemingly irresistible boom in development and unceasing expropriation of human labor by the forces of global capital. These developments cannot but incite the arbitrary displacement and destruction of peoples and places. Metro Manila and many parts of the country today look like war zones: streets pulled up to give way to yet more flyovers, traffic at a standstill as if to serve as a cruel counterpoint to the promises of mobility and modernity, the continuing humiliation and at times death of overseas contract workers, blighted shanties clinging to the walls of gleaming suburban "villages." Even as peace accords are signed and rebellions are tamed, kidnappings abound as entrepreneurship by other means and state instrumentalities from the police to Congress are used shamelessly to promote personal interests as if in belated emulation of the Marcoses, whose presence continues to permeate the body politic in more ways than one.

Ocampo, in his own way, has sought to parry the thrusts of such events, introjecting the past into the present as a corrective to varieties of official and popular mystifications. It is perhaps not unreasonable to suppose that the manner in which we retrieve the past will determine the ways in which we will remember the present and so save it from its violent banalities and everyday injustices. Ambeth Ocampo has had much to say and contribute to this task. With each collection of essays, he continues the necessary task of calling on the specters of the past, tacking between the blowing winds of developmentalism and flowing lahar of Philippines 2000.

8 "Your Grief Is Our Gossip"
Overseas Filipinos and Other Spectral Presences

Circulation sweats money from every pore.... Money haunts the sphere of circulation and constantly moves around within it.—*Karl Marx*, CAPITAL

This chapter grows out of an effort to understand nationalism as a kind of affect productive of a community of longing. My concern lies in the emergence of nationalist sentiment (as distinct from the institutionalization of nationalist ideology and its accompanying disciplinary technologies) in and through the work of mourning particular and exemplary deaths amid the collusion of the state with transnational capital.[1] Focusing on events in the Philippines in the mid-1990s particularly with regard to the flows of immigrants and overseas contract workers, I inquire into nationalist attempts at containing the dislocating effects of global capital through the collective mourning for its victims.

This labor of mourning, however, tends to bring forth the uncanny nature of capitalist development itself on which the nation-state depends. The moral economy of grieving is persistently haunted by the circulation of money. Hence, while nationalist mourning is borne by the desire of the living to defer to the dead, thereby giving rise to the sensation of each belonging to the other, it also anticipates its own failure amid the relentless commodification of everyday life. Often, the form which that anticipation takes, especially in a society saturated by commercially driven mass media, is gossip. As I hope to show, mourning and gossip together generate the structures of feeling specific (but not limited) to Philippine nationalism: the tensions—which is to say the sensation—of becoming Filipino at the start of the twenty-first century.

Workers for the World In 1994, an article in the *Los Angeles Times* described overseas Filipinos in the following way:

Distinctive among the huddled masses of global economic migration, overseas Filipinos represent the elite, high end of the labor market. They are generally well-educated and usually accomplished speakers of English. But like other itinerant workers, they lack opportunities in the dysfunctional Philippine economy. So women with college degrees serve as maids in Tokyo and Hongkong.... Semiskilled laborers toil in Kuwait while Filipino seamen ply the oceans on the world's ships. Filipino business graduates dominate the middle-management ranks of many multinational corporations in Southeast Asia, earning wages they couldn't dream of at home.[2]

Comprising an army of flexible workers, Filipinos abroad simultaneously signify the failure of the Philippine nation-state to contain its excess population *and* the success of global capitalism in absorbing and accommodating this failure. From the point of view of the *Los Angeles Times*, they can best be regarded as both the product and producers of surplus: sheer labor power immediately translatable into a universally understood form of value. Though they originate from the Philippines, they can, thanks to the workings of global capital, now return to the nation in a form that is at once abstract and exterior to it. Indeed, as Filipino-American newspaper publisher Alex Esclamado put it, "Remittances by overseas Filipinos [estimated in 1995 to be about $6 billion annually] to their families are now considered direct foreign aid ... that can have a radical effect on people's lives—building houses in depressed rural villages, paying off medical bills, sending little brothers and sisters and cousins to school."[3]

As "foreign" sources of "aid," overseas Filipinos come to occupy ambiguous positions. Neither inside nor wholly outside the nation-state, they hover on the edges of its consciousness, rendering its boundaries porous with their dollar-driven comings and goings. In this sense, they take on the semblance of spectral presences whose labor takes place somewhere else but whose effects command, by their association with money, a place in the nation-state. As extruded parts of the body politic, the traces of their bodies continue to circulate, producing "radical effects on people's lives." For this reason, overseas Filipinos now increasingly represent novel elements in local understandings of "cultural transformations" and "national development." Their absence becomes an integral feature of vernacular narratives regarding what it means to be modern.

How, then, is the modernity of overseas Filipinos understood in the Philippines? While the Filipino population has had a long history of migrations, it is only in the last twenty-five years that the massive, state-encouraged movements of workers and immigrants have become part of the nation's everyday life.[4] What are the ways in which "foreign" Filipinos are rendered socially legible by the nation-state and its critics? How do the differentially articulated locations of Filipinoness—for example, as contract workers on the move, as immigrant professionals anxious for suburbanized assimilation, or as members of racialized and hyphenated minorities—pose limits to the particularizing reach of a Filipino nationalist imaginary? In what follows, I offer some provisional observations on the peculiar conjunction of "overseas" with "Filipino" in the late twentieth century. While recognizing the diversity of overseas Filipino lives, I will limit my focus in this chapter on two significant terms for designating them in the Philippines: *balikbayan*, or immigrant Filipinos primarily from North America who periodically visit the motherland, and overseas contract workers (ocw) who are employed on a contractual basis in such places as the Middle East, Europe, and East and Southeast Asia.

A Nationalism Deferred It was the Marcos regime in the mid-1970s that coined the term *balikbayan* to describe immigrant Filipinos primarily from North America who periodically visit the motherland. The term joins the Tagalog words *balik* (to return) and *bayan* (town, and at least from the late nineteenth century on, nation). As a balikbayan, one's relationship to the Philippines is construed in terms of one's sentimental attachments to one's hometown and extended family rather than one's loyalty to the nation-state.[5] At the same time, being a balikbayan depends on one's permanent residence abroad. It means that one lives somewhere else and that one's appearance in the Philippines is temporary and intermittent, as if one were a tourist.

Indeed, the Marcos regime's interest in overseas Filipinos was part of its plan to spur the tourist industry both as a generator of foreign exchange and showcase for its putative accomplishments. Offering a combination of bargain airfares, tax breaks, and other incentives, the Philippine government encouraged dollar-earning Filipinos, especially from North America, to visit the country and see for themselves the results of martial law. Living in close proximity to the sources of capital, balikbayans were treated like tourists in their land of origin. As consumers of the Philippines, balikbayans, like other foreign visitors, were to be accorded deference and generously accommodated by local officials.

For the balikbayans, the Philippines was served up as a collection of consumable goods orchestrated by the Department of Tourism. Tourist spots, native handicrafts, and local food were packaged as fragments of the bayan available for purchase. Alienated from the nation, balikbayans returned to encounter commodified versions of their origins now similarly rendered alienable as tourist objects destined for other places. Under the general rubric of tourism, their strangeness was reworked into a manageable, if not entirely familiar, presence by the state.

That the state succeeded in domesticating balikbayans into tourists can partly be seen in the Filipino nationalist unease about them. Nationalist writers often distinguish those who return from working temporary jobs in the Middle East and Asia from those who visit from the United States. Whereas overseas contract workers (OCWS) are seen to return from conditions of near abjection, balikbayans are frequently viewed to be steeped in their own sense of superiority, serving only to fill others with a sense of envy. The well-known journalist Conrado de Quiros, for example, writes about those balikbayans from the United States

who force us each year to make an apologia for the indolence of the Filipinos. They're the ones who sally forth to bedazzle the natives. They queue up in East or West Coast airports with tons and tons of baggage, many of them containing groceries for relatives who can't wait to have a taste of America....[6]

They bring us stories about how much life in America has proved what the *Reader's Digest* says it is. They also bring us homilies, delivered with the proselytizing zeal of Thomasites, which are forceful for their use of contrasts. It's too hot in the Philippines. It's nice to snuggle by the hearth in America. There's grime and smog in our streets. You can't drive without anti-pollutants in the States. Filipino drivers are maniacs. American drivers follow traffic rules. . . . You defer too much to authority here. You can talk man-to-man even with the president of the United States.[7]

De Quiros compares the balikbayans to the Thomasites, the first group of U.S. schoolteachers who arrived in the Philippines at the beginning of this century and who figure in nationalist narratives not as benevolent instructors but as purveyors of the miseducation of the Filipinos. Thanks to the Thomasites and those who came in their wake, Filipinos were led to think of themselves as if they were North Americans; that is, as other than who they were supposed to be.[8] Balikbayans as Thomasites are thus positioned as neocolonizers whose ambitions lie in setting themselves apart from the rest of the so-called natives rather than affiliating with them. In that sense, balikbayans emerge as figures to be envied. Their easy association with Western consumer products and access to a powerful state apparatus in the United States mark them as different: they represent the fulfillment of Filipino desires realizable only outside the Philippines. What adds to their difference is this: they are unable to respond to the envy of others with a show of empathy. While they seem to possess everything, they are in fact missing something: a sense of humility as shown by their inability to defer to those who lack what they have. Indeed, they do nothing else but point out what it is the Philippines lacks as compared to the United States, thereby appearing shameless and arrogant.

Yet that shamelessness, or what in Tagalog is commonly referred to as *walang hiya*,[9] is less a cultural trait than part of a historical legacy. De Quiros continues:

And then you realize that the physical fact of Filipinos migrating abroad is really just the tip of the iceberg. . . . Most of us are expatriates right *here* in our own land. America is our heartland whether we get to go there or not. Nothing demonstrates this better than that the balikbayan *does* succeed in bedazzling the natives. If he flaunts his wares, it's simply because he knows the audience will lap it up. . . . It's the lack of any sense of nationhood, of being Filipino among us that makes expatriation the most preferred option of all. . . . But surely there's a tragedy in seeing the fundamental question of one's life as nothing more than which country can provide a better living? Surely there must be more to life than this? (140)

The shamelessness of the balikbayan turns out to be the "tragedy" that is shared by the majority of Filipinos still caught up in colonial delusions. Balikbayans are disconcerting not only because they seem to corroborate the terms of colonial hegemony; they also mirror the "failure" of nationalism to retain and control the excess known as overseas Filipinos. For the nationalist writer, balikbayans seem to escape rather than confirm the hope that Filipinos as Filipinos would choose to "belong to this particular earth, this particular time"; that rather than leave this "benighted life," they would instead "*do* something about our benightedness" (de Quiros, 141). Not only are balikbayans akin to U.S. colonizers; even more dismaying is their similarity to the collaborators of the past. Their departure amounts to a kind of betrayal of national particularity. Yet, the fact that they are merely enacting a historical role laid out before them makes them far more intimate with the people who they leave behind. Proof of this is the fact that balikbayans are envied. They are recognized for what they are. It isn't the case that their interests diverge from the people, but rather they, not the nationalist intellectuals, set the terms for the articulation of those interests. It is this negative insight that haunts de Quiros's essay.

While the state accords balikbayans a place as touristic consumers identifiable with foreign currency and international legitimacy, the nationalist writer regards them as tragic reflections of the nation's failure to materialize itself as the locus of a people's desire. Through the figure of the balikbayan, de Quiros manages to mark the pathos and poignancy of a nationalism deferred as part of the condition of being a Filipino today. As we shall see, it is precisely this pathos-laden notion of nationalism and the politics of deference it implies that finds expression in the figure of the other overseas Filipino: the ocw.

The "New Heroes" When the balikbayan program was inaugurated in the early martial law years, its original targets, as we saw, were immigrants from North America who then made up the largest pool of overseas Filipinos. By the early 1980s, changes in the global economy increased the demand for skilled and semiskilled Filipino workers in many parts of the Middle East, Asia, and western Europe. Unlike the earlier group of Filipino-Americans, this later group was bound by temporary contracts to foreign employers in international locales. These workers came to be known in the Philippines by a particular name: OCWS, or overseas contract workers.

Unlike Filipinos in the United States—who generally tended to assimilate either as professional middle-class suburbanites or, in the case of the second generation, ethnicized, hyphenated Filipino-Americans[10]— OCWS rarely ever expect to remain permanently in their host country. Forever consigned to positions of relative subservience and marginality by the terms of their contract, as well as by virtue of their exclusion from the linguistic and religious communities of their employers, OCWS can only exist as sheer labor power, supplementary formations to the imagined communities of their bosses. Rather than ask for the rights of citizenship, as Filipino immigrants in North America are wont to do, OCWS tend instead to seek good earnings within maximally safe and minimally abusive environments. They are less interested in influencing legislation or the terms of political representation within the country of their employ—they leave that up to the activist NGOS and church groups to which they have occasional recourse—as they are with securing the material and symbolic means with which to maintain ties of reciprocity and obligatory exchanges with their extended kin groups at home.[11] It is perhaps for this reason that OCWS often refer to their travels as a kind of "adventure," or in Tagalog, as *pakikipagsapalaran* and *pagbabakasakali*.[12] To go abroad is to find one's fortune (*palad*) as well as to take risks (*magbakasakali*). One seeks to convert the products of one's labor into gifts with which to endow one's kin at home, thereby gaining their respect and recognition. At the same time, one also risks uncertain conditions and the prospect of becoming alienated abroad and at home.

Subject to the daily pressures and exploitative demands of an alien working environment and taxed by their efforts to negotiate with or, more commonly, evade the apparatus of a state hostile or indifferent to their situation, OCWS often relate lives of loneliness, deprivation, and abuse. It isn't surprising, then, that they should be accorded a status distinct from that of the balikbayans. Rather than regarded as tourists for whom the Philippines can only exist as a set of commodified objects or failed versions of nationalist modernity, OCWs are recognized as national heroes. Hence, when President Cory Aquino, whose administration was a major beneficiary of dollar remittances by OCWs, addressed a group of domestic helpers in Hong Kong in 1988, she began by telling them, "Kayo po ang mga bagong bayani" ("You are the new heroes").[13]

To understand how it is that OCWs rather than Filipino immigrants to North America came to be considered heroes, it is necessary to ask about the ways in which heroism has historically been construed in the Philippines. As with all modern nation-states, the Philippines traces its official genealogy to a line of male founders, beginning with the "first Filipino," the Chinese mestizo Jose Rizal. As the historian Reynaldo Ileto has convincingly demonstrated, much of the history of Filipino nationalism in the twentieth century has been articulated with reference as much to the purported life of Rizal as to his suffering and death at the hands of Spanish colonial rulers. Invested with a messianic aura, Rizal proved to be far more potent in his death than he was when alive. Numerous revolutionary groups—from Andres Bonifacio's Katipunan to the peasant armies and rebel churches in the southern Tagalog regions—rallied around his name.[14]

Rizal's potency rested on his ability to evoke populist visions of utopic communities held together by an ethos of mutual caring, the sharing of obligations (*damayan*), and the exchange of pity (*awa*). These notions were reminiscent of the great themes set by the widely popular narrative of Jesus Christ's passion translated into various vernaculars (collectively known, as previously mentioned, as *Pasyon*) since the eighteenth century. Recognizing the power of Rizal's memory, U.S. colonial and Filipino national elites collaborated in monumentalizing his absence—for example, in the erection of the Rizal monument at the place of his execution in 1912—as they sought to regulate both the sites and occasions of its commemoration.

It was precisely this image of Rizal in conjunction with the suffering Christ—figures at once pathetic and prophetic—that was mobilized to explain the events that began with the assassination of Ninoy Aquino in 1983 and ended with the People Power Revolt in 1986 that ousted the Marcoses from power. Ninoy and Rizal seemed to merge into a single narrative frame that harked back to the themes of the *Pasyon:* of innocent lives forced to undergo humiliation at the hands of alien forces;

of unjustified deaths both shocking and public; of massive responses of pity and prayer that would, in mobilizing alternative communities of resistance, finally drive away the forces of oppression and pave the way for some kind of liberation. In place of the class-based militancy of the National Democratic Front and Communist Party of the Philippines, this particular narrative drew on cross-class religiosity, positing a sacred hierarchy within which all other hierarchies would be subsumed and reordered.

Predicated on the logics of suffering and sacrifice, the political culture of People Power and subsequent regime of Cory Aquino thrived on the notion of pity rather than equal rights to legitimate their claims to power and moral certainty. As such, Cory Aquino's administration fashioned an ideal of deference and subordination to an ultimately ineffable because transcendent source as the basis for alleging worldly authority. Where the Marcoses depicted themselves as secular modernists presiding over expansive and monumental national projects, Cory Aquino came across as the stoic widow given to prayer, repeatedly turning to her dead husband and her Savior in the midst of right-wing coup attempts and the rampages of anticommunist death squads. On bended knees, she asked only to be an instrument of a higher will. Her obedience was the basis of her power. It was precisely during this moment in Philippine history that ocws—increasingly made up by the mid-1980s of women going abroad as domestic helpers, mail-order brides, and sex workers—came to be known as the new heroes.

The Economy of Pity By encoding ocws as national heroes, Aquino and her successor, Fidel Ramos, have sought to contain the anxieties attendant on the flow of migrant labor, including the emotional distress over the separation of families and the everyday exploitation of migrants by job contractors, travel agents, and foreign employers. As I suggested earlier, such conditions point to the inability of the state to provide for its people. Repeatedly, Philippine embassies abroad have come under criticism from ocw advocates, especially women's groups, for their failure to safeguard the security of Filipinos abroad. Rather than a source of national pride, embassies have become national embarrassments.

Such embarrassment (in Tagalog, hiya) periodically surfaces in the Philippine press, which exists primarily to record the voices of the

Filipino middle class and national elites. Anecdotes are retailed about the Europeans equating the word *Filipino* with domestic helpers, or Filipino tourists being asked by OCWs in Singapore shopping malls or Madrid parks if they, too, are on their day off. In these stories, Filipino elites as well as nationalists feel themselves incapable of maintaining the boundaries of class difference as they are associated with an ethnically marked group of service workers. Embarrassment arises from their inability to keep social lines from blurring (thereby rendering problematic their position as privileged representatives of the nation) and maintaining a distinction between Filipino as the name of a sovereign people and Filipino as the generic term for designating a subservient class dependent on foreign economies.

Anxieties about the instability of and confusion over the term *Filipino* arises most dramatically, however, over news reports about abuses suffered by OCWs at the hands of employers from Saipan to Saudi Arabia.[15] One such event was the recent execution of domestic helper Flor Contemplacion in Singapore. Arrested and subsequently convicted for the double murder of another Filipina domestic, Delia Maga, and the child of the latter's employer in 1991, Contemplacion was sentenced to death on the basis of evidence that to most Filipinos at least, appeared to be of dubious validity. Despite numerous and desperate requests for clemency, the Singaporean courts ordered her execution on March 17, 1995. Her death aroused widespread outrage and anguish, mobilizing mass actions unseen since the People Power Revolt of 1986. For example, in a piece remarkable for its typicality, one journalist sees in the case of Contemplacion an event that "encompasses all the abuse that the nation has had to endlessly endure. . . . The long lines at foreign embassies; the treatment at immigration counters endured by rich and poor Filipino passport holders alike. . . . Patronizing lectures from Mr. Lee Kuan Yew. Memories of Japan's behavior during World War II. . . . On and on. . . . We are mad and we won't take it anymore." Similarly, another editorial writer referred to Contemplacion as the "Filipino Everyman: the lowly peon driven by poverty to seek a life abroad, risking loneliness, abuse and terror to feed his [sic] family, and trying as best as he [sic] can to stay standing amid the swirling storm around him. [sic]."[16]

Whereas anecdotes of being mistaken abroad for OCWs produce embarrassment, incidents of state execution ignite a surge of nationalist identification. The link between Contemplacion and the nation had to do with her innocence, presumed widely by Filipinos, and her suffering in the name of her family. Reduced to an abject entity by outside forces, she could then be converted into an object of pity. Her death could thus be used to "assuag[e] the ravages of the lack of referents" brought about by the conjunction of overseas and Filipino.[17] That Contemplacion was a woman, and that OCWs by virtue of their subordinate position to foreign employers come across as feminized within the gendered contexts of nation-state formations, further reinforced the sense of public pity and outrage. For as we saw earlier, the question of heroism, at least since Cory Aquino, had less to do with asserting sovereignty as with affirming ties of indebtedness to a network of relations and declaring subordination to a transcendent realm of possibilities. In that sense, it had already taken what we might think of as a feminized aspect.

In such a context, authority ideally arises from deference. With deference, pity replaces envy. This is perhaps one way in which we can understand the popular identification with an abused and executed OCW. The figure of Contemplacion appeared to furnish a benign basis for reconsolidating the imaginative borders of the Philippines. Whereas OCWs find a living and sometimes die abroad, they not only return to but are usually buried in their bayan, or homeland. Obscure and anonymous while alive, death provides them with a new identity. Thus are they given a place in the nation as figures who enact the replacement of envy with pity. It is this substitution that differentiates OCWs from balikbayans. Where the latter arouse envy and so flaunt their failure to defer to the nation, the former are abused and even killed for deferring to the interests of their families. In dying, they can lay claim to respect. In this way are the roles of OCWs as sources of money and providers of sheer labor power mythologized. Their deaths open up a different kind of national wishfulness, one where the nation is founded on mourning rather than so-called development. It is an image of a nation that draws nostalgically from the events of 1983–1986 when the dead—all the dead—could compel the attention and respect of the living.

It is important to note that the collective rage over Contemplacion's execution was directed not only at the Singaporean government but also at the Philippine state, especially the officials at the Department of Foreign Affairs and President Ramos himself. It was as if to say that those on top were not doing what they should do: showing compassion, in one case, and looking after the welfare of its citizens abroad, in the other. It meant that the nation-state and foreign capital had failed this time to account for Filipinos abroad. The death of Contemplacion showed how, at times, OCWs were treated as mere excess. Such anger was not a call for the abolition of external dependency. Rather, it was about rectifying the discrepancy between employers and employee, foreigners and Filipinos, the state and the people, whether at home or abroad, thereby stabilizing the differences between them. If only Singapore had taken pity; if only the Ramos government had taken care. It is this desire, massively resurgent in the nation's post-Marcos political culture, for a social order and forms of inequality based on pity and mutual deference to that which lies outside of one that momentarily came to a crisis—and urgently called out for containment—in the death of Flor Contemplacion.

But as we shall see, nationalist attempts to account for Contemplacion's death and the plight of OCWs would themselves flounder. Flor's ghost could only be fitfully mapped onto Ninoy's.

Mourning and Money   Flor Contemplacion's death drew attention to the contrast between a developmentalist understanding of OCWs as sheer labor power essential to inducing the flow of capital, on the one hand, and the nationalist critique of their plight as the unjust effects of state-sponsored developmentalism itself, on the other. Yet, President Ramos's official statements suggested that such differences could be easily negotiated. Acknowledging OCWs as new heroes meant that he could regard them as "our best contributions to the world" whose fate in the hands of abusive employers and foreign legal systems should not be allowed to "adversely affect our long-term and continued growth and prosperity." At the same time, President Ramos could also lament Contemplacion's fate, seeing in her death the beginning "of our own soul-searching.... We have been reborn as a national family, mindful of our obligations to care for one another, especially for those without the means to sustain or protect themselves."[18] Hence could the state marshal the rhetoric of pity in order to further its policies of development.

Nonetheless, there existed another mode of addressing the dilemma of OCWs that simultaneously confirmed and exceeded those of developmentalism and nationalism: show business, centered around movies and movie stars. Showbiz talk, as it is commonly known in the country, appeared alongside the journalistic accounts and opinion columns of major newspapers. In the midst of daily demonstrations and the hearings of the Gancayco Commission—a government-appointed body assigned to investigate the circumstances surrounding the deaths of Contemplacion and the Filipina maid that she was accused of murdering, Delia Maga—newspapers reported the attempts of movie producers to purchase the rights to Contemplacion's story. Talk revolved around the large sum—over two million pesos—that was offered to the Contemplacion family and speculations on which stars would play the roles of Flor and Delia.[19]

Nationalist writers reacted with cynicism and outrage at this showbiz talk. One writer, for example, criticized "the movie people" and "their entrepreneurial sensibilities. Somebody's death is their financial windfall, very much like a mortician.... The film industry has again exposed itself to be beyond and without shame."[20] The shamelessness of movie producers comes from their eagerness to capitalize on death. For this and other writers, remaking death into movies can only result in the corruption of the work of mourning. OCWs from this perspective are doubly victimized: first, by foreign employers who use up their labor while they are alive; and second, by movie producers who plunder their memories once they are dead. Both respond to the sacrifices of OCWs with money. And money leads not to the recognition of the worker but only to the generation of more money. As one labor activist put it, "If there's anything more tragic than brutal and unjustified death in the hands of the merciless Singaporeans, it is the 'true-to-life' flick about it that's bound to be produced.... With the first, you lose your life. With the second, you lose your honor and reputation as well."[21]

Even the dead are not safe from the speculations of the living. While the corpse may be idealized as a figure of respect, thereby generating a sense of community based on the circulation of pity, it is also endangered by the potential intrusions of other interests. And because such interests speak only in terms of money, they remain essentially alien to the task of memorialization. Columnist Raul J. Palabrica stresses this reductive tendency of movies in their portrayal of social issues when he writes, "Never mind if the victims are trivialized.... The pleasant ring of the cash register is more important than the adverse social effects of the commercialization of crime stories."[22] Movies speak in the language of money, and this language's sound has the effect of drowning out and flattening the voices of victims and their advocates.

At the same time, however, the singular soundings of cash turn out to be mediated by another kind of speech: gossip. Palabrica accuses movie producers of wanting to profit from the tragedies of Contemplacion and Maga by calling attention to the gossip and scandals surrounding their stories, such as "the extramarital escapade of Contemplacion's husband . . . the pregnancy of Contemplacion's teenage daughter, the dispute between Contemplacion's parents and her husband over the disposition of money," and so forth. In this way, movie producers "exaggerate" and "distort" events in order to "put more spice and color in their productions."[23] Rather than portray events, they retail gossip.

What is the nature of gossip? How is it related to the work of mourning and the circulation of money?

We might approach the question of gossip by first situating it in relation to other forms of speech. As we saw in chapter 4, the workings of rumor, like that of gossip, differ from other sorts of rhetoric in Philippine history.[24] The circulation of rumor calls forth an anonymous and ephemeral community of hearers and speakers joined by their common imaginings of scenarios that might otherwise remain hidden or unknown. Unlike the rhetoric of nationalism, however, whether on the register of collaboration or resistance, rumors cannot serve as the basis for consolidating social identities to the extent that they do not allow for an accounting of the epistemological and ethical bases for identification. Put another way, rumor and gossip give rise to the prospect of politics divorced from identity.

The salience of gossip to the work of mourning can be seen in the remarkably astute ethnography of funeral rituals and spirit mediums in a Bicol town (southeast of Manila) during the late 1980s by the anthropologist Fenella Cannell. Funeral rites, she notes, entail embalming the corpse and laying it out for several days in an open casket for visitors to see. Of particular interest to the visitors is the corpse's facial expression. Embalming the corpse, in part, has to do with managing its outward features so that it has the look of one at peace, freed from social obligations and physical distress. Such is done to assuage the fear often expressed among the living of seeing on the corpse the signs of something amiss, of things out of place: debts unpaid, obligations unmet, desires unfulfilled. The worry associated with seeing the dead, therefore, is linked to the possibility of being confronted with the illegible traces of its sufferings: of a prior violence that resists being read in terms of the living's expectations of perfect return and reciprocation on death.[25]

The forms that such anxieties take among the living usually includes gossip. As Cannell writes, the facial expression of the corpse is "often the subject both of open discussion at the wake and of private gossip and dark insinuation after leaving it."[26] Here, gossip participates in the work of mourning. Embalming the corpse by way of chemical sanitation and cosmetic enhancement is meant to make it recognizable to the living not as the person him or herself but as his or her image. In this sense, embalming is integral to the work of mourning. It sets the dead apart from the living and renders the corpse available as an object of public display and a subject for collective pity.[27]

Still, the view of the corpse, regardless of how well embalmed it is, occasions comments that invariably include gossip. It is as if gossip about what might have happened to the corpse conjures the possibility that embalming might fail to formalize its appearance. Just as it seeks to secure the place of the corpse as a figure in repose and deserving of respect, embalming seems also to raise thoughts about the corpse's instability and potential to infuse fear among the living. It is this contagious potential of the corpse—the possibility that it may not be fully at rest—that gossip in part seeks to anticipate.

Cannell points out that in the impoverished, lowland Christian setting she is describing, visits from the souls of the dead are expected, especially by their kin. Such visits are regarded as highly charged and potentially dangerous in that the returning souls may trigger misfortune, illness, and even death. It is in this sense that the corpse's contagiousness is regarded: as one death leading potentially to others. Hence arises the problem of controlling the visits of the dead, regulating and domesticating their return through various ritual means.[28]

The fear of death's contagiousness is further aggravated by the belief in the presence of malevolent spirits in search of corpses. Chief among these is the *aswang*, or viscera sucker. Various prohibitions (*palihis*) are enforced throughout the wake so as to ward off the dangers posed by an aswang, who is thought to literally consume its victims from inside out. Using its long snout and tongue to poke through cracks and openings in the house, an aswang is said to penetrate the corpse and devour its entrails. Keeping constant vigil over the corpse is thus a way for the living to fend off the threats of an alien force whose spectral presence looms over the scene of mourning.[29]

The corpse, then, comes across as a scandalous presence. It is neither fully dead nor alive; it is a figure of respect but also vulnerability; publicly displayed, it is contained yet potentially contaminating. Embalming, vigils, ritual prayers, and the like are meant to promote the memorialization of the dead and thereby account for its scandalous presence. Yet such practices also give rise to the possibility of their failure. Thus the necessity of figures such as the aswang that trope the sense of the uncanny that lingers in funerals. Aswangs arguably function like gossip: both are conjured up as ways to organize and so give shape to the thoughts and behavior of the living when confronted with the dead. That is to say, they postulate the outer limits of mourning, mapping an imagined terrain of asociality where speech might fail to coalesce into discourse and the corpse, in its contagiousness, can no longer provide the basis for pity. Instead, it can only occasion fear and the multiplication of further deaths. Located at the interstices of mourning and its possible failure, such phenomena as gossip and aswangs convey the persistently problematic location of the dead among the living.

Given this relationship between mourning and gossip, we can now return to the nationalist critique of showbiz talk regarding Flor Contemplacion. Earlier, I suggested that her death became a way of trying to make sense of the seeming contradiction between "overseas" and "Filipinos" in the post-Marcos period. The displays of anger and expressions of pity reproduced the sense and sensation of a nation in mourning and of mourning as the labor specific to the engendering of nationhood. Overseas workers could be reconciled as fragments of the nation whose travels and labors were not merely selfish acts of escape or betrayal but reflections of the courage and willingness of a people to sacrifice and, if need be, die for one another. Nationalist mourning sought to rescue ocws from the realm of global capitalist production and resituate their bodies as the exilic incarnations of contemporary patriotism.

The most remarkable enactment of these notions came during Contemplacion's funeral. From the massive crowds that attended her wake to the prominent religious leaders who were allies of Ninoy and Cory Aquino presiding over the burial rites, Contemplacion's funeral bore a canny resemblance to that of Ninoy's.[30] The journalist Conrado de Quiros has written what is perhaps one of the more telling accounts of the funeral wake for Contemplacion. His reflections are worth following at some length for their elucidation of the politics of mourning, beginning with its sound:

> It wasn't just the whole neighborhood [in San Pablo, Laguna] that had turned out to see Contemplacion one last time [but] the whole nation. . . . The body of a martyr is the strongest loudspeaker there is. . . . You stood on that street in San Pablo last Saturday night, assailed by the assorted smells of a mass of humanity demanding to occupy one small space of earth all at once, and you knew this was bigger than all the agitators combined could make it. Here was an outpouring of anger and grief and compassion from the bosom of the earth. This was not drawn from outside, this was spread from inside, as spontaneously as pity from a wounded heart, as violently as phlegm from congested lungs.[31]

At the wake, the "mass of humanity" in all its sensuous heterogeneity is given form by the presence of Contemplacion's corpse. Her body, however, was not simply offered for viewing. As the "strongest loudspeaker," it was also the locus of a demand to be heard. In her deathly silence, she seems most able to furnish a kind of lingua franca for mobilizing the masses, transforming them into something "bigger" and other than themselves. Responding to the call of the dead, de Quiros imagines the people speaking in a common language whose features consist of the elemental sounds of grieving: the wailing, violent coughing, and spitting that accompanies crying. Such a language consists less of locating what comes from outside; it is more of an anguished exteriorization of what comes from inside. Thus, it is a kind of speech that signals the identification of the living with the dying through the former's incorporation of the latter's unaccounted pain.

Expressing pity for the dead means heeding their call; but it also entails speaking in the dead's place, articulating the pain that is traced on their remains. Those who grieve give voice to the dead; but at the same time, the sound of grieving is associated with the voiding of excess, the violent release of "phlegm from congested lungs." Such an imagery suggests that taking on the language of the dead so as to speak on their behalf also brings up the possibility of being overcome by such an identification, thereby rendering oneself unable to speak at all. How so?

The language of the dead, de Quiros suggests, has to do with the silence emanating from the wounds of a violated body. In comparing Contemplacion's death with that of Ninoy Aquino's, he writes that what the two had in common was that they gave rise to "more than the shouts of rage"; their deaths also released the "sound of silence breaking."

Ninoy's death broke the silence of muzzled mouths. The hole in his head became the mouth of the nation, the cracks in his skull became the screams of a wounded land. Contemplacion's death broke the silence of fear and trembling. The welt around her neck became the mouth of a volcano, the ruptured veins in her face the screams of a strangled race.... Here in Contemplacion's corpse, frozen in the stillness of death, they found their voice. Here in the prison of her coffin, they found a quiver in their vocal chords ... and let out a primal scream.[32]

The deaths of Ninoy and Flor allow for a speech that had once been repressed. It is a speech that consists of the sounds of rupture: screams, volcaniclike eruptions, quivers, and tremblings whose "primal" quality convey something of their uncontrollable and involuntary nature. Ninoy and Flor share something in common: their ability to furnish, in their deaths, a second language whose appropriation by the living allows them not so much to speak as to successfully evoke the attempt at speaking as one people in the face of loss. In their sorrow, the living speak collectively not in their "own" language but in that of the dead.[33]

It is important to note in this connection that the corpse of Ninoy Aquino was displayed without the benefit of a mortician's makeup. His family wanted the "world to see what they [the Marcos regime] had done to him."[34] Breaking with convention, Ninoy's family laid his body out in the same bloody state that it had been found at the site of his assassination. Similarly, the corpse of Contemplacion bore the visible marks of the rope used to hang her, while photographs of Delia Maga's strangled and beaten body taken by Singaporean authorities for autopsy purposes had been circulated by the Philippine media during the Gancayco Commission hearings. Such corpses could not but arouse fear and anger among those who viewed them. Bearing the marks of unwarranted and unaccounted for suffering, these corpses relayed a history of violated bodies that resonated with the everyday violence of dictatorship, development, and dispossession experienced by the body politic.[35]

Confronted by disfigured corpses, the living find themselves in the midst of deaths out of place. The dead appear to be not quite dead and so threaten to blur the line that separates them from the living. Mourning the dead, the living are drawn to identify with their history of degradation, taking on the shame that is written on each corpse's visage. But doing so raises the danger of becoming an extension of the corpse, as in de Quiros's imagery of bullet holes and welts on the dead serving as equivalents of the mouths of the living. In this case, the living could find themselves speaking not in place of the dead but as if they were themselves dying. It is at such moments of potential contagion that the work of mourning is imperiled. Unable to redraw the difference between the living and dead, public performances of pity and rage over the deaths of Ninoy and Flor threatened instead to result in an excess of identification.

In Aquino's case, such an excess of identification found its resolution in the EDSA revolt and expulsion of the Marcoses. As I argued earlier, the sense of loss created by his death was consolidated into a basis for his widow's authority. In Contemplacion's case, however, the sense of loss generated by her execution could not be sublated. Both the Singaporean and Philippine governments seemed inadequate referents of nationalist rage. And often, rage itself was displaced into masculinist guilt, as nationalist writers took to confessing the nation's culpability in sending "our women to live bestial lives abroad" in order "to keep the economy floating."[36]

It was difficult, then, to definitively assign blame for Contemplacion's death since it seemed to implicate everyone to a greater or lesser degree. Consequently, the sense of generalized grieving, while spurring a series of demonstrations, did not culminate in the spectacular even if temporary undoing of social hierarchy as in the case of the EDSA uprising. It is useful to mention in this regard that despite the nationalist denunciations of the plight of Filipina domestic helpers abroad, the conditions of maids at home (most of whom are themselves migrants from impoverished provincial villages) remained largely obscured and unnoticed.

Indeed, other than the resignation of a number of officials in the Department of Foreign Affairs, a brief diplomatic breach between Singapore and the Philippines, and a flurry of popular demands for and official gestures at reforming the policies meant to protect ocws, Contemplacion's death has had relatively little effect in challenging the current order of things. Whereas Ninoy's death transformed the work of mourning into a national undertaking aimed against an authoritarian regime, Flor's death seems to have eluded nationalist closure.[37]

The sound of mourning described by de Quiros at Contemplacion's funeral could not be transformed into a signal for the arrival of a different social order. Instead, it threatened to become a language devoid of content. In imitating the language of the dead, the living, in this instance, could only repeat the sounds of the corpse's imagined anguish without, however, finding a place for it in the world. Articulating loss as sheer loss, the work of mourning Contemplacion and other ocws remained incomplete and indefinitely deferred. It is in the midst of mourning's—perhaps inevitable—inadequacy that gossip circulates. Securing the limits of grief, gossip set about retailing and thereby domesticating the scandal of death out of place.

Show Biz Talk As we saw previously, one of the major purveyors of gossip in the Philippines is show business. It is in the first instance an industrial media complex that includes producers, directors, actors, and technicians. It also counts on the significant work of movie scribes who serve as publicists for movie stars and the film and television projects they appear in. With very rare exceptions, mass-mediated discussions about entertainment in the Philippines takes the form of gossip or show biz talk usually in Taglish, the hybrid form of Tagalog, English, and Spanish that serves as the lingua franca of the marketplace.[38]

To get a sense of the role of gossip in relation to mourning, I want to consider the writings of Inday Badiday, one of the most recognized movie scribes in the country today.[39] Her radio and television shows attract a wide following and her show biz column, *Face to Face*, appears regularly in the *Philippine Daily Inquirer*, one of the country's leading newspapers of record and home to the columns of several respected journalists.

In the days leading up to the funeral of Contemplacion, Badiday wrote a series of columns on the movie deals being made around her story. Referring to Contemplacion's death as "a very hot issue," Badiday calls Flor's corpse a "superstar whose story has all the ingredients of a sure blockbuster."[40] Acknowledging that the dead isn't quite dead, Badiday echoes the interest of film producers. Through movies, the dead is brought back to life and made to work again. Yet, the labor of the dead consists precisely in reassuring the living. There is a sense in which films enlist the help of the dead in their own mourning. The camera takes the place of the living and views the corpse, rendering its disfigured body into a set of melodramatic narratives available for mechanical reproduction. It recounts what the living, in such close proximity to the dead, may not be able to say. In this way, movies can claim to extend the logic of mourning. Badiday adds that a film on Contemplacion will have the effect of preserving her memory, keeping "our new superstar" in the "limelight for a long time." Such would have "a positive effect on the general public, including the government. . . . Talk about consolations!"[41]

By keeping Contemplacion's memory alive, movies will provide a place for her death: they would serve as virtual spaces for keeping her corpse—and more precisely, the thoughts that her corpse give rise to—on display. Films will provide the stories that can be made to fill the void left by the appearance of her wounded body. By portraying the ghastliness of her alienation while alive, movies can contain, in all senses of the word, the ghostliness of her demise. Thus do films appear to be coextensive with nationalist attempts at idealizing death, converting the corpse into a site for the circulation of pity and a language of commonality.

What movies aim to produce, however, is less a nation of mourners as an audience of consumers. The potential blockbuster value of Contemplacion's death—that is, its ability to mobilize the crowd—means that it would already have been subjected to the calculations of the box office. Once the deals for the stories of Contemplacion and Maga were struck, they became as Badiday writes, "show biz properties." In this way, showbiz departs from nationalist desire: it translates the silence of the corpse into the language of money.

That translation requires as the condition of its mass appeal and popular recognition the labor of movie stars. Showbiz assumes that without stars, movies will go largely unseen and therefore unprofitable. Indeed, the most significant effect of the deaths of domestic helpers in foreign places, according to Badiday, is that their stories will furnish vehicles with which to boost the careers of certain stars. Within days of the funeral, the announcement was made that the once popular but fading star Nora Aunor would play the role of superstar Contemplacion.[42]

Thanks to the dead, stars can come back from a dying career. At the same time, identifying with the dead allows the stars to bring them back to life. Movies, then, seem capable of sustaining in the marketplace the enduring fantasy of perfect reciprocity between the living and dead analogous to that of nationalist mourning. Nevertheless, the economy of the marketplace differs from the economy of pity in at least one respect. In the marketplace, identities are never stable: consumers can slide into the position of the consumed while the dead live mechanically transformed and enhanced. Whereas mourning seeks to reestablish the line between the living and dead, movies tend to blur this distinction by commodifying both.

It is the potential for such confusion that is registered and given form by gossip. "Unlike real life," Badiday observes, "juicy items are essential ingredients to spice up the film versions and sustain the interest of the movie going public."[43] Gossip, like spices, is an essential supplement in the preparation of stories for consumption. Dependent on historical events, gossip nonetheless leads a parasitic existence that threatens to distort such events. Badiday again:

> Will Flor Contemplacion and Delia Maga ever rest in peace? People are telling and talking about all sorts of stories about them . . . stories that can sway opinions, alter beliefs, confuse the public, raise biting and disturbing questions like: Were Flor and Delia close friends? Would Efren [Flor's husband] remarry? Would Flor's mother commit suicide if a film on her daughter pushed through? When did Efren stop loving Flor? Did she have a boyfriend in Singapore? Sounds like show biz questions? Even the serious columns in newspapers and tabloids carry juicy items about Flor and Delia. Nothing wrong with that of course. The writers and editors could always say it's what the readers want; such items attract good readership.[44]

Worth remarking in this passage is its odd tone, mixing titillation with apologia. It suggests the inherent instability of gossip as it migrates from the entertainment sections to the front page, from showbiz talk to "serious columns." Even nationalist attempts to condemn gossip, as we saw earlier, require alluding to, if not relaying, its existence. Gossip as such is contagious, insinuating itself into other forms of writing and speech without itself becoming a separate and distinguishable discourse. By raising questions to which there may not be any answers, gossip also suspends conventions of referentiality, thereby opening up new realms of speculation. Did Flor and Delia have a lesbian affair? Did Efren, Flor's husband, have an incestuous affair with his teenage daughter? Is Efren making millions from selling his dead wife's story? And what exactly did he do with that envelope of money that President Ramos gave him? Indeed, even the Gancayco Commission appointed by President Ramos in its official investigations entertained, and hence circulated, all sorts of rumors and conspiracy theories regarding the deaths of Flor and Delia that implicated even the former head of Singapore, Lee Kwan Yew.[45]

What is disturbing about gossip is that not only does it raise biting and unanswerable questions; it also triggers a potentially limitless series of speculations. It is perhaps this combination of the highly speculative with the potentially limitless that lends gossip a scandalous aspect. It does not know where to stop, nor does it care to. It therefore produces the opposite effect of pity: suspicion, disrespect, disbelief, and so forth. And within the context of show biz, gossip invariably reveals the circulation of money in place of pity: it is money that seeks to resuscitate the dead, co-opting both the corpse and its family through the attraction of the star.

In the funerals described by Fenella Cannell in rural Bicol, money always had a place assigned to it: as part of the donations (*abuloy*) given by friends and relatives of the bereaved family in order to help with the costs of the funeral. Money could, in this way, be converted into a gift.[46] But in show biz talk, movies and the gossip they generate suggest that money is simultaneously out of place and all over the place. Not unlike the aswang, money comes across as a radically alien presence, inserting itself into the cracks of discourse and spaces of identification. Just as money possesses the movie star, it threatens likewise to possess the corpse and turn it into show biz property.

It is in light of money's spectrality that we can perhaps understand the popular interest in show biz talk. Gossip anticipates even as it is driven by the constant yet dispersed presence of money. The promiscuity and liquidity of gossip mimic, and so signal the approach of, money as it seeks to capitalize on the crisis of mourning. It is not surprising that people should greet gossip with a mixture of avidity and anxiety. For gossip alerts one to the workings of money and the danger it poses not only to the dead but to the living as well. Lingering on the borders of mourning, gossip intimates in the most prosaic forms the violence of development. It is in this sense that gossip anticipates the inadequacy of mourning and so inoculates one against its failure. Gossip thus continues the work of mourning, albeit in its commodified form. The commodification of mourning, though, does not foreclose the occasional eruption of mourning for commodified labor, as testified to by recent events and continuing anxieties about the conditions of OCWs. There is, then, the necessity of recognizing the doubleness of gossip: its capacity to simulate yet sustain the fate of memory in a global capitalist economy. It offers a way, however banal and lurid, of speaking in the face of the unspeakable, of arousing popular interest both indeterminate and wholly calculable, when confronted with the disfigured corpses of migratory laborers such as those of Delia Maga and Flor Contemplacion.

Notes

Introduction: Episodic Histories

1   For extended discussions of the predicament of area studies in the post–cold war era, see Vicente L. Rafael, "The Cultures of Area Studies in the United States," *Social Text* 41 (winter 1994): 91–112; Charles Hirschman, Charles Keyes, and Karl Hutterer, eds., *Southeast Asian Studies in the Balance: Reflections from America* (Ann Arbor, Mich.: Association of Asian Studies, 1992); and Arif Dirlik, ed., *What Is in a Rim? Critical Perspectives on the Pacific Region Idea* (Boulder, Colo.: Westview Press, 1993).
2   See chapter 8 of this volume.
3   For the sharpest critiques of the willful amnesia surrounding Philippine centennial celebrations, see Reynaldo Ileto, *Filipinos and Their Revolution: Event, Discourse, and Historiography* (Quezon City, Philippines: Ateneo de Manila University Press, 1998), 239–51; and Ambeth Ocampo, *The Centennial Countdown* (Pasig City, Philippines: Anvil Publishing, Inc., 1998).
4   See particularly chapters 5, 6, 7, and 8 herein for a discussion of contemporary nationalism in the Philippines. One might usefully think of the history of revolution and counterrevolution in the Philippines in relation to that of its neighbor, Indonesia. See, for example, Benedict Anderson, *Java in a Time of Revolution: Occupation and Resistance, 1944–1946* (Ithaca, N.Y.: Cornell University Press, 1972); and James T. Siegel, *Fetish, Recognition, and Revolution* (Princeton, N.J.: Princeton University Press, 1997), and *A New Criminal Type in Jakarta: Counter-Revolution Today* (Durham, N.C.: Duke University Press, 1998).
5   Here I am thinking of the works of such latter-twentieth-century writers as Horacio de la Costa, S.J., Resil Mojares, Reynaldo Ileto, Renato Constantino, John Schumacher, Doreen Fernandez, Carmen Guerrero-Nakpil, and Nick Joaquin, about whom more will be said below. The greatest of all Filipino essayists—one whose greatness precisely grew out of the turbulent times he was addressing—was Jose Rizal. It should be noted, however, that these "episodic" writers have at some point in their lives also produced (and continue to work on) "epic" works, most of which are cited throughout the pages that follow.
6   The word *irony* is derived from the Greek *eirōneia*, meaning simulated ignorance. One who is an *eiron* is a dissembler. According to the *Oxford English Dictionary*, irony refers to "the expression of one's meaning by language of opposite or different tendency, especially [the] simulated adoption of another's point of view or laudatory tone for purpose of ridicule; [the] ill-timed or perverse arrival of [an] event or circumstance [that] in itself [is] desirable, as if in mockery of the fitness of things; [the] use of language that has an inner meaning for a privileged audience and an

outer meaning for the person addressed or concerned (occasionally including [the] speaker, cf. tragic irony)."

These various modes of irony, as we shall see, figure considerably in the chapters to come. As the trope of noncoincidence and willful dissimulation, irony's power lies in its capacity to suggest other realms of meaning that have been repressed inasmuch as it points to those moments when meaning fails altogether. Hence, its political salience lies in its ability not only to evade totalizing claims to power but also to delineate the limits of resistance to such power. Attending to the ironic is one way of calling attention to the fissures within language—for example, between what a text says and how it says it—that relay and reflect the fissures in the consciousness and behaviors of those who deploy it. To do so is to point to those moments that resist closure, when neither one nor the other has the last word, and thus, final control over the means for the production of meaning and determination of history. In this way, attention to the ironic can never be merely an aesthetic pose (even if it takes aesthetics seriously), or worse, a retreat to sheer relativism. Rather, it is a way of arriving at a more objective view of the world where facts themselves are messy and unstable, subject to ongoing interpretations and contests, stubbornly resistant and at odds with any single political will or cultural articulation. Facts are what are given under conditions that we did not choose but that we actively remake, that can be approached ironically and allegorically as the remains of a past radically exterior to ourselves, and thereby, the guarantee of futures whose horizons have yet to be discerned. To the commonplace notion of irony as a mode of skepticism, and therefore of negative critique, then, one can add that it is also a figure of radical hope, of possibilities still unthought and histories that cannot be foreclosed. For a useful discussion of irony, see Paul de Man, "The Concept of Irony," in *Aesthetic Ideology* (Minneapolis: University of Minnesota Press, 1996), 163–84, and "The Rhetoric of Temporality," in *Blindness and Insight: Essays in the Rhetoric of Contemporary Criticism* (Minneapolis: University of Minnesota Press, 1983), 187–228.

7   In this regard, it is worth asking if there is a Tagalog equivalent for the word *irony*. Pedro Serrano-Laktaw, *Diccionario Tagalog-Hispano* (Manila: Imprenta de Santos y Bernal, 1914), 2:1309, 1336) gives it as *tuya*, synonymous with *tudyo*, which can mean a kind of blunder, a provocation, or stupidity. In its verb form, it means to jeer, scold, pull each other's hair in jest, ridicule, or let loose stupidities against one another. To speak ironically in Tagalog, then, is to commit an error and provoke a response, perhaps in the form of a scolding, to poke fun and tease one another. Irony is thus associated with play. As such, it involves risks—embarrassment and error, for example—but also the promise of pleasure. There is no telling where irony will lead you, and it is this uncertainty—with all its attendant risks and pleasures—that underwrites this book.

8   See "Expedition of Ruy Lopez de Villalobos, 1541–1546," in *The Philippine Islands, 1493–1898*, ed. Emma Blair and James Robertson, 55 vols. (1905; reprint, Mandaluyong, Rizal: Cacho Hermanos, Inc., 1973), 2:47, 70–71. See also William Henry Scott, *Barangay: Sixteenth Century Philippine Culture and Society* (Quezon City,

Philippines: Ateneo de Manila University Press, 1994), 6. Also useful is Nicolas Cushner, *Spain in the Philippines* (Quezon City, Philippines: Ateneo de Manila University Press, 1974).

9 See Alfred McCoy and Ed. J. De Jesus, eds., *Philippine Social History: Global Trade and Local Transformations* (Quezon City, Philippines: Ateneo de Manila University Press, 1982); Jonathan Fast and Jim Richardson, *Roots of Dependency: Political and Economic Revolution in Nineteenth Century Philippines* (Quezon City, Philippines: Foundation for Nationalist Studies, 1979); and the important work of Filomeno V. Aguilar Jr., *Clash of Spirits: The History of Power and Sugar Planter Hegemony on a Visayan Island* (Quezon City, Philippines: Ateneo de Manila University Press, 1998).

10 Nick Joaquin, "Bulls and Geography," in *Culture and History: Occasional Notes on the Process of Philippine Becoming* (Manila: Solar Publishing Corp., 1988), 95, 97. For one of the more lucid accounts of the Philippine colony in the seventeenth century, see Horacio de la Costa, *Jesuits in the Philippines, 1581–1768* (Cambridge, Mass.: Harvard University Press, 1961).

11 William Henry Scott notes that Spanish accounts from the seventeenth century at times made mention of indios Filipinos to differentiate the local populace from the indios in the New World, even as they reserved the term *Negritos* to refer to the darker and shorter Aeta groups, largely un-Christianized, who lived as hunters and gatherers in the colonial peripheries and the equally derogatory term *moros* for the Islamicized groups in the south. In the late eighteenth century, the engraver Francisco Suarez refers to himself as indio Filipino. All of which points to the fact that the juridical category "Filipino" used to refer to Spaniards born in the Philippines was not always continuous with local everyday usages. And it is precisely this discontinuity between the juridical and the everyday that made Filipino available for rearticulation and redeployment by late-nineteenth-century nationalists like Jose Rizal, who by 1887 could say of the Philippine community in Madrid, "Creoles, mestizos, and Malays, we simply call ourselves Filipinos" (Scott, *Barangay*, 6–7).

12 Benedict Anderson, *The Spectre of Comparisons: Nationalism, Southeast Asia, and the World* (London: Verso, 1998), 65, 232–33, 257–58.

13 See Vicente L. Rafael, *Contracting Colonialism: Translation and Christian Conversion in Tagalog Society under Early Spanish Rule* (Durham, N.C.: Duke University Press, 1993).

14 See Andrew Gonzalez, *Language and Nationalism: The Philippine Experience Thus Far* (Quezon City, Philippines: Ateneo de Manila University Press, 1980), and the special issue of *Solidarity* that he edited, reprinted as *The Role of English and Its Maintenance in the Philippines* (Manila: Solidaridad Publishing House, 1988).

15 We can readily see this constant movement between assimilation and separation in almost all the writings of Jose Rizal, the so-called father of the Filipino nation, but most instructively in his two great novels, *Noli me Tangere* (Berlin: Berliner Buchdruckerei-Aktien-Gesellschaft, 1887) and *El Filibusterismo* (Ghent: F. Meyer-Van Loo, 1891).

16 Another irony: whereas in the past Hong Kong was an important base of anti-

colonial activities for *ilustrados* like Rizal and later Aguinaldo and his junta, it has become in our time the site for the densest concentration of Filipina domestic workers outside the Philippines. "Filipina" in Hong Kong today is nearly always synonymous with maid.

17 See Ambeth Ocampo, *The Centennial Countdown* (Pasig City, Philippines: Anvil Publishing, Inc., 1998), 59–64.

18 For details, see Teodoro Agoncillo, *Revolt of the Masses: The Story of Bonifacio and the Katipunan* (Quezon City: University of the Philippines Press, 1956), and *Malolos: The Crisis of the Republic* (Quezon City: University of the Philippines Press, 1960). See also the highly problematic work of Glenn A. May, *Inventing a Hero: The Posthumous Re-creation of Andres Bonifacio* (Quezon City, Philippines: New Day Press, 1997).

19 See Reynaldo Ileto, *Pasyon and Revolution: Popular Movements in the Philippines, 1840–1910* (Quezon City: Ateneo de Manila University Press, 1979); David Sturtevant, *Popular Uprisings in the Philippines 1840–1940* (Ithaca, N.Y.: Cornell University Press, 1976); Michael Cullinane, "Ilustrado Politics: The Response of the Filipino Educated Elite to American Colonial Rule, 1898–1907" (Ph.D. diss., University of Michigan, 1989); Peter Stanley, *A Nation in the Making: The Philippines and the United States, 1899–1921* (Cambridge, Mass.: Harvard University Press, 1974); Stuart Creighton Miller, *Benevolent Assimilation: The American Conquest of the Philippines, 1899–1903* (New Haven, Conn.: Yale University Press, 1982); Milagros Guerrero, "Luzon at War: Contradictions in Philippine Society, 1898–1902" (Ph.D. diss., University of Michigan, 1977); and William Henry Scott, *Ilocano Responses to American Aggression, 1900–1901* (Manila: New Day Press, 1986).

20 The more instructive Spanish accounts of the revolution include Manuel Sastrón, *La Insurrecion en Filipinas y Guerra Hispano-Americana en el Archipielago* (Madrid, 1901); Jose M. del Castillo, *El Katipunan, o el Filibusterismo en Filipinas* (Madrid, 1897); Juan Caro y Mora, *La Situacion del Pais*, 2d ed. (Manila, 1897); and the documents found in Wenceslao E. Retana, ed., *Archivo del Bibliofilo Filipino*, 5 vols. (Madrid, 1892), esp. 3:332–60.

21 Ileto, *Pasyon and Revolution*.

22 Ibid.

23 All of this is incisively analyzed in Benedict Anderson, "Cacique Democracy in the Philippines: Origins and Dreams," in *Discrepant Histories: Translocal Essays on Filipino Cultures*, ed. Vicente L. Rafael (Philadelphia, Pa.: Temple University Press, 1995), 3–47.

24 See Ileto, *Pasyon and Revolution*, 107–8; and Rafael, *Contracting Colonialism*, chap. 6.

25 EDSA is the acronym for Epifanio de los Santos Avenue, the highway (formerly known as Highway 54) where some of the more important, largely nonviolent engagements occurred between the military and anti-Marcos opposition during the People Power Revolt in 1986.

26 Joaquin, *Culture and History*, 249–53. I thank Doreen Fernandez for this reference.

1 White Love: Census and Melodrama in the U.S. Colonization of the Philippines

1 Dean C. Worcester, *The Philippines Past and Present*, 2 vols. (New York: Macmillan Publishing Co., 1914), 1:308. Subsequent references are cited in the text.
2 The most useful historical accounts of the war include Stuart Creighton Miller, *Benevolent Assimilation: The American Conquest of the Philippines, 1899–1903* (New Haven, Conn.: Yale University Press, 1982); Leon Wolff, *Little Brown Brother* (Garden City, N.Y.: Doubleday, 1982); Russell Roth, *Muddy Glory: America's "Indian Wars" in the Philippines, 1899–1935* (West Hanover, Mass.: Christopher Publishing House, 1981); Reynaldo Ileto, *Pasyon and Revolution: Popular Movements in the Philippines, 1840–1910* (Quezon City, Philippines: Ateneo de Manila University, 1979); and Glenn A. May, *Battle for Batangas* (New Haven, Conn.: Yale University Press, 1991). An indispensable source for primary documents relating to the war is John R. M. Taylor, ed. *The Philippine Insurrection against the United States*, 5 vols. (Quezon City, Philippines: Eugenio Lopez Foundation, 1971).
3 See also Peter Stanley, "'The Voice of Worcester Is the Voice of God': How One American Found Fulfillment in the Philippines," in *Reappraising an Empire: New Perspectives on Philippine-American History*, ed. Peter Stanley (Cambridge, Mass.: Harvard University Press, 1984), 117–41. Though critical of Worcester's career and imperialism in general, Stanley was drawn into an implicit identification with Worcester's plight as a fellow U.S. academic whose work on the fringes of empire was analogous to that of a scholar working on a "peripheral field" such as Philippine studies (see 137, 140). For a recent biography of Worcester, see Rodney Sullivan, *Exemplar of Americanism: The Philippine Career of Dean C. Worcester* (Ann Arbor, Mich.: Center for South and Southeast Asian Studies, University of Michigan, 1991).
4 Cited in Miller, *Benevolent Assimilation*, 213, 216.
5 Cited in Adjutant General of the Army, *Correspondence Relating to the War with Spain* (Washington, D.C.: U.S. Government Printing Office, 1902), 2:1352–53.
6 Cited in Paul A. Kramer, "The Pragmatic Empire: U.S. Anthropology and Colonial Politics in the Occupied Philippines, 1898–1916" (Ph.D. diss., Princeton University, 1998), 149–50.
7 Cited in Adjutant General, *Correspondence*, 2:859. For related documents, see also the appendix in Worcester, *The Philippines*, 2:975; and *Report of the Philippine Commission to the President* (Washington, D.C.: U.S. Government Printing Office, 1900–1901), 1:3–4.
8 *Report of the Philippine Commission*, 1:4.
9 Ibid.
10 Cited in Adjutant General, *Correspondence*, 2:859.
11 *Report of the Philippine Commission*, 1:4–5.
12 William Howard Taft, *The Philippine Islands: An Address Delivered before the Chamber of Commerce of the State of New York* (New York, 1904), 6–9.
13 Woodrow Wilson, *Constitutional Government in the United States* (New York: Co-

lumbia University Press, 1921), 52–53. For a critical history of the relays linking civilization, gender, and race in the late-nineteenth and early-twentieth-century United States that inform the ideology of benevolent assimilation, see Gail Bederman, *Manliness and Civilization: A Cultural History of Gender and Race in the United States, 1880–1917* (Chicago: University of Chicago Press, 1995), esp. 170–216.

14 A great deal of U.S. postwar journalism and scholarship on the Philippines still resonates with these notions of benevolent assimilation. For a recent example, see the Pulitzer Prize–winning book by Stanley Karnow, *In Our Image: America's Empire in the Philippines* (New York: Ballantine Books, 1989); for a trenchant critique of this book, see Michael Salman, "In Our Orientalist Imagination: Historiography and the Culture of Colonialism in the U.S.," *Radical History Review* 50 (spring 1991): 221–32. See also the recent critical appraisal of American historical scholarship on the Philippines by Reynaldo Ileto, *Knowing America's Colony: A Hundred Years from the Philippine War*, Occasional Papers Series, no. 13 (Honolulu: Center for Philippine Studies, 1999).

15 See, for instance, the important work of Reynaldo Ileto, "Orators and the Crowd: Philippine Independence Politics, 1910–1914," in *Reappraising an Empire: New Perspectives on Philippine-American History*, ed. Peter Stanley (Cambridge, Mass.: Harvard University Press, 1984), 85–113; and Paul A. Kramer's insightful social history of the early colonial period, "The Pragmatic Empire." See also Warwick Anderson, "'Where Every Prospect Pleases and Only Man Is Vile': Laboratory Medicine as Colonial Discourse," *Critical Inquiry* 18, no. 3 (spring 1992): 506–29; Sullivan, *Exemplar of Americanism;* and Michael Salman, "The United States and the End of Slavery in the Philippines, 1898–1914: A Study of Imperialism, Ideology, and Nationalism," 2 vols. (Ph.D. diss., Stanford University, 1993).

My discussion of the interruption of the colonial state's wish for the totalizing representation of the subjects of supervision is found below in my section on the seditious Tagalog plays. We can infer some aspect of this desire of the state from a careful and selective reading of the works of Glenn A. May, *Social Engineering in the Philippines* (Westport, Conn.: Greenwood Press, 1980); Peter Stanley, *A Nation in the Making: The Philippines and the United States, 1899–1921* (Cambridge, Mass.: Harvard University Press, 1974); Ruby Paredes, ed., *Philippine Colonial Democracy* (Quezon City, Philippines: Ateneo de Manila University Press, 1989); Michael Cullinane, "Ilustrado Politics: The Response of the Filipino Educated Elite to American Colonial Rule, 1898–1907" (Ph.D. diss., University of Michigan, 1989); and Norman Owen, ed., *Compadre Colonialism: Philippine-American Relationship, 1898–1946* (Ann Arbor, Mich.: Center for South and Southeast Asian Studies, 1971), to mention only a few.

16 U.S. Bureau of the Census, *Census of the Philippine Islands*, 4 vols. (Washington, D.C.: U.S. Government Printing Office, 1905). Subsequent references are cited in the text.

17 For helpful accounts of the origins and significance of the modern census, especially in the formation of colonial and nation-states, see Benedict Anderson, "National-

ism, Identity, and the Logic of Seriality," in *The Spectre of Comparisons: Nationalism, Southeast Asia, and the World* (London: Verso, 1998), 29–45; Paul Starr, "The Sociology of Official Statistics," in *The Politics of Numbers*, ed. William Alonso and Paul Starr (New York: Russell Sage Foundation, 1987), 7–57; and W. Stull Holt, *The Bureau of Census: Its History, Activities, and Organization* (New York: AMS Press, 1929).

18 See also Onofre D. Corpuz, "The Population of the Archipelago, 1565–1898," in *The Roots of the Filipino Nation* (Quezon City, Philippines: Aklahi Foundation, Inc., 1989), 1:515–70.

19 Kramer, "The Pragmatic Empire," chapters 1 and 2.

20 See this book's introduction, 9–13.

21 Ibid., esp. chapters 2, 3, and 5. See also Owen, *Compadre Colonialism*; Bonifacio Salamanca, *The Filipino Reaction to American Rule, 1901–1913* (Norwich, Conn.: Shoestring Press, 1968); Onofre D. Corpuz, *The Bureaucracy in the Philippines* (Quezon City: University of the Philippines Press, 1957); Stanley, *A Nation in the Making*; Cullinane, "Ilustrado Politics"; and Paredes, *Philippine Colonial Democracy*.

22 Benedict Anderson, *Imagined Communities: Reflections on the Origins and Spread of Nationalism in the Philippines*, 2d ed. (London: Verso, 1991), 166. See also Thongchai Winichakul, *Siam Mapped: A History of the Geo-Body of Siam* (Honolulu: University of Hawaii Press, 1993). I have also profited considerably from the fine essay by Alan J. Sekula, "The Body and the Archive," *October* 39 (winter 1986): 3–64, on the intertwined history of photography and statistics in the conceptualization of populations as domains of state intervention. In addition, see the classic essay on the colonial census by Bernard Cohn, "The Census, Social Structure, and Objectification in South Asia," in *An Anthropologist among Historians* (Delhi: Oxford University Press, 1987), 224–54.

23 See Worcester, *The Philippines*, chapters 20–25.

24 The notion that the archipelago was populated by different waves of migration was put forth by the European ethnologist and close friend of Jose Rizal, Ferdinand Blumentritt, in the 1890s. His work was then translated into English and popularized in a number of U.S. magazines after the United States took control in the Philippines. For other U.S. formulations of the theory of racial migrations, see Dean C. Worcester, *The Philippine Islands and Their People* (New York: Macmillan Publishing Co., 1898), 473–82; *A Pronouncing Gazetteer and Geographical Dictionary of the Philippine Islands* (Washington, D.C.: U.S. Government Printing Office, 1902); and William Cameron Forbes, *The Philippine Islands* (Boston: Houghton Mifflin Co., 1928), 1:586–90. For a concise review of the archeological evidence that decisively repudiates the wave migration theory, see William Henry Scott, *Prehispanic Source Materials for the Study of Philippine History*, rev. ed. (Quezon City, Philippines: New Day Press, 1984), 31–32, 143–44.

25 As with the colonial state, so with the colonial gaze: its wish for mastery was subject to compromise, uncertainties, and contingencies located in the embodied existence of U.S. officials living in an alien tropical context, on the one hand, and the body

politic of a colonial society dependent on the collaboration of nonwhite others, on the other. As Warwick Anderson has argued, the white gaze was far from steady, at times seeming to be no more than a series of uncertain glances. See his essay, "The Trespass Speaks: White Masculinity and Colonial Breakdown," *American Historical Review* 102 (December 1997): 1343–70. In this regard, see also the diaries of William Cameron Forbes at the Houghton Library, Harvard University.

26 The image of the census—indeed of the entirety of colonial government reports—as a series of dioramas in an imperialist museum of native history was suggested to me by Donna Haraway's essay, "Teddy Bear Patriarchy: Taxidermy in the Garden of Eden, New York City, 1908–1936," in *Primate Visions: Gender, Race, and Nature in the World of Modern Science* (New York: Routledge, 1989), 26–58. For a critique of ethnological photographs, see chapter 4 of this book. And for an astute analysis of the spectacular failure of one such attempt to display the dreams of empire in the St. Louis Exposition of 1904, see Kramer, "The Pragmatic Empire," chap. 4.

27 The citation from the colonial Supreme Court appears in Arthur Stanley Riggs, *The Filipino Drama* (Manila: Ministry of Human Settlements, 1981), xi; originally written in 1904. Riggs's book contains both the original Tagalog texts of the seditious dramas as well as their English translation, accompanied by the author's instructive, even if at times hysterical, ramblings on the threats posed by such plays to the U.S. regime. Subsequent references are cited in the text. I thank Doreen Fernandez for making this book available to me and her many insights on nationalist theater during this period.

Other useful background materials on the nationalist plays can be found in Cullinane, "Ilustrado Politics," 173–83; E. Arsenio Manuel, *Dictionary of Philippine Biography* (Quezon City, Philippines: Filipiniana Publications, 1970), 2:371–83; and Amelia Lapena-Bonifacio, *The Seditious Tagalog Playwrights: Early American Occupation* (Manila: Zarzuela Foundation of the Philippines), 1972. Also helpful in understanding the larger historical setting of the nationalist dramas are Wenceslao E. Retana, *Noticias historico-bibliograficas del teatro en Filipinas desde sus origines hasta 1898* (Madrid: Libreria General de Victoriano Suarez, 1909); Nicanor Tiongson, *Kasaysayan ng komedya sa Pilipinas, 1766–1982* (Manila: Integrated Research Center, De la Salle University, 1982); Doreen Fernandez, *Palabas: Essays on Philippine Theater History* (Quezon City, Philippines: Ateneo de Manila University Press, 1996), 60–103, and *The Iloilo Zarzuela* (Quezon City,Philippines: Ateneo de Manila University Press, 1978); Edna Manlapaz, ed., *Aurelio Tolentino: Selected Writings* (Quezon City, Philippines: Ateneo de Manila University Press, 1975); and Resil Mojares, *Origins and Rise of the Filipino Novel: A Generic Study of the Novel until 1940* (Quezon City: University of the Philippines Press, 1983), and *Theater in Society, Society in Theater: The Social History of a Cebuano Village, 1840–1940* (Quezon City, Philippines: Ateneo de Manila University Press, 1985).

28 For a description of the social context of late-nineteenth-century theatrical performances, see the novel by Jose Rizal, *Noli me Tangere* (Berlin: Buchdruckerei-Aktien-Gesellschaft, 1887), chapters 27–29. See also Tiongson, *Kasaysayan ng komedya;* and

Fernandez, *Palabas*, 60–103. As Fernandez points out, state support for theater did not materialize until the mid-1970s, and even then such support was miserly and undependable, to say the least.

29 Ileto, *Pasyon and Revolution*.

30 For a nuanced discussion of how popular notions of Kalayaan (as mentioned earlier, associated with the perfect reciprocity between a mother and child) varied considerably from North American and Filipino elites' understanding of independence as originating from the actions of the state, see Ileto, *Pasyon and Revolution*, 197–258, and "Orators and the Crowd."

31 For a more detailed discussion of notions of reciprocal indebtedness in Tagalog society, see Vicente L. Rafael, *Contracting Colonialism: Translation and Christian Conversion in Tagalog Society under Early Spanish Rule* (Durham, N.C.: Duke University Press, 1993), 84–135; as well as chapter 5 of this volume.

32 It is useful to remember here that unlike neighboring Indonesia, the Philippines does not have an extensive record of anti-Chinese violence. The last anti-Chinese riots, largely sponsored by the Spaniards, occurred in the seventeenth century. In the 1896–1897 revolution itself, Chinese were at times targeted by some of the fighters, but equally important was the fact that a number of Chinese also figured among the revolutionary troops. See Edgar Wickberg, *The Chinese in Philippine Life, 1850–1898* (New Haven, Conn.: Yale University Press, 1965), for an illuminating discussion on the place of the Chinese in Philippine history.

33 For another discussion of the role of women in shaping nationalist discourse in the Philippines, especially those who become overseas contract workers today, see chapter 8 of this volume.

34 For a preliminary discussion of the problematic place of the father in the thinking of first-generation Filipino nationalists, see Vicente L. Rafael, "Nationalism, Imagery, and the Filipino Intelligentsia of the Nineteenth Century," in *Discrepant Histories: Translocal Essays on Filipino Cultures*, ed. Vicente L. Rafael (Philadelphia, Pa.: Temple University Press, 1995), 133–58.

35 The ways in which such desires for reciprocity would come under crisis and become subject to political manipulation in the post–World War II era is taken up in chapter 5 of this volume.

2 Colonial Domesticity: Engendering Race at the Edge of Empire, 1899–1912

1 Helen Taft, *Recollections of Full Years* (New York: Dodd, Mead, and Co., 1914), 214.

2 A partial list of the growing literature on the constitutive relationship between imperialism and bourgeois domesticity, especially with regard to the emergence of a modern female subjectivity, might include the following: Rosemary Marangoly George, "Homes in the Empire, Empires in the Home," *Cultural Critique* (winter 1993–1994): 95–127; Jenny Sharpe, *Allegories of Empire: The Figure of Woman in the Colonial Text* (Minneapolis: University of Minnesota Press, 1993); Anna Davin, "Imperialism and Motherhood," *History Workshop* 5 (1978): 9–65; Ann Stoler, "Car-

nal Knowledge and Imperial Power: Gender, Race, and Morality in Colonial Asia," in *Gender at the Crossroads of Knowledge: Feminist Anthropology in the Postmodern Era*, ed. Micaela Di Leonardo (Berkeley: University of California Press, 1991), 51–101; Vron Ware, *Beyond the Pale: White Women, Racism, and History* (London: Verso, 1992); Nupur Chaudhuri and Margaret Strobel, eds., *Western Women and Imperialism: Complicity and Resistance* (Bloomington: University of Indiana Press, 1992); Sara Suleri, *The Rhetoric of English India* (Chicago: University of Chicago Press, 1992); Margaret Strobel, *European Women and the Second British Empire* (Bloomington: Indiana University Press, 1991); and Gail Bederman, *Manliness and Civilization: A Cultural History of Gender and Race in the United States, 1880–1917* (Chicago: University of Chicago Press, 1995).

3   Symptomatic of such a view is Stanley Karnow, *In Our Image: America's Empire in the Philippines* (New York: Ballantine Books, 1989). See also David Joel Steinberg, *The Philippines: A Singular and a Plural Place*, 2d ed. (Boulder, Colo.: Westview Press, 1990).

4   See, for example, the important collection of essays edited by Amy Kaplan and Donald E. Pease, *Cultures of United States Imperialism* (Durham, N.C.: Duke University Press, 1993), for a sense of the emergent interest in reexamining the national history and historiography of the United States through the lens of imperialist legacies. Of course, the writings of William Appleman Williams, Richard Drinnon, and Michael Rogin, to name only a few, have served as indispensable guideposts for thinking through the imperial sources of U.S. domestic culture and politics. More recent and iconoclastic revisions of the history of U.S. rule in the Philippines include Paul A. Kramer, "The Pragmatic Empire: U.S. Anthropology and Colonial Politics in the Occupied Philippines, 1898–1916" (Ph.D. diss., Princeton University, 1998); Warwick Anderson, "Colonial Pathologies: American Medicine in the Philippines, 1898–1921" (Ph.D. diss., University of Pennsylvania, 1992); and Michael Salman, "The United States and the End of Slavery in the Philippines, 1898–1914: A Study of Imperialism, Ideology, and Nationalism," 2 vols. (Ph.D. diss., Stanford University, 1993). See also Vicente L. Rafael, ed., *Discrepant Histories: Translocal Essays on Filipino Cultures* (Philadelphia, Pa.: Temple University Press, 1995).

5   Richard Drinnon, *Facing West: The Metaphysics of Indian Hating and Empire Building* (New York: New American Library, 1980).

6   See, for example, Donna Haraway, "Teddy Bear Patriarchy: Taxidermy in the Garden of Eden, New York City, 1908–1936," in *Primate Visions: Gender, Race, and Nature in the World of Modern Science* (New York: Routledge, 1989), 3–51; Amy Kaplan, "Romancing the Empire: The Embodiment of American Masculinity in the Popular Historical Novel of the 1890s," *American Literary History* 2, no. 4 (winter 1990): 659–90; Susan Jeffords, *The Remasculinization of America: Gender in the Vietnam War* (Bloomington: Indiana University Press, 1989); and Bederman, *Manliness and Civilization*.

7   See the following essays by Ann Stoler: "Carnal Knowledge and Imperial Power"; "Rethinking Colonial Categories: European Communities and the Boundaries of

Rule," in *Colonialism and Culture*, ed. Nicholas Dirks (Ann Arbor: University of Michigan Press, 1992), 319–52; and "Sexual Affronts and Racial Frontiers: European Identities and the Cultural Politics of Exclusion in Colonial Southeast Asia," *Comparative Studies in Society and History* 34 (July 1992): 514–51.

8   Imperialism as a progressive and modernizing force was (and continues to be) a staple feature of many areas of U.S. thinking and has often been woven into the rhetoric of abolitionism (seeing in colonial rule, for example, the means to end the last vestiges of local forms of slavery in the Philippines), Christian conversion, and what one governor-general, William Cameron Forbes, termed the "romance of business." See, for instance, Salman, "The United States and the End of Slavery"; and Kramer, "The Pragmatic Empire."

9   According to the *Census of the Philippine Islands* (4 vols. [Washington, D.C.: U.S. Government Printing Office, 1905]), out of a total population of 7.6 million in the Philippines in 1903, whites from the United States made up about one-fifth of 1 percent, or a total of 8,135 people. Out of this number, 6,920 were males and 1,215 were females—that is, women constituted only 14.9 percent of the entire U.S. community in 1903. Those numbers would actually go down by the next census, in 1918, though the male-female ratio within the white North American community would remain stable. There were, of course, other whites, including some 3,888 Spaniards, 667 English, and smaller numbers of French and Germans. See *Census*, 2:14–15, 44.

10 I borrow the term *beneficial republicanism* from the Reverend Wallace Radcliffe, cited in Stuart Creighton Miller, *Benevolent Assimilation: The American Conquest of the Philippines, 1899–1903* (New Haven, Conn.: Yale University Press, 1982), 171.

11 See, for example, the publisher's preface to *An Army Woman in the Philippines*, by Caroline S. Shunk (Kansas City, Mo.: Franklin Hudson Publishing, 1914); preface by her husband, Albert Jenks, to *Death Stalks the Philippine Wilds*, by Maude Huntley Jenks (Minneapolis, Minn.: Lund Press, 1951); preface to *Recollection of Full Years*, by Helen Taft (New York: Dodd, Mead, and Co., 1914); and preface in the U.S. edition to *An Englishwoman in the Philippines*, by Campbell Dauncy (New York: E. P. Dutton, 1906).

12 Mary H. Fee, *A Woman's Impressions of the Philippines* (Chicago: A. C. McClurg and Co., 1910), 44. Subsequent references are cited in the text.

13 Edith Moses, *Unofficial Letters of an Official's Wife* (New York: Appleton and Co., 1908), 310. Subsequent references are cited in the text. For a brilliant study of European and Euro-American travel accounts, to which this essay is indebted, see Mary Louise Pratt, *Imperial Eyes: Travel Writing and Transculturation* (New York: Routledge, 1992).

14 For exemplary white masculinist accounts of the United States in the Philippines, see Dean C. Worcester, *The Philippines Past and Present*, 2 vols. (New York: Macmillan Publishing Co., 1914; and William Cameron Forbes, *The Philippine Islands*, 2 vols. (Boston: Houghton Mifflin Co., 1928).

15 Nona Worcester, 1909, Bentley Historical Collection, University of Michigan, Ann Arbor, 7. Subsequent references are cited in the text.

16   Caroline S. Shunk, *An Army Woman in the Philippines* (Kansas City, Mo.: Franklin Hudson Publishing, 1914), 28. Subsequent references are cited in the text.
17   Alice Byram Condict, *Old Glory and the Gospel in the Philippines* (Chicago: Fleming and Revelle Co., 1901), 67.
18   Given these fantasies of white female bodies potentially besieged by the contaminating proximity of nonwhite ones—fantasies so widespread in the United States at this time—one might have expected the emergence of a racial hysteria among the white community in the colony that—as in the British, Dutch, and French colonies, as well as on the U.S. mainland—would have led to a spate of legislation regulating sexual relations across the color line. Yet such did not happen in the Philippines. No antimiscegenation laws were ever enacted in the colony, and despite informal practices of racial segregation, no Jim Crow laws ever made it across the Pacific. Indeed, colonial accounts are full of instances of people from the United States socializing with mostly upper-class Filipinos. Given the extremely small number of U.S. residents in the colony—less than one-fifth of 1 percent at its peak in 1903—and the imperative of attracting the collaboration of Filipinos—especially in the colonial administration—the institutionalization of racial segregation would have been impossible. It is perhaps because of the absence of a clearly demarcated color line that racist discourse became even more important in marking out a sense of bodily and cultural integrity among colonizers from the States. See Vicente L. Rafael, "Mimetic Subjects: Engendering Race at the Edge of Empire," *differences: A Journal of Feminist Cultural Studies* 7, no. 2 (1995): 127–49.
19   For this discussion of domestic architecture, I am indebted to Gillian Brown, *Domestic Individualism: Imagining the Self in Nineteenth-Century America* (Berkeley: University of California Press, 1990), 71–72; and Witold Rybczynski, *Home: A Short History of an Idea* (New York: Penguin, 1986).
20   Fernando N. Zialcita and Martin I. Tinio, *Philippine Ancestral Houses* (Quezon City, Philippines: CGF Books, 1980), 6, 19. See also Resil Mojares, *Casa Gorordo in Cebu: Urban Residence in a Philippine Province, 1860–1920* (Cebu, Philippines: Ramon Aboitiz Foundation, 1983).
21   Dauncy, *An Englishwoman*, 339.
22   The containment of these threats is the special task of domestic technology, much of which was detailed in the various domestic manuals, household tips, and civics textbooks that were published, especially after 1912, advising North American and elite Filipina women on how to manage their households and supervise their servants. Mimicking the language of military and bureaucratic operations, these manuals conceive of home management as a continuous process of mapping the sites of surveillance and intervention. Domesticity comes across as the routine and rationalized administration of violence with which to reproduce the boundaries between the inside and outside, the pure and polluted. See, for example, Mrs. Samuel Gaches, *Good Cooking and Health in the Tropics* (Manila: Bureau of Printing, 1922); and Alice M. Fuller, *Housekeeping: A Textbook for Girls in the Public and Intermediate Schools of the Philippines* (Manila: Bureau of Printing, 1917).

23 Clearly, the mistress-servant relation of the sort I will be writing about is not unique to colonial Philippine society, in part because of the globalization of a certain Western bourgeois style of living that associated domestic respectability with the discrete but efficient presence of servants. But as we shall see, the specificity of the racial and gender configuration of servitude in the islands under U.S. rule bears striking contrasts as well as similarities to the dynamics of domestic labor between white middle-class women and their immigrant, African American, Asian, and Latino servants in the United States. See, for example, David Katzman, *Seven Days a Week: Women and Domestic Service in Industrializing America* (New York: Oxford University Press, 1977); Phyllis Palmer, *Domesticity and Dirt: Housewives and Domestic Servants in the United States, 1920–1945* (Philadelphia, Pa.: Temple University Press, 1989); Judith Rollins, *Between Women: Domestics and Their Employers* (Philadelphia, Pa.: Temple University Press, 1985); Daniel Sutherland, *Americans and Their Servants: Domestic Service in the United States from 1800–1920* (Baton Rouge: Louisiana State University Press, 1981); Evelyn Nakano Glenn, *Issei, Nisei, War Bride: Three Generations of Japanese American Women in Domestic Service* (Philadelphia, Pa.: Temple University Press, 1986); and Mary Romero, *Maid in the U.S.A.* (New York: Routledge, 1992). For a useful African comparison with the Philippine case, especially in the matter of male servants, see Karen Tranberg Hansen, *Distant Companions: Servants and Employers in Zambia, 1900–1985* (Ithaca, N.Y.: Cornell University Press, 1989).

24 See *Census*, 2:101. The question of why domestic labor was monopolized by men rather than women in the Philippines during this period is a complex one that cannot be answered in the space of this chapter.

25 Winnifred Hubble, Unpublished Papers, 1907–1908, Bentley Historical Collection, University of Michigan, Ann Arbor.

26 Maude Huntley Jenks, *Death Stalks the Philippine Wilds*, ed. Carmen Nelson Richards (Minneapolis, Minn.: Lund Press, 1951), 90.

27 For a provocative study of the relation between mimesis, modernity, and colonial relations, see Michael Taussig, *Mimesis and Alterity: A Particular History of the Senses* (New York: Routledge, 1993). See also Walter Benjamin, "On the Mimetic Faculty," in *Reflections: Essays, Aphorisms, Autobiographical Writings*, ed. Peter Demetz, trans. Edward Jephcott (New York: Harcourt Brace Jovanovich, 1978), 333–36.

28 Here, it is useful to note that the late-nineteenth and early-twentieth-century middle-class norms of the United States posited the necessity of servants as a way to signal respectability. That is, the presence of servants served as an important indication of the functioning of a patriarchal regime that positioned women as wives in charge of managing the domestic sphere through the labor of servants. As David Katzman writes of the period from the 1880s to the 1920s, "Throughout the United States, then, middle class life-style required servants, whether for the comforts provided or as an indication of the family's status to the community" (*Seven Days a Week*, 149). It is less a question of whether many of these women had previously utilized servants back in the States, thus making servants in the Philippines seem like

a thrilling and gratifying novelty. Rather, domestic servitude and the political and symbolic economy attendant on it were integral parts of the notion of respectability constitutive of bourgeois hegemony in North America and Western Europe—a hegemony that would, of course, spread to the colonies.

The point here is that the very claim to bourgeois respectability was indissociable from the claim to transcend the demands of manual labor, including that of domestic work, in favor of managerial work. Again, at stake in the notion of respectability as the distancing of oneself from manual labor is, as alluded to above, the ability to disavow and repress one's embodiment so crucial in the formation of white identity. What this suggests is that it is impossible historically to dissociate the formation of bourgeois identity from the encoding of whiteness as the *unmarking* of the body. And that the colonial context I examine here is but one way of specifying this observation.

29 There still remains the question of how native servants understood their own subject position. The workings of white mimicry in North American women's accounts suggest that, to rephrase Gayatri Spivak's claim, only certain subalterns can speak, and then only at the expense of others. Yet, in the autobiography of Filipino writer Carlos Bulosan, there is an account of his having worked briefly as a servant for a woman librarian from the United States in Bagiuo in the 1920s. It is through Miss Mary Strandon that Bulosan is introduced to both English and North American literature. Later, he tries to reciprocate her affection by seeking out her family in Iowa to give them a copy of his book. And while a migrant laborer on the West Coast, Bulosan also writes about working with his brother for a short time as a servant for a wealthy family in Los Angeles; he leaves after being insulted by the mistress. Bulosan's rescripting of colonial domesticity, his fractured and complex relations with white women in both the Philippines and United States, and the refashioning of the notion of benevolent assimilation in conjunction not with an imperialist ethos but toward realizing a socialist project are matters that deserve to be treated in another essay. See Carlos Bulosan, *America Is in the Heart* (1943); reprint, Seattle: University of Washington Press, 1973), 67–75, 140–43.

3 The Undead: Notes on Photography in the Philippines, 1898–1920s

1 Malek Alloula, *The Colonial Harem*, trans. Myrna Godzich and Wlad Godzich (Minneapolis: University of Minnesota Press, 1986), 5.

2 See, for example Donna Haraway, *Primate Visions: Gender, Race, and Nature in the World of Modern Science* (New York: Routledge, 1989), 1–18, 26–58; Mary Louise Pratt, *Imperial Eyes: Travel Writing and Transculturation* (New York: Routledge, 1992); and Alan J. Sekula, "The Body and the Archive," *October* 39 (winter 1986): 3–64. I do not mean to suggest that all these works are alike and say the same thing, only that they have been among some of the more powerful and persuasive reformulations of photography's sociohistorical significance, furnishing indispensable touchstones for critiques of photography's colonial usages.

3 See, for example, the engaging book by Benito M. Vergara Jr., *Displaying Filipinos:*

Photography and Colonialism in Early-Twentieth-Century Philippines (Quezon City: University of the Philippines Press, 1995).

4   I borrow the term *compulsory visibility* from Michel Foucault, *Discipline and Punish: The Birth of the Prison*, trans. Alan Sheridan (New York: Vintage Books, 1979).

5   For a recent discussion of the use of photography in U.S. ethnological surveys conducted between 1900 and 1905, and the commercial uses, cultural effects, and political debates that such photographs instigated, see Paul A. Kramer, "The Pragmatic Empire: U.S. Anthropology and Colonial Politics in the Occupied Philippines, 1898–1916" (Ph.D. diss., Princeton University, 1998). See also Vergara, *Displaying Filipinos*.

6   For example, ethnological photographs along with live specimens of Filipino types were displayed at the St. Louis Exposition of 1904. For a critical history of these exhibits, see Robert Rydell, *All the World's a Fair: Visions of Empire at American International Exhibitions, 1876–1916* (Chicago: University of Chicago Press, 1984), and *World of Fairs: The Century-of-Progress Exposition* (Chicago: University of Chicago Press, 1993). Also useful is Eric Breitbart, *A World on Display: Photographs from the St. Louis World Fair, 1904* (Albuquerque: University of New Mexico Press, 1997), which contains among other things tourist snapshots of the fair that show Igorot men watching other native types on display. For an astute account of the political and commercial failure of the St. Louis Exposition to promote the aims of the colonial government to publicize its accomplishments in the Philippines and the desire of exposition officials to make a profit, see Kramer, "The Pragmatic Empire," 200–252.

7   For a more detailed discussion of this theme, as well as references to other important works along this line, see chapter 1 of this volume.

8   These photographs appear in such government publications as *Census of the Philippine Islands*, 4 vols. (Washington, D.C.: U.S. Government Printing Office, 1905); *Annual Reports of the Philippine Commission, 1901–1908* (Washington, D.C.: U.S. Government Printing Office, 1902–1909); and in Dean C. Worcester, *The Philippines Past and Present*, 2 vols. (New York: Macmillan Publishing Co., 1914).

9   See Foucault, *Discipline and Punish;* and a number of works on colonialism inspired by this book, most notably Timothy Mitchell, *Colonizing Egypt* (Berkeley: University of California Press, 1991); and Allan Feldman, *Formations of Violence: The Narrative of the Body and Political Terror in Northern Ireland* (Chicago: University of Chicago Press, 1991).

10 See, for example, General Oscar Fitzhalan Long's photographic album, "Our New Possessions in the Philippines," with photographs by James David Givens, Bancroft Library, University of California, Berkeley; F. Tennyson Neely, *Fighting in the Philippines: Authentic and Original Photographs* (Chicago, 1899; Marrion Wilcox, ed., *Harper's History of the War in the Philippines* (New York: Harper and Brothers, 1900); William S. Bryan, ed., *Our Islands and Their People as Seen with Camera and Pencil* (New York: N. D. Thompson and Publishing, 1899; and Stuart Creighton Miller, *Benevolent Assimilation: The American Conquest of the Philippines, 1899–1903*

(New Haven, Conn.: Yale University Press, 1982). As Jonathan Best has noted, some of these photographs were used as postcards, while others illustrated battles not even related to the Philippines, such as those of the Mexican Revolution. See his *A Philippine Album: American Era Photographs, 1900–1930* (Makati City, Philippines: Bookmark, Inc., 1998), 213.

11 This detail comes from Daniel B. Schirmer, *Republic or Empire? American Resistance to the Philippine-American War* (Cambridge, Mass.: Schenkman Publishing Co., 1972), 143.

12 I am grateful to Geoffrey Klingsporn for alerting me to this history in his unpublished essay, " 'A Harvest of Death': War, Photography, and History" (1998), 3–6. Also suggestive is Alan Trachtenberg's stunning observations on war photography in *Reading American Photographs: Images as History, Matthew Brady to Walker Evans* (New York: Hill and Wang, 1989), 71–118.

13 Did the photographs of Filipino dead also lend themselves to ironic readings on the part of U.S. viewers? Certainly. James David Givens, for example, captions one such photograph as "War is Hell," which seems to resonate with the "harvest of war" motif associated with Civil War photographs. And anti-imperialists used these pictures to illustrate what they felt was the unwarranted brutality of the war. Yet, as I discuss below, there is something about these photographs that escapes both triumphalist and ironic readings insofar as they bring to mind an event, death, whose eventfulness, as conveyed by photographs, defies interpretive closure.

14 Roland Barthes, *Camera Lucida: Reflections on Photography*, trans. Richard Howard (New York: Hill and Wang, 1981), 79.

15 Here, we might note that among the Filipino nationalist elites who were part of the colonial state, there arose a tremendous outcry over the use of photographic images of Igorots and other non-Christian Filipinos for display in the St. Louis Exposition and, later on, in a series of lantern slide lectures given by Dean Worcester in several U.S. cities as part of his campaign for the indefinite retention of the Philippines by the United States. In all cases, Filipino elites reacted with anger and embarrassment at the thought that the world would regard the "savage" and "dog-eating" Igorots as representative of the country as a whole. To counter this impression, the Filipino colonial assembly passed a law in 1914 to ban the possession and display of "naked Filipinos" (see Kramer, "The Practical Empire," 332–45). It is difficult to tell what the effects of such a ban were or how enforceable it proved to be. But it is instructive to note that to this day, one can travel to the Cordilleras and pose with older Igorots dressed in "traditional" costumes for a nominal fee, suggesting that the ghost of colonial ethnology, far from being exorcised, still lingers in the country.

16 To my knowledge, there is as yet no work comparing painting to photography in the Philippines or in any other part of Southeast Asia. There is instead what appears to be a modernist bias that divides cultural production in the region between so-called traditional or high art (those aesthetic forms deemed uncorrupted by colonial influences or the Western cultural industries) and popular or low culture (products of colonial domination and industrial developments). For a recent example of this

modernist treatment of art history, see Juan T. Gatbonton, Jeannie E. Javelosa, and Lourdes Ruth R. Roa, eds., *Art in the Philippines* (Pasig City, Philippines: Crucible Workshop, 1992).

17 There is as yet no book-length account of the social and cultural history of photography in the Philippines or, as far as I know, the Southeast Asian region. But see Vergara, *Displaying Filipinos*; John Silva, *Colonial Philippines: Photographs, 1860–1910* (exhibition catalog, Lowie Museum of Anthropology, University of California, Berkeley, 9–11 May 1987), and "Nineteenth Century Photography," in *The World of 1896* (Makati City, Philippines: Bookmark, Inc., 1998), 138–43; and Best, *A Philippine Album*. The connection between nineteenth-century portraiture and studio photography is evident in the nature of the poses and kinds of backdrops used in both media, phenomena that of course were quite common in many other parts of the world. But as Walter Benjamin has argued, photography soon came to evacuate the sense of the subject's presence that painting seemed to convey, freeing the image from its ties to its original context. For this reason, the photographic image could migrate, appearing in conjunction with other images in other contexts in ways that paintings, tied to a specific place, could not. See Walter Benjamin, "A Short History of Photography," in *One Way Street and Other Writings*, trans. Edmund Jephcott and Kingsley Shorter (London: New Left Books, 1979), 240–57.

18 E. Aguilar Cruz, "Vintage Photographs," in *Being Filipino*, ed. Gilda Cordero-Fernando (Quezon City, Philippines: GCF Books, 1981), unpaginated. The photographs that follow as illustrations here are taken from the collection that appear in Cruz's text. What is his connection to these photographs? Were they relatives or friends, or were these simply part of a larger collection of Filipiniana art that the author was known to be fond of? Cruz does not tell us. But the origins of these photographs and identity of their subjects are precisely the least interesting aspect of these portraits, as I hope to show. The fact that Cruz was drawn to them, and that the editors of this book—like us, its present readers—felt compelled to attend to them without knowing who the subjects were, says something about the communicative power of photographic portraits that surpasses the specific identities of their subjects.

19 My remarks on photographic portraits as gifts spring from my understanding of Marcel Mauss's classic work, *The Gift: Forms and Functions of Exchange in Archaic Societies* (New York: W. W. Norton, 1977).

20 See Vicente L. Rafael, "Nationalism, Imagery, and the Filipino Intelligentsia in the Nineteenth Century," in *Discrepant Histories: Translocal Essays on Filipino Cultures*, ed. Vicente L. Rafael (Philadelphia, Pa.: Temple University Press, 1995), 133–58.

21 Again, Roland Barthes in *Camera Lucida* is suggestive in this matter: "The photograph is literally an emanation of the referent. From a real body which was there proceed radiations which ultimately touch me, who am here; the duration of transmission is insignificant; the photograph of the missing body . . . will touch me like the delayed rays of a star. A sort of umbilical cord links the body of the photographed to my gaze; light, though impalpable, is here a carnal medium, a skin I

share with anyone who has been photographed" (80). Given the weird ontological status of photographs, it is small wonder that they cannot be reduced, as I have been arguing, to transparent historical documents. This is perhaps what we might deduce, among other things, from Barthes's earlier statement in the same book: "Photography evades me" (4).

22 Barthes, *Camera Lucida*, 85–119.

4 Anticipating Nationhood: Identification, Collaboration, and Rumor in Filipino Responses to Japan

1 Mariano Ponce, *Cartas Sobre la Revolucion, 1897–1900* (Manila: Bureau of Printing, 1932), 121–23. Note that this particular letter was addressed to Felipe Agoncillo, also an ambassador of the revolutionary government and uncle of Teodoro Agoncillo, a nationalist historian, about whom more will be said below. For other admiring remarks on Japan by Ponce, see also 125–26, 148–49, 230, 240.

2 Jose Rizal, *One Hundred Letters of Jose Rizal* (Manila: Philippine National Historical Society, 1949), 343. For a sketch of Rizal's fascination with Japan, see Leon Maria Guerrero, *The First Filipino* (Manila: National Historical Commission, 1974), 194–96.

3 See Reynaldo Ileto, *Pasyon and Revolution: Popular Movements in the Philippines, 1840–1910* (Quezon City, Philippines: Ateneo de Manila University Press, 1976), 254, 298–99. See also David Sturtevant, *Popular Uprisings in the Philippines, 1840–1940* (Ithaca, N.Y.: Cornell University Press, 1976).

4 Rizal, *One Hundred Letters*, 119; see also 21, 103.

5 See Benedict Anderson, *Imagined Communities: Reflections on the Origins and Spread of Nationalism*, 2d ed. (London: Verso, 1991). See also my extended gloss on Anderson in Vicente L. Rafael, "Nationalism, Imagery, and the Filipino Intelligentsia in the Nineteenth Century," in *Discrepant Histories: Translocal Essays on Filipino Cultures*, ed. Vicente L. Rafael (Philadelphia, Pa.: Temple University Press, 1995), 133–56.

6 Anderson, *Imagined Communities*, 82 ff.

7 See Peter Stanley, *A Nation in the Making: The Philippines and the United States, 1899–1921* (Cambridge, Mass.: Harvard University Press, 1974); and especially Reynaldo Ileto, "Orators and the Crowd: Philippine Independence Politics, 1910–1914," in *Reappraising an Empire: New Perspectives on Philippine-American History*, ed. Peter Stanley (Cambridge, Mass.: Harvard University Press, 1984).

8 The standard guide to the social history of the Philippines is Alfred McCoy and Ed. J. De Jesus, eds., *Philippine Social History: Global Trade and Local Transformations* (Quezon City, Philippines: Ateneo de Manila University Press, 1982).

9 See Benedict Anderson, "Cacique Democracy in the Philippines: Origins and Dreams," in *Discrepant Histories: Translocal Essays on Filipino Cultures*, ed. Vicente L. Rafael (Philadelphia, Pa.: Temple University Press, 1995), 3–47, for a succinct summary of these developments.

10 See Theodore Friend, *Between Two Empires: Philippine Ordeal and Development*

from the Great Depression through the Pacific War, 1929-1946 (New Haven, Conn.: Yale University Press, 1965).

11 See Benedict Kerkvliet, *The Huk Rebellion: A Study of Peasant Revolt in the Philippines* (Berkeley: University of California Press, 1977), chap. 3; and Anderson, "Cacique Democracy," 13-15.

12 Jose P. Laurel, *War Memoirs* (Manila: Lyceum Press, 1962), 22. The standard text on the politics of collaboration, although consumed by reified notions of "Filipino culture and values," is David Joel Steinberg, *Philippine Collaboration in World War II* (Ann Arbor: University of Michigan Press, 1967).

13 See Nick Joaquin, *The Aquinos of Tarlac: An Essay on History as Three Generations* (Manila: Cacho Hermanos, 1983), 169. See also Claro M. Recto, *Three Years of Enemy Occupation* (Manila: People's Publishers, 1946), 76.

14 Laurel, *Memoirs*, 48. For similar sentiments, see also Recto, *Three Years*; and Armando J. Malay, *Occupied Philippines* (Manila: Filipiniana Book Guild Series, 1967).

15 Cited in Joaquin, *Aquinos*, 158-59. See also Recto, *Three Years*, 79; and David Joel Steinberg, "Jose P. Laurel: A 'Collaborator' Misunderstood," *Journal of Asian Studies* 24 no. 4 (1965): 651-65.

16 Cited in Malay, *Occupied Philippines*, 193.

17 Ibid., 163-64, 165-66, 171-75, 184-90. See also Jose P. Laurel, "The Inaugural Address of President Jose P. Laurel, October 14, 1943," appendix f of *The Fateful Years: Japan's Adventure in the Philippines, 1941-1945*, by Teodoro Agoncillo (Quezon City, Philippines: R. P. Garcia Publishing Co., 1966), 2:1000-1011.

18 See Teodoro Agoncillo, *The Fateful Years: Japan's Adventure in the Philippines, 1941-1945* (Quezon City, Philippines: R. P. Garcia Publishing Co., 1966), 2:350, 443, 454. See also Victor Gosengfiao, "The Japanese Occupation: 'The Cultural Campaign,'" in *Rediscovery: Essays in Philippine Life and Culture*, ed. Cynthia Lumbera and Teresita Maceda (Quezon City, Philippines: National Bookstore, 1977), 170-83. For an overview of Japanese cultural policies and Filipino responses to them, see Gina Barte, ed., *Panahon ng Hapon: Sining sa Digmaan/Digmaan Sa Sining* (Manila: Museo ng Kalinangan Pilipino, 1992).

19 Andrew Gonzalez, *Language and Nationalism: The Philippine Experience Thus Far* (Quezon City, Philippines: Ateneo de Manila University Press, 1980), 28-33. My remarks on language under U.S. colonial rule are culled from Gonzalez's book. It should also be noted that the vernacular languages, particularly Tagalog in the Manila area, played an important role as a language of protest during the period of U.S. rule. It was precisely during the first decade of U.S. occupation that the country witnessed a flowering of vernacular literature, especially novels, poetry, and dramas framed by anticolonial, proindependence sentiments. A number of bilingual, vernacular-Spanish newspapers appeared periodically as well. The combination of U.S. repression of nationalist sentiments combined with the gradual cooptation of the Filipino intelligentsia into the colonial state worked to keep the vernaculars at the periphery of official discourse.

20 As Jorge B. Vargas put it, "I never felt at any time guilty of any culpable cooperation

21 with the Japanese military occupation in any way" (cited in Malay, *Occupied Philippines*, 6).
21 Recto, *Three Years*, 15–16. See also Renato Constantino and Letizia Constantino, *The Philippines: The Continuing Past* (Manila: Foundation for Nationalist Studies, 1978), 117.
22 On Japanese notions of race and empire, see John Dower, *War without Mercy: Race and Power in the Pacific War* (New York: Pantheon Books, 1986).
23 Laurel, *Memoirs*, 57.
24 Teodoro Agoncillo (1912–1985) also coauthored (along with Milagros C. Guerrero) what has become the standard college textbook in Philippine history and certainly one of the most influential books to have shaped nationalist historiography in the postwar period, *History of the Filipino People* (Quezon City, Philippines: R. P. Garcia Publishing Co., 1960). Born in Batangas to a family whose name is closely attached to the revolution, Agoncillo was educated at the University of the Philippines, established by the United States. He turned to writing and literary criticism before becoming a historian—at a time when the study of history was largely the province of amateurs and public intellectuals. After the war, he served on the faculty of the history department at the University of the Philippines, holding the chair for many years. For a series of telling interviews with Agoncillo, see Ambeth Ocampo, *Talking History: Conversations with Teodoro A. Agoncillo* (Manila: De La Salle University Press, 1995).
25 Agoncillo, *Fateful Years*, vi–vii.
26 Martin Heidegger, *Being and Time*, trans. John Macquarrie and Edward Robinson (New York: Harper and Row, 1962), 213. I thank Jim Siegel for referring me to this source and many other ideas regarding the workings of rumor.
27 *Rumor* is from the Latin for noise. It is also interesting to note in this connection the laws passed by the New Regime criminalizing the spread of rumors as an indication of rumors' subversive potential (see Agoncillo, *Fateful Years*, 311–12).
28 Agoncillo, *Fateful Years*, 51, 54.
29 Ibid., 297–98.
30 Ibid., viii.
31 Ibid., vii.
32 Ibid., 161.
33 Ibid., 160.
34 Ibid., 588–89.
35 Ibid., 310. See also Constantino, *The Philippines*, 57.
36 Agoncillo, *Fateful Years*, 400.
37 Ibid., 584–85.

5 Patronage, Pornography, and Youth: Ideology and Spectatorship during the Early Marcos Years

1 *Malacañang: A Guidebook* (Quezon City, Philippines: Kayumangi Press, 1986), 13. For various lowland versions of this myth, see Francisco Demetrio, *Myths and*

Symbols Philippines (Manila: National Bookstore, 1978), 41–43. See also Remedios F. Ramos et al., Si Malakas and Si Maganda (Manila: Jorge Y. Ramos, 1980). I am grateful to Doreen Fernandez and Ambeth Ocampo for bringing the commissioned rewriting of the legend to my attention. For a recent study of the Marcos's political imaginary, surprisingly the first book-length treatment of the topic, see James Hamilton-Paterson, *America's Boy: The Marcoses and the Philippines* (London: Granta Books, 1998).

2   Numerous accounts of the Marcoses on the campaign trail can be found in various Philippine magazines and newspapers. For this chapter, I have relied on a series of essays by Kerima Polotan in the *Philippine Free Press* (hereafter *FP*): "Marcos '65: The Inside Story of How Marcos Captured the Presidency," 29 March 1969, 50–60; "The Men, the Method," 5 April 1969, 4, 54–62; and "The Package Deal," 12 April 1969, 2–3, 46–51. See also Carmen Navarro-Pedrosa, *The Untold Story of Imelda Marcos* (Manila: Bookmark, 1969), esp. chap. 15; Napoleon G. Rama and Quijano de Manila, "Campaigning with Marcos and Osmeña," *FP*, 30 August 1969, 2–4, 181–82; and Filemon V. Tutay, "Marcos vs. Osmena: 'Nakakahiya,'" *FP*, 20 September 1969, 2–3, 64–72.

3   Rama and de Manila, "Campaigning with Marcos," 2.

4   Navarro-Pedrosa, *The Untold Story*, 216.

5   I should note that the discussion that follows begs the question of the history of private life in the Philippines. How did such a divide between the private and public emerge? What is the history of notions of intimacy and their relationship to class and gender identities, on one hand, and colonial and nationalist discourses, on the other? Was there an architecture of privacy, a costuming of publicity, especially in bourgeois life? I have begun to signal these themes in my earlier discussion of women from the United States in the colonial Philippines (see chapter 2), but the task of systematically retracing a history of privacy in the Filipino middle classes has yet to be undertaken. Here, I can only offer some inferences and conjectures that hopefully will invite revisions from future scholars.

6   For accounts of the Marcos romance, see Hartzell Spence, *Marcos of the Philippines* (New York: World Publishing Co., 1969), 237–67. Originally, this book appeared as *For Every Tear a Victory* (New York: McGraw-Hill, 1964). The publication of Spence's book occasioned considerable criticism from Filipino journalists, who claimed that his glorification of Ferdinand Marcos often came at the expense of racially tinged put-downs of his fellow Filipinos' capacities. See, for example, Quijano de Manila, *Reportage on Politics* (Manila: National Bookstore, 1981), 213–32. For biographies of Imelda Marcos, see Navarro-Pedrosa, *The Untold Story*, chapters 11–12; Kerima Polotan, *Imelda Romualdez Marcos* (New York: World Publishing Co., 1969), 79–82; Katherine Ellison, *Imelda: Steel Butterfly of the Philippines* (New York: McGraw-Hill, 1988); and Beatriz Romualdez Francia, *Imelda and the Clans: A Story of the Philippines* (Manila: Solar Publishing, 1988). For interviews with the Marcoses from their Hawaiian exile, see "Marcos Remembers," *Asia Week*, 5 July 1987, 28–33; and "Imelda and Ferdinand Marcos," *Playboy*, August 1987, 51–61. The romance

between Ferdinand and Imelda was also of central importance in the Marcos-commissioned campaign movies, *Iginuhit ng Tadhana* (*Drawn by Destiny*) in 1965 and *Pinagbuklod ng Langit* (*Joined by Heaven*) in 1969. I have not, unfortunately, been able to locate copies of these films, but see Napoleon Rama, "The Election Campaign in Review," *FP*, 15 November 1969, 5.

7 Spence, *Marcos*, 217.
8 Cited in ibid., 207.
9 Ibid., 240.
10 Navarro-Pedrosa, *The Untold Story*, 153.
11 Cited in ibid., 154.
12 Spence, *Marcos*, 5.
13 Ibid., chapters 3–6.
14 Ibid., 194.
15 Ibid., 28.
16 See, for example, Charles C. McDougal, *The Marcos File* (San Francisco, Calif.: San Francisco Publishers, 1987), 5–108.
17 Navarro-Pedrosa, *The Untold Story*, xv.
18 Polotan, "Marcos '65," 59.
19 Navarro-Pedrosa, *The Untold Story*, 203.
20 Polotan, "Marcos '65," 56.
21 Polotan, "The Men, The Method," 59–60.
22 Joe Guevarra, cited in Navarro-Pedrosa, *The Untold Story*, 156.
23 Navarro-Pedrosa, *The Untold Story*, 216.
24 Ibid., 222–23.
25 Rosario Mencias Querol, "What Are First Ladies For?" *Weekly Graphic* (hereafter *WG*), February 1965, 87.
26 *WG*, 30 December 1970, 1.
27 See Walter Benjamin, "The Work of Art in the Age of Mechanical Reproduction," in *Illuminations*, ed. Hannah Arendt, trans. Harry Zohn (New York: Schocken Books, 1969), 217–52.
28 Joe Quirino, "Another Kind of Bomba," *FP*, 6 December 1969, 18.
29 Petronilio Bn. Daroy, "The New Films, Sex, and the Law on Obscenity," *WG*, 30 December 1970, 7–9. The quote comes from Quirino, "Another Kind of Bomba," 16.
30 Quirino, "Another Kind of Bomba," 16.
31 Ibid., 18.
32 Ibid.
33 This is not to say that bombas met with no protest. The Catholic Church and various women's groups on both the Left and Right protested the ready availability of bombas and other forms of what they considered pornographic material. Periodic seizures of movies and raids of movie houses were made, and sidewalk cleanup campaigns were routinely ordered, especially during election time, by local officials to rid the cities of so-called smut. Nonetheless, the commercial profitability of pornography in the country meant that such materials were bound to return, calling

forth further campaigns of suppression and so on around the circle. There is as yet no study of the relationship between censorship and pornography in the Philippines, and like many other aspects of Philippine modernity, an examination of this relationship undoubtedly would deepen our understanding of postwar political culture.

34 Polotan, *Imelda*, 87.
35 Ibid., 86, 184, 220.
36 The most succinct and perspicacious analysis of the Marcos regime can be found in Benedict Anderson, "Cacique Democracy in the Philippines: Origins and Dreams," in *Discrepant Histories: Translocal Essays on Filipino Cultures*, ed. Vicente L. Rafael (Philadelphia, Pa.: Temple University Press, 1995), 3–47. See also Primitivo Mojares, *The Conjugal Dictatorship of FerdinandImelda Marcos* (San Francisco, Calif.: Union Square Publishers, 1976); Gary Hawes, *The Philippine State and the Marcos Regime* (Ithaca, N.Y.: Cornell University Press, 1987), esp. chapters 1–5; and John Bresnan, ed., *Crisis in the Philippines* (Princeton, N.J.: Princeton University Press, 1986), chapters 4–7.
37 This sense of national culture as a series of gifts coming from above is arguably a legacy of the history of colonialism informed by the ideology of white love that I discussed in chapter 1. There is therefore nothing remotely "indigenous" about it. In this connection, it is worth noting that the practice of patronage that has long characterized contemporary Philippine politics—most recently under the rubric of cronyism—has never been a Filipino monopoly. Spanish and U.S. colonial offices were all appointive so that they were routinely obtained on the basis of patronage and, in at least the Spanish case, outright purchase. Hence it is historically inaccurate, if not ethnocentric, on the part of an earlier generation of North American scholarship to cite the putatively regressive practices of patronage in Philippine politics as the source of much corruption while conveniently forgetting that the overwhelming majority of officeholders under the U.S. colonial state—from governor-generals to ethnologists—owed their positions to powerful friends on top just as they used their positions to dispense favors and make friends among those below. For examples of these, see Paul A. Kramer, "The Pragmatic Empire: U.S. Anthropology and Colonial Politics in the Occupied Philippines, 1898–1916" (Ph.D. diss., Princeton University, 1998); and Michael Cullinane, "Ilustrado Politics: The Response of the Filipino Educated Elite to American Colonial Rule, 1898–1907" (Ph.D. diss., University of Michigan, 1989). Thus was Philippine modernity under the Marcoses neocolonial in every way.
38 The literature on the history and structure of patronage in the Philippines is considerable and uneven. Most explorations written from the 1960s through the 1980s tend to treat the topic as part of a reified field of Filipino values. The more significant (and also symptomatic) works include Mary Hollnsteiner, *The Dynamics of Power in a Philippine Municipality* (Quezon City: University of the Philippines Press, 1963); Theodore Friend, *Between Two Empires: Philippine Ordeal and Development from the Great Depression through the Pacific War, 1929–1946* (New Haven, Conn.: Yale

University Press, 1965); David Joel Steinberg, *Philippine Collaboration in World War II* (Ann Arbor: University of Michigan Press, 1967); Carl Lande, *Leaders, Factions, and Parties: The Structure of Philippine Politics* (New Haven, Conn.: Yale Southeast Asian Studies, 1964); Onofre D. Corpuz, *The Philippines* (Englewood Cliffs, N.J.: Prentice-Hall, 1965), esp. 93–140; Kit G. Machado, "From Traditional Faction to Machine: Changing Patterns of Political Leadership and Organization in Rural Philippines," *Journal of Asian Studies* 33, no. 4 (August 1974): 523–47; and Amando Doronilla, "The Transformation of Patron-Client Relations and Its Political Consequences in Post-War Philippines," *Journal of Southeast Asian Studies* 16, no. 1 (March 1985): 99–116.

The more astute attempts to critique culturalist analysis of patronage include Resil Mojares, *The Man Who Would Be President: Serging Osmeña and Philippine Politics* (Cebu City, Philippines: Maria Cacao, 1986); Benedict Kerkvliet, *The Huk Rebellion: A Study of Peasant Revolt in the Philippines* (Berkeley: University of California Press, 1977); and Reynaldo Ileto, *Pasyon and Revolution: Popular Movements in the Philippines, 1840–1910* (Quezon City, Philippines: Ateneo de Manila University Press, 1979). The vicissitudes of patronage under U.S. colonial rule is thematized in Peter Stanley, ed., *Reappraising an Empire: New Perspectives on Philippine-American History* (Cambridge, Mass.: Harvard University Press, 1984); Ruby Paredes, ed., *Philippine Colonial Democracy* (Quezon City, Philippines: Ateneo de Manila University Press, 1989); and Cullinane, "Ilustrado Politics." For more contemporary accounts, see the essays in Alfred McCoy's edited collection, which bears the unfortunately essentializing title *An Anarchy of Families: State and Family in the Philippines* (Quezon City, Philippines: Ateneo de Manila University Press, 1994). For a discussion of patronage during the Spanish colonial period, see Vicente L. Rafael, *Contracting Colonialism: Translation and Christian Conversion in Tagalog Society under Early Spanish Rule* (Durham, N.C.: Duke University Press, 1993), esp. chapters 3 and 4.

39 Kerkvliet, *The Huk Rebellion*, 1–25, 250–60, 266–69.
40 See Lande, *Leaders, Factions, and Parties*, 15–18, 24–25, 72–75, 62–68, 79–81, 111–14; and Machado, "From Traditional Faction to Machine." One of the most useful guides to the economic and social processes that underpinned such a transition are the essays in Alfred McCoy and Ed. J. De Jesus, eds., *Philippine Social History: Global Trade and Local Transformations* (Quezon City, Philippines: Ateneo de Manila University Press, 1982).
41 See especially Mojares, *The Man Who Would Be President*, 71–81, for a succinct summary of the importance of money in Philippine politics.
42 Polotan, *Imelda*, 195, 233–34.
43 Ibid., 235.
44 Ibid., 237.
45 "The Three Images of Imelda," *FP*, 13 December 1969, 92–94. By the second half of the 1970s, however, the *Free Press* had become a strident critic of the Marcoses, who were rumored to be plotting to perpetuate their power indefinitely by running Imelda for president, changing constitutional provisions that barred Marcos from

seeking a third term in office, and possibly even declaring martial law, which of course he did in 1972.

46   Polotan, *Imelda*, 212.

47   "Three Images," 92–93. Subsequent references are cited in the text.

48   I indicate some of the more recent manifestations of the postwar, neocolonial aesthetic of patronage and the contradictions symptomatic of nationalist modernity in the chapters that follow. See also Vicente L. Rafael, "Fishing, Underwear, and Hunchbacks: Humor and Politics in the Philippines, 1886 and 1983," *Bulletin of Concerned Asian Scholars* 18, no. 3 (1986): 2–7.

49   See Quijano de Manila, "Woman of the Year," *FP*, 11 January 1969, 33; Isabelo T. Crisostomo, "Imelda for President?" *FP*, 12 December 1970, 18–19, 141–44; Napoleon G. Rama, "Imelda, the Presidency, the Nacionalistas—and the People," *FP*, 19 December 1970, 5, 52–54; and Ben Trio Rufin, "Is Imelda Really Running for President in 1972?" *FP*, 2 October 1971, 1.

50   Cited in Quijano de Manila, "Parthenon or Pantheon?" *FP*, 22 February 1969, 73.

51   My understanding of the liminal status of youth in society has benefited from the writings of Benedict Anderson, *Java in a Time of Revolution: Occupation and Resistance, 1944–1946* (Ithaca, N.Y.: Cornell University Press, 1972), chap. 1; and James T. Siegel, *Solo in the New Order: Language and Hierarchy in an Indonesian City* (Princeton, N.J.: Princeton University Press, 1986), chap. 8.

52   For historical sketches of the Kabataang Makabayan and student activism of the 1960s, see Benjamin Pimentel, *Rebolusyon! A Generation of Struggle in the Philippines* (New York: Monthly Review Press, 1991), 45–62; William Chapman, *Inside the Philippine Revolution: The New People's Army and Its Struggle for Power* (New York: W. W. Norton, 1987), 68–78; and Alex Magno, *A Nation Reborn*, vol. 9 of *Kasaysayan: The Story of the Filipino People* (Hong Kong: Asia Publishing Company, 1998), 82–83, 143–47, 227–37. See also Amadis Maria Guerrero, "Siege at Congress: A Sidelight," *WG*, 11 February 1970, 10–11; and Roy H. Hizon, "The Left in the Sixties," *WG*, 25 February 1970, 10–13. There is as yet no book-length treatment of the early days of the youth movement.

53   See Pimentel, *Rebolusyon!* 45–93; and Jose Maria Sison, *Philippine Society and Revolution* (Manila: Pulang Tala Publications, 1971). The intellectual groundwork for Sison's understanding of Philippine conditions was laid out by such nationalist scholars as Renato Constantino, Lorenzo Tanada, and before them, Claro M. Recto.

54   See, for example, the interviews in Pimentel, *Rebolusyon!*

55   In 1966, for instance, violent clashes occurred as youth groups rallied against the war in Vietnam during the visit of President Lyndon Johnson and allied heads of state for the Manila Summit. See Magno, *A Nation Reborn*, 82–86; Hizon, "The Left in the Sixties"; and Quijano de Manila, "Anarchs in Academe," *FP*, 7 September 1968, 68–71.

56   In Philippine societies, circumcision among males is a sign of maturity. It is therefore highly insulting to refer to an adult male as uncircumcised.

57   Jose F. Lacaba, "The January 26 Confrontation" and "And the January 30 Insurrection," *FP*, 7 February 1970, 45. Subsequent references are cited in the text. These two

articles as well as other reports were later gathered by Lacaba in his book, *Days of Disquiet, Nights of Rage: The First Quarter Storm and Other Related Events* (Manila: Salinlahi Publications, 1982). For other accounts of the First Quarter Storm, see Pimentel, *Rebolusyon!;* and Magno, *A Nation Reborn.*

58 Kerima Polotan, "The Long Week," *FP,* 7 February 1970, 32A.
59 Cited in Quijano de Manila, "To Sir with Love and Irony," *FP,* 14 February 1970, 68.
60 See Quijano de Manila, "The President States His Side," *FP,* 7 March 1970, 2–3, 43–48. Marcos, of course, was not entirely wrong. Leaders of the KM and other radical student groups were, in fact, affiliated with the Communist Party of the Philippines headed by Jose Maria Sison. Many of them would join the CPP's armed wing, the New People's Army. With the increasing formalization and militarization of leftwing opposition, the earlier "wild" nature of the youth movement would come under party discipline. For critical accounts of the role of the Communist Party in recent Philippine history, see the essays in Patricio N. Abinales, ed., *The Revolution Falters: The Left in Philippine Politics after 1986* (Ithaca, N.Y.: Southeast Asia Program Publications, Cornell University, 1996).

6 Taglish, or the Phantom Power of the Lingua Franca

1 Jessica Hagedorn, *Dogeaters* (New York: Penguin Books, 1990), 3–4. Subsequent references are cited in the text.
2 My remarks on the workings of classical notions of film spectatorship in the erasure of social differences for the sake of producing a "national" audience attuned to a culture of consuming images are indebted to Miriam Hansen, *Babel and Babylon: Spectatorship in American Silent Film* (Cambridge, Mass.: Harvard University Press, 1991), esp. chap. 3. I am also indebted to Walter Benjamin's essay, "The Work of Art in the Age of Mechanical Reproduction," in *Illuminations,* ed. Hannah Arendt, trans. Harry Zohn (New York: Schocken Books, 1969), 217–52.
3 See Edgar Wickberg, "The Chinese Mestizo in Philippine History," *Journal of Southeast Asian History* 5 (March 1964): 62–100, and *The Chinese in Philippine Life, 1850–1898* (New Haven, Conn.: Yale University Press, 1965). See also the brilliant novels of Jose Rizal, *Noli me Tangere* (Berlin: Berliner Buchdruckerei-Aktion-Gesellschaft, 1887) and *El Filibusterismo* (Ghent: F. Meyer-Van Loo, 1891); and for a succinct historical overview of the formation of the mestizo elite, see Benedict Anderson, "Cacique Democracy in the Philippines: Origins and Dreams," in *Discrepant Histories: Translocal Essays on Filipino Cultures,* ed. Vicente L. Rafael (Philadelphia, Pa.: Temple University Press, 1995), 3–47.
4 For an elaboration of the question of envy and revenge, especially as it arises from a felt sense of exclusion from the upper reaches of colonial society among Filipino ilustrado men, see Vicente L. Rafael, "Translation and Revenge: Castilian and the Origins of Nationalism in the Philippines," in *The Places of History: Regionalism Revisited in Latin America,* ed. Doris Sommer (Durham, N.C.: Duke University Press, 1999), 214–35.
5 Here, it is important to note that the Filipino nation-state conjured by mestizos/as,

especially those with Chinese ancestry, has historically involved regarding the Chinese as a foreign, albeit essential element in the national order. For the odd place of the Chinese in contemporary Philippine life, see Caroline S. Hau, "'Who Will Save Us from the Law?': The Criminal State and the Illegal Alien in Post-1986 Philippines," in *Figures of Criminality in Indonesia, the Philippines, and Colonial Vietnam*, ed. Vicente L. Rafael (Ithaca, N.Y.: Cornell Southeast Asia Program Publications, 1999), 128–51. For a series of essays that explicate the role of mestizo qualities in the history of the Philippine Revolution, see Nick Joaquin, *A Question of Heroes: Essays in the Criticism of Key Figures of Philippine History* (Makati, Philippines, Ayala Museum, 1977).

6   For late-nineteenth-century examples of mestizo uses of Taglish—more specifically, the mixing of Tagalog and Spanish—see the two great novels of the Chinese mestizo national hero of the Philippines, Rizal, *Noli me Tangere*, and *El Filibusterismo*. The political stakes of Taglish in this case were, of course, far different from those contained in the work of New York–based Filipina author Jessica Hagedorn.

7   See Vicente L. Rafael, *Contracting Colonialism: Translation and Christian Conversion in Tagalog Society under Early Spanish Rule* (Durham, N.C.: Duke University Press, 1993), for a fuller discussion of the languages of Spanish colonial rule.

8   Ibid.

9   Andrew Gonzalez, *Language and Nationalism: The Philippine Experience Thus Far* (Quezon City, Philippines: Ateneo de Manila University Press, 1980), 155–62. Also useful is the special issue of *Solidarity* on the future of English in the Philippines, reprinted as Andrew Gonzalez, ed., *The Role of English and Its Maintenance in the Philippines* (Solidaridad Publishing House, 1988). What is abundantly obvious in all these discussions on language is that like the nineteenth-century ilustrados and the Spanish clerical authorities before them, Filipino elites remain invested in the maintenance of a linguistic hierarchy as a way of regulating the social hierarchy.

10 Teodoro Agoncillo and Milagros C. Guerrero, *History of the Filipino People* (Quezon City, Philippines: R. P. Garcia Publishing Co., 1960), 535–36. Oddly, Agoncillo readily slipped into Taglish himself during interviews and most likely while teaching his classes at the University of the Philippines. See Ambeth Ocampo, *Talking History: Conversations with Teodoro A. Agoncillo* (Manila: De La Salle University Press, 1995). Indeed, as I have argued in connection with the workings of rumor in chapter 4, it is possible to see a kind of Taglish sensibility in Agoncillo's books, as in the case of his two-volume account of the Japanese occupation of the Philippines, *The Fateful Years: Japan's Adventures in the Philippines, 1941–1945* (Quezon City, Philippines: R. P. Garcia Publishing Co., 1966).

11 See, for example, the essays in Gonzalez, *The Role of English*. That Taglish seems to elude official codification does not mean that it is wholly carnivalesque. It is possible to render a formal account of Taglish grammar and syntax apart from its sociohistorical uses. What is instructive, however, is the relative disinterestedness or seeming inability of Filipino academics and officials to do so. As will become apparent below, the codification of Taglish in recent years has been most effectively

carried out by the market, especially in the film and advertising industries. I thank James Clifford for pushing me to clarify this matter.

12   Jose F. Lacaba, "Notes on Bakya, Being an Apologia of Sorts for Filipino Mass Cult," in *Readings in Filipino Cinema*, ed. Rafael Maria Guerrero (Manila: Experimental Cinema of the Philippines Publications, 1983), 117–23. Originally published in the *Philippine Free Press* in 1970, this essay has been widely anthologized in college textbooks on Filipino culture.

13   The mimetic response of the middle class to bakya speech recalls here the mimicking of native servants' speech by American women in chapter 2. The stakes in such a move, however, could not be more different, as we shall see below.

14   Lacaba, "Notes on Bakya," 121.

15   We can see contemporary manifestations of bakya English and its capacity to invoke interest, and so serve as the basis for a politics of dis-identification, in the stories and jokes regarding the career of Joseph "Erap" Estrada, once a popular action star in Filipino films of the 1950s to 1970s and currently the thirteenth president of the republic of the Philippines. These jokes have now been collected in the national best-seller, *ERAPtion: How to Speak English without Really Trial* (Manila: Oxford Printing Corporation, 1994), and fully endorsed by Estrada himself as a calculated attempt to boost his popularity.

16   See Jose F. Lacaba, "Movies, Critics, and the Bakya Crowd," in *Readings in Filipino Cinema*, ed. Rafael Maria Guerrero (Manila: Experimental Cinema of the Philippines Publications, 1983), 175–81.

17   See Vicente L. Rafael, "Fishing, Underwear, and Hunchbacks: Humor and Politics in the Philippines, 1886 and 1983," *Bulletin of Concerned Asian Scholars* 18, no. 3 (1986): 2–7.

18   Nonoy Marcelo, *Ikabod* (Manila: Solar Publishing House, 1987), 196. Subsequent references are cited in the text.

19   One historical precedent for this sort of linguistic practice premised on the interruption of a second language by a first (and vice versa) can be seen in the literature of *ladino* writers from the seventeenth century, such as Tomas Pinpin discussed in my *Contracting Colonialism*, especially chapter 2.

20   Anderson, "Cacique Democracy," 3–50.

21   For useful accounts of the history of the Filipino film industry, see Clodualdo del Mundo Jr., *Native Resistance: Philippine Cinema and Colonialism, 1898–1941* (Manila: De La Salle University Press, 1998); Emmanuel Reyes, *Notes on Philippine Cinema* (Manila: De La Salle University Press, 1989); Lolita R. Lacuesta, ed., *Beyond the Mainstream: The Films of Nick de Ocampo* (Pasig City: Anvil Publishing, Inc., 1997); and the essays in Clodualdo del Mundo Jr., ed., *Philippine Mass Media: A Book of Readings* (Manila: Communication Foundation of Asia, 1986). See also the essays in Rafael Maria Guerrero, ed., *Readings in Philippine Cinema* (Manila: Experimental Cinema of the Philippines Publications, 1983). Also informative are J. Eddie Infante, *Inside Philippine Movies, 1970–1990* (Quezon City, Philippines: Ateneo de Manila University Press, 1991); and Isagani Cruz, *Movie Time* (Manila: National Bookstore,

1984). I am grateful to Enrique Bonus for providing me with these sources. It is instructive to note how Philippine cinema is doubly localized by the fact that there has been to date almost no foreign, especially from the United States, scholarship on Filipino cinema.

22 The different conditions of exhibition and consumption of Filipino movies, as they travel from a national to a diasporic audience, are reproduced in film or video formats, are encountered in metro Manila mega-malls or the smaller, ghettoized spaces of video stores in ethnic strip malls in the United States, is a subject that needs to be explored at greater length and requires a separate essay.

23 Both movies were produced by Regal Films. The first was written and directed by Jose Javier Reyes; the second by the popular writer Lualhati Bautista and directed by Joey Romero. My choice of these films is, in the end, arbitrary. They seemed to typify a range of Filipino movies that I had seen between 1994 and 1996, and they were easily accessible to me through a local Filipino video rental place in San Diego, California, where I live.

24 Reyes, *Notes on Philippine Cinema*, 58–59. See also Joel David, *The National Pastime: Contemporary Philippine Cinema* (Pasig City, Philippines: Anvil Publishing, Inc., 1990), 88–93. Also useful for an understanding of the historical specificity of Filipino gay culture are the essays by Martin Manalansan, "Speaking of AIDS: Language and the Filipino 'Gay' Experience in America," and Fenella Cannell, "The Power of Appearances: Beauty, Mimicry, and Transformation in Bikol," both in *Discrepant Histories: Translocal Essays on Filipino Cultures*, ed. Vicente L. Rafael (Philadelphia, Pa.: Temple University Press, 1995), 193–221 and 223–58 respectively. See also Neil C. Garcia and Danton Remoto, eds., *Ladlad: An Anthology of Philippine Gay Writing* (Pasig City, Philippines: Anvil Publishing, Inc., 1994).

25 It is useful to note that in the contemporary Philippines, the bakla is not the only figure pressed into the service of representing so as to repress the disruptive possibilities of Taglish. There is also the figure of the mestiza colegiala, or convent-educated young woman (specifically from the Assumption school), whose Taglish has been the subject of numerous parodies in the press as well as in academic and elite circles. Her sense of privilege is often seen to result in ignorance, reflected in her inability to speak proper Tagalog and thus her need to resort to Taglish. The tone of the parodies, however, are for the most part laced with envy for precisely the class privileges associated with her speech. As we saw in the *Ikabod* example, this gives the colegiala Taglish a certain erotic allure.

26 See Virgilio Almario, "Cinderella Superstar: The Life and Legend of Nora Aunor," Quijano de Manila, "Mr. Box-Office," Denise Chou Allas, "Dolphy: The Way of a Clown," and Julie Y. Daza, "The Eddie Rodriguez Syndrome," all in *Readings in Philippine Cinema*, ed. Rafael Maria Guerrero (Manila: Experimental Cinema of the Philippines Publications, 1983), 135–43, 144–56, 157–69, and 170–74 respectively.

27 The *Oxford English Dictionary* notes that *glamour*, the power to enchant or bewitch with physical beauty, is etymologically related to *gramarye*, that is, magic or necromancy, by way of *grammar* from the old French *gramaire*, learning.

28   That movie stars and media celebrities, beginning with actor Joseph "Erap" Estrada, now comprise the newest generation of political elites in the Philippines should come as no surprise, given the preceding discussion on their role as the locus for the dissemination of a language of national longing that is simultaneously the echo of capitalist desire. And as we saw in the previous chapter, many of the conditions for the reception of stars into politics had already been laid out with the emergence of Imelda and Ferdinand Marcos in the public eye in the mid-1960s.

7 Writing History after EDSA

1   For a succinct account of the history of the popular press during the martial law period and leading up to the events of 1986, see Melinda Quintos de Jesus, "The Media: High on Verve, Low on Substance," in *Duet for EDSA: Looking Back, Looking Forward*, ed. Lorna Kalaw-Tirol (Manila: Foundation for Worldwide People Power, Inc., 1995), 193–218. A useful survey of protest theater during the Marcos years and after is Doreen Fernandez, *Palabas: Essays on Philippine Theater History* (Quezon City, Philippines: Ateneo de Manila University Press, 1996), 104–52. See also Mark R. Thompson, *The Anti-Marcos Struggle: Personalistic and Democratic Transition in the Philippines* (New Haven, Conn.: Yale University Press, 1995); and for the important role of the NDF during these years, see Joel Rocamora, *Breaking Through: The Struggle within the Communist Party of the Philippines* (Pasig City, Philippines: Anvil Publishing, Inc. 1994).

2   One indication of the importance of newspaper writers in the post-EDSA public sphere is the sheer number of books that have appeared containing compilations of their past columns. Such collections suggest that the very act of writing a daily newspaper column, whatever its contents or reach, is considered historically significant in and of itself when seen against the repressive policies of the Marcos regime. The fact that a readership, not to mention a market (however relatively small), for their writing exists seems to suggest that columnists play a role that can, at times, run counter to that of the movie star's (especially the movie star turned politician) in the cultural politics of the country. The post-EDSA nature of this phenomenon is indicated by the relative absence of newspaper column compilations prior to 1986. Aside from the occasional collections of Carmen Guerrero-Nakpil's work, for example, or the stray collection of articles by Joe Guevarra, newspaper columns were not regarded as anything but disposable by newspaper readers. One way to get a sense of the significance of columnists' new place in post-EDSA society is to peruse the impressive series of collections published by Anvil Publishing, Inc. (Pasig City, Philippines)—the same press that has published most of Ocampo's books—under the much-praised leadership of Karina A. Bolasco. To name only a few: Conrado de Quiros, *Flowers from the Rubble* (1990); Sheila S. Coronel, *Coups, Cults, and Cannibals: Chronicles of a Troubled Decade, 1982–1992* (1993); Jo-Ann Q. Maglipon, *Primed: Selected Stories, 1972–1992* (1993); Sylvia Mendez Ventura, *Ragtime in Kamuning: Sari-Sari Essays* (1992); Randy David, *Public Lives: Essays on Selfhood and Social Solidarity* (1998); and Jessica Zafra, *Planet of the Twisted* (1998).

3   See the essays in the following collections by Ambeth Ocampo, all published by Anvil Publishing, Inc.: *Looking Back* (1990); *Rizal without the Overcoat* (1990); *Aguinaldo's Breakfast* (1993); *Bonifacio's Bolo* (1995); *Mabini's Ghost* (1995); and *Luna's Moustache* (1997).
4   See especially Ambeth Ocampo's latest collection, *The Centennial Countdown* (Pasig City, Philippines: Anvil Publishing, Inc., 1998), which contains some of the most perspicacious and pointed critiques of state-sponsored and popularly held myths of the revolution and its counterrevolutionary aftermath.
5   In his approach to the sensorium of historical artifacts, Ocampo has learned a great deal from his mentors, Teodoro Agoncillo, E. Aguilar Cruz, and Doreen Fernandez.
6   This term, a piece of neocolonial science fiction kitsch if there ever was one, was coined by former President Fidel Ramos to highlight the developmentalist ambitions of his regime.
7   For a historical account of the linguistic hierarchy characteristic of the contemporary Philippines, see chapter 6 above.
8   For a discussion of ilustrado attempts to vernacularize Spanish and their political consequences, see Vicente L. Rafael, "Translation and Revenge: Castilian and the Origins of Nationalism in the Philippines," in *The Places of History: Regionalism Revisited in Latin America*, ed. Doris Sommer (Durham, N.C.: Duke University Press, 1999), 214–35.
9   It is worth noting here that Ocampo himself has been attached to academic institutions over the years, including the history departments of the University of the Philippines, De La Salle University, and as of 1999, the Ateneo de Manila University. It is not therefore the case that he stands in direct opposition to academic institutions; only that his writing tends to appeal to a popular readership in direct proportion to its marginalization by professional historians.
10 Such stands in contrast to the more tendentious mistranslations of Rizal's novels, for example, by Leon Maria Guerrero. For an account of the political history and social implications of Guerrero's mistranslations, see Benedict Anderson, "Hard to Imagine," in *The Spectre of Comparisons: Nationalism, Southeast Asia, and the World* (London: Verso, 1998), 235–62.
11 El Shaddai is a conservative Catholic group whose meetings are styled after born-again, fundamentalist Protestant sects. It is headed by self-styled prophet and former insurance salesperson Mike Velarde. His mass following has made him a formidable political force, and he has been a strong supporter of President Joseph Estrada.

8 "Your Grief Is Our Gossip": Overseas Filipinos and Other Spectral Presences

The title of this chapter comes from a quote accidentally found on a button in a local record store in San Diego, California.

1   See Benedict Anderson's suggestion of nationalism's intrinsic dependence on death as a means of "command[ing] . . . profound emotional legitimacy" in *Imagined Communities: Reflections on the Origins and Spread of Nationalism* 2d ed. (London:

Verso, 1991), 4, 10–11, 204–6. See also my essay, "Nationalism, Imagery, and the Filipino Intelligentsia of the Nineteenth Century," in *Discrepant History: Translocal Essays on Filipino Cultures*, ed. Vicente L. Rafael (Philadelphia, Pa.: Temple University Press, 1995), 133–58.

2 Karl Schoenberger, "Living off Expatriate Labor," *Los Angeles Times*, 1 August 1994, 1.
3 Cited in ibid., A16.
4 For a succinct review of the literature dealing with Filipino immigration to the United States, see Catherine C. Choy, "The Export of Womanpower: A Transnational History of Filipino Nurse Migration to the United States" (Ph.D. diss., University of California, Los Angeles, 1998). See also the essays edited by Filomeno V. Aguilar Jr. under the heading "Filipinos as Transnational Migrants" in the special issue of *Philippine Sociological Review* 44, nos. 1–4 (December–January 1996); the essays edited by Jonathan Okamura based on the theme "Filipino American History, Identity, and Community in Hawai'i" in the special issue of *Social Process in Hawai'i* 37 (1996); Jonathan Okamura, "The Filipino American Diaspora: Sites of Space, Time, and Ethnicity," in *Privileging Sites: Positions in Asian American Studies*, ed. Gary Okihiro (Pullman, Wash.: Washington State University Press, 1997), 387–400; Su Cheng Chan, *Asian Americans: An Interpretive History* (Boston: Twayne Publishing, 1991); and Yen Le Espiritu, "The Intersection of Race, Ethnicity, and Class: The Multiple Identities of Second-Generation Filipinos," *Identities* 1, no. 2 (1994): 249–73, and *Filipino-American Lives* (Philadelphia, Pa.: Temple University Press, 1995).
5 For drawing me to reflect on the affective politics of nationalism, I thank Brian Mussumi, whose dense and yet to be published essay, "The Political Economy of Belonging and the Logic of Relation," has been richly suggestive.
6 Among the "tons and tons of baggage" that de Quiros refers to are large boxes commonly known as balikbayan boxes, a staple feature of balikbayan identity for the last twenty-five years. Supplanting the discarded boxes of computer equipment, canned goods, and Pampers diapers that were used in the 1970s and early 1980s to pack gifts (*pasalubongs*) that visiting immigrants felt obliged to bring back to their relatives in the Philippines, standardized cardboard versions marked "balikbayan box" began to be manufactured by Filipino-American entrepreneurs in the mid-1980s. As with the found boxes used in an earlier period, balikbayan boxes conform to airline regulations on the maximum allowable size of checked baggage. Large enough to contain the quantities and varieties of pasalubongs, balikbayan boxes are also cheap and disposable alternatives to more costly suitcases.

Such boxes are the material evidence of immigrant success as much as they are symbolic of the promise of immigration itself. Thus do they constitute the materialization of a desire realizable only outside the nation, yet recognizable only within its borders. As such, the balikbayan box is a kind of social hieroglyph indexing a Filipino-American immigrant social formation predicated on the improvisation and subsequent standardization of a hybrid type: a subject at once neocolonial *and* national. I thank Rudy and Cecile Martija, Bayani Rafael, and Rosemary Rafael for shedding light on the matter of balikbayan boxes.

7   Conrado de Quiros, "Bracing for Balikbayans," in *Flowers from the Rubble* (Pasig City, Philippines: Anvil Publishing, Inc., 1990), 139–41. Subsequent references are cited in the text.
8   For the classic formulation of this nationalist critique, see Renato Constantino, *Mis-Education of the Filipino* (Manila, 1966).
9   For discussions of the historical importance of walang hiya, see Reynaldo Ileto, *Pasyon and Revolution: Popular Movements in the Philippines, 1840–1912* (Quezon City, Philippines: Ateneo de Manila University Press, 1979); and Vicente L. Rafael, *Contracting Colonialism: Translation and Christian Conversion in Tagalog Society under Early Spanish Rule* (Durham, N.C.: Duke University Press, 1993), 121–35.
10 See Espiritu, "The Intersection of Race, Ethnicity, and Class," for a lucid account of the cultural transformations of Filipinoness in the late-twentieth-century United States.
11 See, for example, the riveting accounts of OCWs in Japan in Rey Ventura, *Underground in Japan* (London: Jonathan Cape, 1992); and Maria Rosario P. Ballescas, *Filipino Entertainers in Japan: An Introduction* (Quezon City, Philippines: Foundation for Nationalist Studies, 1992). Also instructive are the collected letters from OCWs in Justino Dormiendo, ed., *Nagmamahal, Flor: Mga Liham Mula sa Mga OCW* (Pasig City, Philippines: Anvil Publishing, Inc., 1995).

See also *The Labor Trade: Filipino Migrant Workers around the World* (London: Catholic Institute for International Relations, 1987); and Jane Margold, "Narratives of Masculinity and Transnational Migration: Filipino Workers in the Middle East," in *Bewitching Women, Pious Men: Gender and Body Politics in Southeast Asia*, ed. Aihwa Ong and Michael Peletz (Berkeley: University of California Press, 1995), 274–98. For a recent ethnography of Filipina domestics abroad, see Nicole Constable, *Maid to Order in Hong Kong: Stories of Filipina Workers* (Ithaca, N.Y.: Cornell University Press, 1997).
12 See, for instance, the letters of OCWs in Dormiendo, *Nagmamahal, Flor*.
13 Jo-Ann Q. Maglipon, "DH in HK," in *Primed: Selected Stories, 1972–1992* (Pasig City, Philippines: Anvil Publishing, Inc., 1993), 45–53.
14 See Reynaldo Ileto, *Filipinos and Their Revolution: Event, Discourse, and Historiography* (Quezon City, Philippines: Ateneo de Manila University Press, 1998), esp. chapters 1, 2, 6, 7, and 8, "Tagalog Poetry and the Perception of the Past in the War against Spain," in *Perceptions of the Past in Southeast Asia*, ed. David Marr and Anthony Reid (Singapore: Heineman, 1979), 374–400, and *Pasyon and Revolution*.
15 See, for example, Neferti X. Tadiar, "Filipina Domestic Bodies," *Sojourn: A Journal of Social Issues in Southeast Asia* 12, no. 2 (October 1997): 153–91.
16 The citations appear respectively in Jerry Barrican, "Anybody but Lakas," *Manila Chronicle*, 19 March 1995, 5; and "Rage, Rage," *Philippine Daily Inquirer*, 19 March 1995 (hereafter *PDI*).
17 The quote is from James T. Siegel and Kenji Tsuchiya, "Invincible Kitsch, or as Tourists in the Age of Des Alwi," *Indonesia* 50 (October 1990): 61–76.
18 Cited in *PDI*, 19 March 1995, 12; and the *Straits Times* (Singapore), 17 April 1995

(hereafter *ST*). My thanks to Professors C. J. Wan-Ling and Paul Kratoska for generously providing me with copies of the *Straits Times* (Singapore).
19 *PDI*, 29 March 1995, 1.
20 Cited in Gerard Ramos, "Turning Tragedy into Profit," *PDI*, 28 March 1995, 7.
21 Cited in Teddy Casiño, "Flor Contemplacion (the Movie)," *PDI*, 29 March 1995, 8.
22 Raul J. Palabrica, "Crime Pays for Some Movie Producers," *PDI*, 1 April 1995, 5.
23 Ibid.
24 For a discussion of rumors, gossip, and other forms of idle talk in relation to everyday life, see Martin Heidegger, *Being and Time*, trans. John Macquarrie and Edward Robinson (New York: Harper and Row, 1962), 211–17.
25 Fenella Cannell, *Power and Intimacy in the Christian Philippines* (Cambridge, U.K.: Cambridge University Press, 1999), 137–64. This book, in my opinion, is one of the most important ethnographies published in the postwar period of any lowland Christian society in the Philippines in contemporary times.
26 Ibid., 142.
27 My understanding of the work of mourning is indebted to the classic account by Sigmund Freud, "Mourning and Melancholia," in *The Standard Edition of the Complete Psychoanalytic Works of Sigmund Freud*, ed. and trans. James Strachey (London: Hogarth, 1953–1974), 14:239–60. I have also been aided considerably by the insightful ethnographies of Marilyn Ivy, *Discourses of the Vanishing: Modernity, Phantasm, Japan* (Chicago: University of Chicago Press, 1995), 141–91; and James T. Siegel, *Solo in the New Order: Language and Hierarchy in an Indonesian City* (Princeton, N.J.: Princeton University Press, 1986), 257–76.
28 Cannell, *Power and Intimacy*, 148–51.
29 Ibid., 145–52.
30 Accounts of Contemplacion's funeral and its immediate aftermath can be found in *PDI* and *ST* issues from 27 to 29 March 1995.
31 Conrado de Quiros, "Phenomenon," *PDI*, 27 March 1995, 6.
32 Ibid.
33 To get a sense of the historical origins of death as the locus for reconceiving linguistic and social hierarchy, see Vicente L. Rafael, "Paradise and the Reinvention of Death," in *Contracting Colonialism: Translation and Christian Conversion in Tagalog Society under Early Spanish Rule* (Durham, N.C.: Duke University Press, 1993), 167–209.
34 Doña Aurora Aquino, Ninoy's mother, cited in Socorro Engañe-Sapnit, ed., *Ninoy: Ideals and Ideologies, 1932–1983* (Hong Kong: Sanford Printing Co., 1993), 149; photographs of Ninoy's corpse as it was displayed in public appear on 82–86. My thanks to David and Rina Rafael for providing me with a copy of this book.
35 The communicative force of these corpses within the context of nationalist history resonates, no doubt, with the photographs of the Filipino dead during the Filipino-American War that we saw, or tried to see, in chapter 3.
36 Teodoro Benigno, cited in Nimma Gosh, "Manila Turns Maid's Case into Singapore Bashing," *ST*, 22 March 1995, 27. Guilt itself could metamorphosize into shame then

back into guilt again as in Jessica Zafra's remarks: "Maybe deep down inside our collective psyche, we're ashamed that our people have to go abroad and get pushed around so their families at home can lead decent lives. Maybe we're guilty because we can't take care of our own people, so we allow them to get maltreated in other lands while the dollars they send back fuel our economy" ("The Long Hot Simmer," *Today*, 1 April 1995, B5).

37 Perhaps the most pathetic and manipulative attempt on the part of the state to reclaim the bodies of migrant Filipinas as national heroes is seen in the recent change of their designation from OCWs to overseas Filipino workers (OFWs). The substitution of names does no more than further mystify their contractual and expendable status, obscuring it with a designation thought to be more dignified. Like other migrant Filipinos who move from the provinces to the cities, the plight of OFWs can then be promptly put out of mind.

38 For a discussion of the history of Taglish, see chapter 6 of this volume.

39 Inday Badiday is the pen name of Lourdes Jimenez Carvajal. Raised in an upper-middle-class family in Manila, educated at the University of the Philippines, and sister to the former editor of the *Philippine Daily Inquirer*, she started writing about showbiz in the middle of the 1960s and took on a pen name to save her family from the potential embarrassment of being associated with such working-class proclivities as movie stars and Tagalog films. My thanks to Karina Bolasco and Lulu Reyes for this information.

40 Inday Badiday, "Flor, the Superstar," *PDI*, 25 March 1995, C5.

41 Ibid.

42 See "Nora Plays Die-hard Noranian in Flor Movie," *PDI*, 29 March 1995, 1; and Inday Badiday, "The Other Superstar," *PDI*, 1 April 1995, C2.

43 Inday Badiday, "Flor and Delia's Never-Ending Story," *PDI*, 8 April 1995, D4.

44 Ibid.

45 See "Vicious Rumors," *PDI*, 23 March 1995, 7; and the *ST* issues of 20 and 24 April 1995, which detail the rumors regarding the drugging, torture, and rape of Contemplacion in prison.

46 Cannell, *Power and Intimacy*, 140–55.

Bibliography

NEWPAPERS AND MAGAZINES
Asia Week
Los Angeles Times
Manila Chronicle
Philippine Daily Inquirer
Philippine Free Press
Straits Times (Singapore)
Today
Weekly Graphic

BOOKS, ARTICLES, DISSERTATIONS, AND UNPUBLISHED PAPERS

Abinales, Patricio N., ed. *The Revolution Falters: The Left in Philippine Politics after 1986.* Ithaca, N.Y.: Southeast Asia Program Publications, Cornell University, 1996.

Agoncillo, Teodoro. *The Fateful Years: Japan's Adventure in the Philippines, 1941–1945.* 2 vols. Quezon City, Philippines: R. P. Garcia Publishing Co., 1966.

———. *Malolos: The Crisis of the Republic.* Quezon City: University of the Philippines Press, 1960.

———. *The Revolt of the Masses: The Story of Bonifacio and the Katipunan.* Quezon City: University of the Philippines Press, 1956.

Agoncillo, Teodoro, and Milagros Guerrero. *History of the Filipino People.* Quezon City, Philippines: R. P. Garcia Publishing Co., 1960.

Aguilar, Filomeno V., Jr. *Clash of Spirits: The History of Power and Sugar Planter Hegemony on a Visayan Island.* Quezon City, Philippines: Ateneo de Manila University Press, 1998.

Alloula, Malek. *The Colonial Harem.* Translated by Myrna Godzich and Wlad Godzich. Minneapolis: University of Minnesota Press, 1986.

Anderson, Benedict. "Cacique Democracy in the Philippines: Origins and Dreams." In *Discrepant Histories: Translocal Essays on Filipino Cultures,* edited by Vicente L. Rafael. Philadelphia, Pa.: Temple University Press, 1995.

———, *Imagined Communities: Reflections on the Origins and Spread of Nationalism.* 2d ed. London: Verso, 1991.

———. *Java in a Time of Revolution: Occupation and Resistance, 1944–1946.* Ithaca, N.Y.: Cornell University Press, 1972.

———. *The Spectre of Comparisons: Nationalism, Southeast Asia, and the World.* London: Verso, 1998.

Anderson, Warwick. "Colonial Pathologies: American Medicine in the Philippines, 1898–1921." Ph.D. diss., University of Pennsylvania, 1992.

———. "The Trespass Speaks: White Masculinity and Colonial Breakdown." *American Historical Review* 102 (December 1997): 1343–70.

———. " 'Where Every Prospect Pleases and Only Man Is Vile': Laboratory Medicine as Colonial Discourse." *Critical Inquiry* 18, no. 3 (spring 1992): 506–29.

Ballescas, Maria Rosario P. *Filipino Entertainers in Japan: An Introduction.* Quezon City, Philippines: Foundation for Nationalist Studies, 1992.

Barte, Gina V., ed. *Panahon ng Hapon: Sining sa Digmaan/Digmaan Sa Sining*. Manila: Museo ng Kalinangan Pilipino, 1992.

Barthes, Roland. *Camera Lucida: Reflections of Photography*. Translated by Richard Howard. New York: Hill and Wang, 1981.

Bederman, Gail. *Manliness and Civilization: A Cultural History of Gender and Race in the United States, 1880–1917*. Chicago: University of Chicago Press, 1995.

Benjamin, Walter. *Illuminations*. Edited by Hannah Arendt. Translated by Harry Zohn. New York: Schocken Books, 1969.

———. *One Way Street and Other Writings*. Translated by Edmund Jephcott and Kingsley Shorter. London: New Left Books, 1979.

———. *Reflections: Essays, Aphorisms, Autobiographical Writings*. Edited by Peter Demetz. Translated by Edward Jephcott. New York: Harcourt Brace Jovanovich, 1978.

Best, Jonathan. *A Philippine Album: American Era Photographs, 1900–1930*. Makati City, Philippines: Bookmark, Inc., 1998.

Blair, Emma, and James Robertson, eds. *The Philippine Islands, 1493–1898*. 55 vols. 1905. Reprint, Mandaluyong, Rizal: Cacho Hermanos, Inc., 1973.

Breitbart, Eric. *A World on Display: Photographs from the St. Louis World Fair, 1904*. Albuquerque: University of New Mexico Press, 1997.

Bresnan, John, ed. *Crisis in the Philippines*. Princeton, N.J.: Princeton University Press, 1986.

Brown, Gillian. *Domestic Individualism: Imagining the Self in Nineteenth-Century America*. Berkeley: University of California Press, 1990.

Bryan, William S., ed. *Our Islands and Their People as Seen with Camera and Pencil*. New York: N. D. Thompson and Publishing, 1899.

Bulosan, Carlos. *America Is in the Heart*. 1943. Reprint, Seattle: University of Washington Press, 1973.

Cannell, Fenella. *Power and Intimacy in the Christian Philippines*. Cambridge, U.K.: Cambridge University Press, 1999.

Caro y Mora, Juan. *La Situacion del Pais*. 2d ed. Manila, 1897.

Chan, Su Cheng. *Asian Americans: An Interpretive History*. Boston: Twayne Publishing, 1991.

Chapman, William. *Inside the Philippine Revolution: The New People's Army and Its Struggle for Power*. New York: W. W. Norton, 1987.

Chaudhuri, Nupur, and Margaret Strobel, eds. *Western Women and Imperialism: Complicity and Resistance*. Bloomington: University of Indiana Press, 1992.

Choy, Catherine C. "The Export of Womanpower: A Transnational History of Filipino Nurse Migration to the United States." Ph.D. diss., University of California, Los Angeles, 1998.

Cohn, Bernard. *An Anthropologist among Historians*. Delhi: Oxford University Press, 1987.

Condict, Alice Byram. *Old Glory and the Gospel in the Philippines*. Chicago: Fleming and Revelle Co., 1901.

Constable, Nicole. *Maid to Order in Hong Kong: Stories of Filipina Workers*. Ithaca, N.Y.: Cornell University Press, 1997.

Constantino, Renato, and Letizia Constantino. *The Philippines: The Continuing Past. Manila: Foundation for Nationalist Studies, 1978.

Coronel, Sheila S. *Coups, Cults, and Cannibals: Chronicles of a Troubled Decade, 1982–1992*. Pasig City, Philippines: Anvil Publishing, Inc., 1993.

Corpuz, Onofre D. *The Bureaucracy in the Philippines*. Quezon City: University of the Philippines Press, 1957.

———. *The Philippines*. Englewood Cliffs, N.J.: Prentice-Hall, 1965.

———. *The Roots of the Filipino Nation*. 2 vols. Quezon City, Philippines: Aklahi Foundation, Inc., 1989.

Cruz, E. Aguilar. "Vintage Photographs." In *Being Filipino*, edited by Gilda Cordero-Fernando. Quezon City, Philippines: GCF Books, 1981.

Cruz, Isagani. *Movie Time*. Manila: National Bookstore, 1984.

Cullinane, Michael. "Ilustrado Politics: The Response of the Filipino Educated Elite to American Colonial Rule, 1898–1907." Ph.D. diss., University of Michigan, 1989.

Cushner, Nicolas. *Spain in the Philippines*. Quezon City, Philippines: Ateneo de Manila University Press, 1974.

Dauncey, Campbell. *An Englishwoman in the Philippines*. New York: E. P. Dutton, 1906.

Davin, Anna. "Imperialism and Motherhood." *History Workshop* 5 (1978): 9–65.

de la Costa, Horacio. *Jesuits in the Philippines, 1581–1768*. Cambridge, Mass.: Harvard University Press, 1961.

del Castillo, Jose M. *El Katipunan, o el Filibusterismo en Filipinas*. Madrid, 1897.

del Mundo, Clodualdo, Jr. *Native Resistance: Philippine Cinema and Colonialism, 1898–1941*. Manila: De La Salle University Press, 1998.

———, ed. *Philippine Mass Media: A Book of Readings*. Manila: Communication Foundation of Asia, 1986.

de Man, Paul. *Aesthetic Ideology*. Minneapolis: University of Minnesota Press, 1996.

———. *Blindness and Insight: Essays in the Rhetoric of Contemporary Criticism*. Minneapolis: University of Minnesota Press, 1983.

de Manila, Quijano. *Reportage on Politics*. Manila: National Bookstore, 1981.

Demetrio, Francisco. *Myths and Symbols Philippines*. Manila: National Bookstore, 1978.

de Quiros, Conrado. *Flowers from the Rubble*. Pasig City, Philippines: Anvil Publishing, Inc., 1990.

Dirlik, Arif, ed. *What Is in a Rim? Critical Perspectives on the Pacific Region Idea*. Boulder, Colo.: Westview Press, 1993.

Dormiendo, Justino, ed. *Nagmamahal, Flor: Mga Liham Mula sa Mga OCW*. Pasig City, Philippines: Anvil Publishing, Inc., 1995.

Doronilla, Armando. "The Transformation of Patron-Client Relations and Its Political Consequences in Post-War Philippines." *Journal of Southeast Asian Studies* 16, no. 1 (March 1985): 99–116.

Dower, John. *War without Mercy: Race and Power in the Pacific War*. New York: Pantheon Books, 1986.

Drinnon, Richard. *Facing West: The Metaphysics of Indian Hating and Empire Building*. New York: New American Library, 1980.

Ellison, Katherine. *Imelda: Steel Butterfly of the Philippines*. New York: McGraw-Hill, 1988.

Engañe-Sapnit, Socorro, ed. *Ninoy: Ideals and Ideologies, 1932–1983*. Hong Kong: Sanford Printing Co., 1993.

ERAPtion: How to Speak English without Really Trial. Manila: Oxford Printing Corporation, 1994.

Espiritu, Yen Le. *Filipino-American Lives*. Philadelphia, Pa.: Temple University Press, 1995.

———. "The Intersection of Race, Ethnicity, and Class: The Multiple Identities of Second-Generation Filipinos." *Identities* 1, no. 2 (1994): 249–73.

Fast, Jonathan, and Jim Richardson. *Roots of Dependency: Political and Economic Revolution in Nineteenth Century Philippines*. Quezon City, Philippines: Foundation for Nationalist Studies, 1979.

Fee, Mary H. *A Woman's Impressions of the Philippines*. Chicago: A. C. McClurg and Co., 1910.

Feldman, Allen. *Formations of Violence: The Narrative of the Body and Political Terror in Northern Ireland*. Chicago: University of Chicago Press, 1991.

Fernandez, Doreen. *The Iloilo Zarzuela*. Quezon City, Philippines: Ateneo de Manila University Press, 1978.

———. *Palabas: Essays on Philippine Theater History*. Quezon City, Philippines: Ateneo de Manila University Press, 1996.

Forbes, William Cameron. *The Philippine Islands*. 2 vols. Boston: Houghton Mifflin Co., 1928.

Foucault, Michel. *Discipline and Punish: The Birth of the Prison*. Translated by Alan Sheridan. New York: Vintage Books, 1979.

Francia, Beatriz Romualdez. *Imelda and the Clans: A Story of the Philippines*. Manila: Solar Publishing, 1988.

Freud, Sigmund. "Mourning and Melancholia." In *The Standard Edition of the Complete Psychoanalytic Works of Sigmund Freud*, edited and translated by James Strachey. Vol. 14. London: Hogarth, 1953–1974.

Friend, Theodore. *Between Two Empires: Philippine Ordeal and Development from the Great Depression through the Pacific War, 1929–1946*. New Haven, Conn.: Yale University Press, 1965.

Fuller, Alice M. *Housekeeping: A Textbook for Girls in the Public and Intermediate Schools of the Philippines*. Manila: Bureau of Printing, 1917.

Gaches, Mrs. Samuel. *Good Cooking and Health in the Tropics*. Manila: Bureau of Printing, 1922.

Garcia, Neil C., and Danton Remoto. *Ladlad: An Anthology of Philippine Gay Writing*. Pasig City, Philippines: Anvil Publishing, Inc., 1994.

Gatbonton, Juan T., Jeannie E. Javelosa, and Lourdes Ruth R. Roa, eds. *Art in the Philippines*. Pasig City, Philippines: Crucible Workshop, 1992.

George, Rosemary Marangoly. "Homes in the Empire, Empires in the Home." *Cultural Critique* (winter 1993–1994): 95–127.

Glenn, Evelyn Nakano. *Issei, Nisei, War Bride: Three Generations of Japanese American Women in Domestic Service*. Philadelphia, Pa.: Temple University Press, 1986.

Gonzalez, Andrew. *Language and Nationalism: The Philippine Experience Thus Far*. Quezon City, Philippines: Ateneo de Manila University Press, 1980.

———, ed. *The Role of English and Its Maintenance in the Philippines*. Manila: Solidaridad Publishing House, 1988.

Gosengfiao, Victor. "The Japanese Occupation: 'The Cultural Campaign.'" In *Rediscovery: Essays in Philippine Life and Culture*, edited by Cynthia Lumbera and Teresita Maceda. Quezon City, Philippines: National Bookstore, 1977.

Guerrero, Leon Maria. *The First Filipino*. Manila: National Historical Commission, 1974.

Guerrero, Milagros C. "Luzon at War: Contradictions in Philippine Society, 1898–1902." Ph.D. diss., University of Michigan, 1977.

Hagedorn, Jessica. *Dogeaters*. New York: Penguin Books, 1990.

Hamilton-Paterson, James. *America's Boy: The Marcoses and the Philippines*. London: Granta Books, 1998.

Hansen, Karen Tranberg. *Distant Companions: Servants and Employers in Zambia, 1900–1985*. Ithaca, N.Y.: Cornell University Press, 1989.

Hansen, Miriam. *Babel and Babylon: Spectatorship in American Silent Film*. Cambridge, Mass.: Harvard University Press, 1991.

Haraway, Donna. *Primate Visions: Gender, Race, and Nature in the World of Modern Science*. New York: Routledge, 1989.

Hau, Caroline S. " 'Who Will Save Us from the Law?': The Criminal State and the Illegal Alien in Post-1986 Philippines." In *Figures of Criminality in Indonesia, the Philippines, and Colonial Vietnam*, edited by Vicente L. Rafael. Ithaca, N.Y.: Cornell Southeast Asian Program Publications, 1999.

Hawes, Gary. *The Philippine State and the Marcos Regime*. Ithaca, N.Y.: Cornell University Press, 1987.

Heidegger, Martin. *Being and Time*. Translated by John Macquarrie and Edward Robinson. New York: Harper and Row, 1962.

Hirschman, Charles, Charles Keyes, and Karl Hutterer, eds. *Southeast Asian Studies in the Balance: Reflections from America*. Ann Arbor, Mich.: Association of Asian Studies, 1992.

Hollnsteiner, Mary. *The Dynamics of Power in a Philippine Municipality*. Quezon City, Philippines: University of the Philippines Press, 1963.

Holt, W. Stull. *The Bureau of Census: Its History, Activities, and Organization*. New York: AMS Press, 1929.

Hubble, Winnifred. Unpublished Papers, 1907–1908. Bentley Historical Collection, University of Michigan, Ann Arbor.

Ileto, Reynaldo. *Filipinos and Their Revolution: Event, Discourse, and Historiography*. Quezon City, Philippines: Ateneo de Manila University Press, 1998.

———. *Knowing America's Colony: A Hundred Years from the Philippine War*. Occasional Papers Series, no. 13. Honolulu: Center for Philippine Studies, 1999.

———. "Orators and the Crowd: Philippine Independence Politics, 1910–1914." In *Reappraising an Empire: New Perspectives on Philippine-American History*, edited by Peter Stanley. Cambridge, Mass.: Harvard University Press, 1984.

———. *Pasyon and Revolution: Popular Movements in the Philippines, 1840–1910*. Quezon City, Philippines: Ateneo de Manila University Press, 1979.

Infante, J. Eddie. *Inside Philippine Movies, 1970–1990*. Quezon City, Philippines: Ateneo de Manila University Press, 1991.

Ivy, Marilyn. *Discourses of the Vanishing: Modernity, Phantasm, Japan*. Chicago: University of Chicago Press, 1995.

Jeffords, Susan. *The Remasculinization of America: Gender in the Vietnam War*.

Bloomington: Indiana University Press, 1989.

Jenks, Albert E. *The Bontoc Igorot*. Manila: Bureau of Public Printing, 1905.

Jenks, Maude Huntley. *Death Stalks the Philippine Wilds*. Edited by Carmen Nelson Richards. Minneapolis, Minn.: Lund Press, 1951.

Joaquin, Nick. *The Aquinos of Tarlac: An Essay on History as Three Generations*. Manila: Cacho Hermanos, 1983.

——. *Culture and History: Occasional Notes on the Process of Philippine Becoming*. Manila: Solar Publishing Corp., 1988.

——. *A Question of Heroes: Essays in the Criticism of Key Figures of Philippine History*. Makati, Philippines: Ayala Museum, 1977.

Kalaw-Tirol, Lorna, ed. *Duet for EDSA: Looking Back, Looking Forward*. Manila: Foundation for Worldwide People Power, Inc., 1995.

Kaplan, Amy. "Romancing the Empire: The Embodiment of American Masculinity in the Popular Historical Novel of the 1890s." *American Literary History* 2, no. 4 (winter 1990): 659–90.

Kaplan, Amy, and Donald E. Pease, eds. *Cultures of United States Imperialism*. Durham, N.C.: Duke University Press, 1993.

Karnow, Stanley. *In Our Image: America's Empire in the Philippines*. New York: Ballantine Books, 1989.

Katzman, David. *Seven Days a Week: Women and Domestic Service in Industrializing America*. New York: Oxford University Press, 1977.

Kerkvliet, Benedict. *The Huk Rebellion: A Study of Peasant Revolt in the Philippines*. Berkeley: University of California Press, 1977.

Klingsporn, Geoffrey. "'A Harvest of Death': War, Photography, and History." Paper, 1998.

Kramer, Paul A. "The Pragmatic Empire: U.S. Anthropology and Colonial Politics in the Occupied Philippines, 1898–1916." Ph.D. diss., Princeton University, 1998.

The Labor Trade: Filipino Migrant Workers around the World. London: Catholic Institute for International Relations, 1987.

Lacaba, Jose F. *Days of Disquiet, Nights of Rage: The First Quarter Storm and Other Related Events*. Manila: Salinlahi Publications, 1982.

——. "Movies, Critics, and the Bakya Crowd." In *Readings in Filipino Cinema*, edited by Rafael Maria Guerrero. Manila: Experimental Cinema of the Philippines Publications, 1983.

——. "Notes on Bakya, Being an Apologia of Sorts for Filipino Mass Cult." In *Readings in Filipino Cinema*, edited by Rafael Maria Guerrero. Manila: Experimental Cinema of the Philippines Publications, 1983.

Lacuesta, Lolita R., ed. *Beyond the Mainstream: The Films of Nick de Ocampo*. Pasig City, Philippines: Anvil Publishing, Inc., 1997.

Lande, Carl. *Leaders, Factions, and Parties: The Structure of Philippine Politics*. New Haven, Conn.: Yale Southeast Asian Studies, 1964.

Lapeña-Bonifacio, Amelia. *The Seditious Tagalog Playwrights: Early American Occupation*. Manila: Zarzuela Foundation of the Philippines, 1972.

Laurel, Jose P. *War Memoirs*. Manila: Lyceum Press, 1962.

Long, Oscar Fitzhalan. Photo album. "Our New Possessions in the Philippines." 1899–1901. With photos by James David Givens. Bancroft Library, University of California, Berkeley.

Machado, Kit G. "From Traditional Faction to Machine: Changing Patterns of Political Leadership and Organization in Rural Philippines." *Journal of Asian Studies* 33, no. 4 (August 1974): 523–47.

Maglipon, Jo-Ann Q. *Primed: Selected Stories, 1972–1992*. Pasig City, Philippines: Anvil Publishing, Inc., 1993.

Magno, Alex. *A Nation Reborn*. Vol. 9, *Kasaysayan: The Story of the Filipino People*. Hong Kong: Asia Publishing Company, 1998.

Malacañang: A Guidebook. Quezon City, Philippines: Kayumangi Press, 1986.

Malay, Armando J. *Occupied Philippines*, Manila: Filipiniana Book Guild Series, 1967.

Manalansan, Martin. "Speaking of AIDS: Language and the Filipino 'Gay' Experience in America." In *Discrepant Histories: Translocal Essays on Filipino Culture*, edited by Vicente L. Rafael. Philadelphia, Pa.: Temple University Press, 1995.

Manlapaz, Edna, ed. *Aurelio Tolentino: Selected Writings*. Quezon City, Philippines: Ateneo de Manila University Press, 1975.

Manuel, E. Arsenio. *Dictionary of Philippine Biography*. 4 vols. Quezon City, Philippines: Filipiniana Publications, 1970.

Marcelo, Nonoy. *Ikabod*. Manila: Solar Publishing House, 1987.

Margold, Jane. "Narratives of Masculinity and Transnational Migration: Filipino Workers in the Middle East." In *Bewitching Women, Pious Men: Gender and Body Politics in Southeast Asia*, edited by Aihwa Ong and Michael Peletz.

Berkeley: University of California Press, 1995.

Marx, Karl. *Capital: A Critique of Political Economy*. Vol. 1. Translated by Ben Fowkes. New York: Vintage Books, 1977.

Mauss, Marcel. *The Gift: Forms and Functions of Exchange in Archaic Societies*. New York: W. W. Norton, 1977.

May, Glenn A. *Battle for Batangas*. New Haven, Conn.: Yale University Press, 1991.

———. *Inventing a Hero: The Posthumous Re-creation of Andres Bonifacio*. Quezon City, Philippines: New Day Press, 1997.

———. *Social Engineering in the Philippines*. Westport, Conn.: Greenwood Press, 1980.

McCoy, Alfred, ed. *An Anarchy of Families: State and Family in the Philippines*. Quezon City, Philippines: Ateneo de Manila University Press, 1994.

McCoy, Alfred, and Ed. J. De Jesus, eds. *Philippine Social History: Global Trade and Local Transformations*. Quezon City, Philippines: Ateneo de Manila University Press, 1982.

McDougal, Charles C. *The Marcos File*. San Francisco, Calif.: San Francisco Publishers, 1987.

Miller, Stuart Creighton. *Benevolent Assimilation: The American Conquest of the Philippines, 1899–1903*. New Haven, Conn.: Yale University Press, 1982.

Mitchell, Timothy. *Colonizing Egypt*. Berkeley: University of California Press, 1991.

Mojares, Primitivo. *The Conjugal Dictatorship of FerdinandImelda Marcos*. San Francisco, Calif.: Union Square Publishers, 1976.

Mojares, Resil. *Casa Gorordo in Cebu: Ur-*

ban Residence in a Philippine Province, 1860–1920. Cebu, Philippines: Ramon Aboitiz Foundation, 1983.

———. The Man Who Would Be President: Serging Osmena and Philippine Politics. Cebu City, Philippines: Maria Cacao, 1986.

———. Origins and Rise of the Filipino Novel: A Generic Study of the Novel until 1940. Quezon City: University of the Philippines Press, 1983.

———. Theater in Society, Society in Theater: The Social History of a Cebuano Village, 1840–1940. Quezon City, Philippines: Ateneo de Manila University Press, 1985.

Moses, Edith. Unofficial Letters of an Official's Wife. New York: Appleton and Co., 1908.

Navarro-Pedrosa, Carmen. The Untold Story of Imelda Marcos. Manila: Bookmark, 1969.

Neely, F. Tennyson. Fighting in the Philippines: Authentic and Original Photographs. Chicago, 1899.

Ocampo, Ambeth. The Centennial Countdown. Pasig City, Philippines: Anvil Publishing, Inc., 1998.

———. Luna's Moustache. Pasig City, Philippines: Anvil Publishing, Inc., 1997.

———. Talking History: Conversations with Teodoro A. Agoncillo. Manila: De La Salle University Press, 1995.

Okamura, Jonathan. "The Filipino American Diaspora: Sites of Space, Time, and Ethnicity." In Privileging Sites: Positions in Asian American Studies, edited by Gary Okihiro. Pullman, Wash.: Washington State University Press, 1997.

Owen, Norman, ed. Compadre Colonialism: Philippine-American Relationship, 1898–1946. Ann Arbor, Mich.: Center for South and Southeast Asian Studies, 1971.

Palmer, Phyllis. Domesticity and Dirt: Housewives and Domestic Servants in the United States, 1920–1945. Philadelphia, Pa.: Temple University Press, 1989.

Paredes, Ruby, ed. Philippine Colonial Democracy. Quezon City, Philippines: Ateneo de Manila University Press, 1989.

Pimentel, Benjamin. Rebolusyon! A Generation of Struggle in the Philippines. New York: Monthly Review Press, 1991.

Polotan, Kerima. Imelda Romualdez Marcos. New York: World Publishing Co., 1969.

Ponce, Mariano. Cartas Sobre la Revolucion, 1897–1900. Manila: Bureau of Printing, 1932.

Pratt, Mary Louise. Imperial Eyes: Travel Writing and Transculturation. New York: Routledge, 1992.

A Pronouncing Gazetteer and Geographical Dictionary of the Philippine Islands. Washington, D.C.: U.S. Government Printing Office, 1902.

Rafael, Vicente L. Contracting Colonialism: Translation and Christian Conversion in Tagalog Society under Early Spanish Rule. Durham, N.C.: Duke University Press, 1993.

———. "The Cultures of Area Studies in the United States." Social Text 41 (winter 1994): 91–112.

———. "Fishing, Underwear, and Hunchbacks: Humor and Politics in the Philippines, 1886 and 1983." Bulletin of Concerned Asian Scholars 18, no. 3 (1986): 2–7.

———. "Mimetic Subjects: Engendering Race at the Edge of Empire." *differences: A Journal of Feminist Cultural Studies* 7, no. 2 (1995): 127–49.

———. "Translation and Revenge: Castilian and the Origins of Nationalism in the Philippines." In *The Places of History: Regionalism Revisited in Latin America*, edited by Doris Sommer. Durham, N.C.: Duke University Press, 1999.

———, ed. *Discrepant Histories: Translocal Essays on Filipino Cultures*. Philadelphia, Pa.: Temple University Press, 1995.

Ramos, Remedios F., et al. *Si Malakas and Si Maganda*. Manila: Jorge Y. Ramos, 1980.

Recto, Claro M. *Three Years of Enemy Occupation*. Manila: People's Publishers, 1946.

Retana, Wenceslao E., ed. *Archivo del Bibliofilo Filipino*. 5 vols. Madrid: Minuesa de los Rios, 1895–1898.

———. *Noticias historico-bibliograficas del teatro en Filipinas desde sus origines hasta 1898*. Madrid: Libreria General de Victoriano Suarez, 1909.

Reyes, Emmanuel. *Notes on Philippine Cinema*. Manila: De La Salle University Press, 1989.

Riggs, Arthur Stanley. *The Filipino Drama*. Manila: Ministry of Human Settlements, 1981. Originally written in 1904.

Rizal, Jose. *El Filibusterismo*. Ghent: F. Meyer-Van Loo, 1891.

———. *Noli me Tangere*. Berlin: Berliner Buchdruckerei-Aktien-Gesellschaft, 1887.

———. *One Hundred Letters of Jose Rizal to his Parents, Brother, Sisters, Relatives*. Manila: Philippine National Historical Society, 1959.

Rocamora, Joel. *Breaking Through: The Struggle within the Communist Party of the Philippines*. Pasig City, Philippines: Anvil Publishing, Inc., 1994.

Rollins, Judith. *Between Women: Domestics and Their Employers*. Philadelphia, Pa.: Temple University Press, 1985.

Romero, Mary. *Maid in the U.S.A.* New York: Routledge, 1992.

Roth, Russell. *Muddy Glory: America's "Indian Wars" in the Philippines, 1899–1935*. West Hanover, Mass.: Christopher Publishing House, 1981.

Rybczynski, Witold. *Home: A Short History of an Idea*. New York: Penguin, 1986.

Rydell, Robert. *All the World's a Fair: Visions of Empire at American International Expositions, 1876–1916*. Chicago: University of Chicago Press, 1984.

———. *World of Fairs: The Century-of-Progress Exposition*. Chicago: University of Chicago Press, 1993.

Salamanca, Bonifacio. *The Filipino Reaction to American Rule, 1901–1913*. Quezon City: University of the Philippines Press, 1957.

Salman, Michael. "In Our Orientalist Imagination: Historiography and the Culture of Colonialism in the U.S." *Radical History Review* 50 (spring 1991): 221–32.

———. "The United States and the End of Slavery in the Philippines, 1898–1914: A Study of Imperialism, Ideology, and Nationalism." 2 vols. Ph.D. diss., Stanford University, 1993.

Sastrón, Manuel. *La Insurrecion en Filipinas y Guerra Hispanno-Americana en el Archipiélago*. Madrid: Imprenta de la sucesora de M. Minuesa de los Rios, 1901.

Schirmer, Daniel B. *Republic or Empire? American Resistance to the Philippine-American War*. Cambridge, Mass.: Schenkman Publishing Co., 1972.
Scott, William Henry. *Barangay: Sixteenth Century Philippine Culture and Society*. Quezon City, Philippines: Ateneo de Manila University Press, 1994.
———. *Ilocano Responses to American Aggression, 1900–1901*. Manila: New Day Press, 1986.
———. *Prehispanic Source Materials for the Study of Philippine History*. Rev. ed. Quezon City, Philippines: New Day Press, 1984.
Sekula, Alan J. "The Body and the Archive." *October* 39 (winter 1986): 3–64.
Serrano-Laktaw, Pedro. *Diccionario Tagalog-Hispano*. 2 vols. Manila: Imprenta de Santos y Bernal, 1914.
Sharpe, Jenny. *Allegories of Empire: The Figure of Woman in the Colonial Text*. Minneapolis: University of Minnesota Press, 1993.
Shunk, Caroline S. *An Army Woman in the Philippines*. Kansas City, Mo.: Franklin Hudson Publishing, 1914.
Siegel, James T. *A New Criminal Type in Jakarta: Counter-Revolution Today*. Durham, N.C.: Duke University Press, 1998.
———. *Fetish, Recognition, and Revolution*. Princeton, N.J.: Princeton University Press, 1997.
———. *Solo in the New Order: Language and Hierarchy in an Indonesian City*. Princeton, N.J.: Princeton University Press, 1986.
Siegel, James T., and Kenji Tsuchiya. "Invincible Kitsch, or as Tourists in the Age of Des Alwi." *Indonesia* 50 (October 1990): 61–76.
Silva, John. *Colonial Philippines: Photographs, 1860–1910*. Exhibition catalog, Lowie Museum of Anthropology, University of California, Berkeley, 9–11 May 1987.
———. "Nineteenth Century Photography." In *The World of 1896*. Makati City, Philippines: Bookmark, Inc., 1998.
Sison, Jose Maria. *Philippine Society and Revolution*. Manila: Pulang Tala Publications, 1971.
Spence, Hartzell. *Marcos of the Philippines*. New York: World Publishing Co., 1969.
Stanley, Peter. *A Nation in the Making: The Philippines and the United States, 1899–1921*. Cambridge, Mass.: Harvard University Press, 1974.
———, ed. *Reappraising an Empire: New Perspectives on Philippine-American History*. Cambridge, Mass.: Harvard University Press, 1984.
Starr, Paul. "The Sociology of Official Statistics." In *The Politics of Numbers*, edited by William Alonso and Paul Starr. New York: Russell Sage Foundation, 1987.
Steinberg, David Joel. "Jose P. Laurel: A 'Collaborator' Misunderstood." *Journal of Asian Studies* 24, no. 4 (1965): 651–65.
———. *Philippine Collaboration in World War II*. Ann Arbor: University of Michigan Press, 1967.
———. *The Philippines: A Singular and a Plural Place*. 2d ed. Boulder, Colo.: Westview Press, 1990.
Stoler, Ann. "Carnal Knowledge and Imperial Power: Gender, Race, and Morality in Colonial Asia." In *Gender at the Crossroads of Knowledge: Feminist Anthropology in the Postmodern Era*, edited by Micaela Di Leonardo. Berkeley: University of California Press, 1991.
———. "Rethinking Colonial Categories:

European Communities and the Boundaries of Rule." In *Colonialism and Culture*, edited by Nicholas B. Dirks. Ann Arbor: University of Michigan Press, 1992.

———. "Sexual Affronts and Racial Frontiers: European Identities and the Cultural Politics of Exclusion in Colonial Southeast Asia." *Comparative Studies in Society and History* 34 (July 1992): 514–51.

Strobel, Margaret. *European Women and the Second British Empire*. Bloomington: Indiana University Press, 1991.

Sturtevant, David. *Popular Uprisings in the Philippines, 1840–1940*. Ithaca, N.Y.: Cornell University Press, 1976.

Suleri, Sara. *The Rhetoric of English India*. Chicago: University of Chicago Press, 1992.

Sullivan, Rodney. *Exemplar of Americanism: The Philippine Career of Dean C. Worcester*. Ann Arbor, Mich.: Center for South and Southeast Asian Studies, University of Michigan, 1991.

Sutherland, Daniel. *Americans and Their Servants: Domestic Service in the United States from 1800–1920*. Baton Rouge: Louisiana State University Press, 1981.

Tadiar, Neferti X. "Filipina Domestic Bodies." *Sojourn: A Journal of Social Issues in Southeast Asia* 12, no. 2 (October 1997): 153–91.

Taft, Helen. *Recollections of Full Years*. New York: Dodd, Mead, and Co., 1914.

Taft, William Howard. *The Philippine Islands: An Address Delivered before the Chamber of Commerce of the State of New York*. New York, 1904.

Taussig, Michael. *Mimesis and Alterity: A Particular History of the Senses*. New York: Routledge, 1993.

Taylor, John R. M., ed. *The Philippine Insurrection against the United States*. 5 vols. Quezon City, Philippines: Eugenio Lopez Foundation, 1971.

Thompson, Mark R. *The Anti-Marcos Struggle: Personalistic and Democratic Transition in the Philippines*. New Haven, Conn.: Yale University Press, 1995.

Tiongson, Nicanor. *Kasaysayan ng komedya sa Pilipinas, 1766–1982*. Manila: Integrated Research Center, De La Salle University, 1982.

Trachtenberg, Alan. *Reading American Photographs: Images as History, Matthew Brady to Walker Evans*. New York: Hill and Wang, 1989.

Ventura, Rey. *Underground in Japan*. London: Jonathan Cape, 1992.

Vergara, Benito M., Jr. *Displaying Filipinos: Photography and Colonialism in Early-Twentieth-Century Philippines*. Quezon City, Philippines: University of the Philippines Press, 1995.

Ware, Vron. *Beyond the Pale: White Women, Racism, and History*. London: Verso, 1992.

Wickberg, Edgar. *The Chinese in Philippine Life, 1850–1898*. New Haven, Conn.: Yale University Press, 1965.

———. "The Chinese Mestizo in Philippine History." *Journal of Southeast Asian History* 5 (March 1964): 62–100.

Wilcox, Marrion, ed. *Harper's History of the War in the Philippines*. New York: Harper and Brothers, 1900.

Wilson, Woodrow. *Constitutional Government in the United States*. New York: Columbia University Press, 1921.

Winichakul, Thongchai. *Siam Mapped: A History of the Geo-Body of Siam*. Honolulu: University of Hawaii Press, 1993.

Wolff, Leon. *Little Brown Brother*. Garden City, N.Y.: Doubleday, 1982.

Worcester, Dean C. *The Philippine Islands and Their People*. New York: Macmillan Publishing Co., 1898.

———. *The Philippines Past and Present*. 2 vols. New York: Macmillan Publishing Co., 1914.

Worcester, Nona. Diary, 1909. Bentley Historical Collection, University of Michigan, Ann Arbor.

U.S. Adjutant General of the Army. *Correspondence Relating to the War with Spain*. 2 vols. Washington, D.C.: U.S. Government Printing Office, 1902.

U.S. Bureau of the Census. *Census of the Philippine Islands*, 1903, 4 vols., Washington, D.C.: U.S. Government Printing Office, 1905.

U.S. Bureau of the Census. *Census of the Philippine Islands, 1918*. 4 vols. Manila: Bureau of Printing, 1920–21.

U.S. Philippine Commission. *Annual Report of the Philippine Commission, 1901–1908*. Washington, D.C.: U.S. Government Printing Office, 1902–1909.

———. *Report of the Philippine Commission to the President*. 4 vols. Washington, D.C.: U.S. Government Printing Office, 1900–1901.

———. *Report of the Taft Philippine Commission*. Washington, D.C.: U.S. Government Printing Office, 1901.

Zialcita, Fernando N., and Martin I. Tinio. *Philippine Ancestral Houses*. Quezon City, Philippines: CGF Books, 1980.

Index

PAGE NUMBERS IN ITALICS INDICATE ILLUSTRATIONS.

Abad, Juan, 44
Aestheticization of politics, 100, 150
Aetas (Negritos), 36, 37, *38*, 78, *78*
Agoncillo, Teodoro, 115–19, 121, 170–71, 173
Agricultural development, 5
Aguinaldo, Emilio, 9–10, 194, 195, 196
Alcuaz, Federico Aguilar, portrait of Imelda Marcos, *146*, *147*, *149*
Alloula, Malek, 77
Anderson, Benedict, 1, 7, 31, 107, 180
Animism: and census classification, 33
Anonymity: and rumor, 217
Anonymous viewing experience, 133–34, 162, 164, 185, 188. *See also* Spectator experience/identity
Anti-Sinitism, 48. *See also* Chinese
Apacible, Galiciano, 196
Aquino, Benigno "Ninoy," 142, 160, 211–12; assassination of, 174; funeral of, 220, *221*; on Imelda Marcos, 151–52; responses to death of, 211–12, 222
Aquino, Corazon "Cory," 211, 212; presidency of, 3, 179–80, 211, 212
Architecture, domestic: and privacy, 65–68
Area studies, 2, 3
Aswang (viscera-sucking spirit), 218–19
Ateneo de Manila University, 153
Aunor, Nora, 189, 225
Avellana, Lamberto, 171

Badiday, Inday, 223–26
Bagobos, *80*

Bakla figures in film, 185–88
Bakya, 171–74
Balikbayans, 206–9, 214
Baltazar, Francisco, 43
Barrows, David Prescott, 20, 21, 27, 35
Barthes, Roland, 76, 90
Bataan: rumors of Japanese defeat at, 118–19
Benevolent assimilation, 21–24, 33–34, 44, 54–55, 61, 81
Benjamin, Walter, 133
Bomba, explained, 132–33
Bomba films, 133, 134–37, 150
Bomba stars, 133, 135–37, 143, 145, 150
Bonifacio, Andres, 9–10, 194, 211
The Bontoc Igorot (Jenks), 79
Bourns, Frank S., 34
Bravo, Claudio, portrait of Imelda Marcos, *144*, *145*, *147*
Britain, 5

Cacique democracy, 180
Cannell, Fenella, 217–19, 226
Capital (Marx), 204
Capitalist economic development, 139–40, 202, 204
Cartoons, political, 174–79, *175*, *178*
Catholic Church/Catholicism, 12, 33–34, 191, 192; and Spanish missionary activity, 8–9, 168
Censorship: of bomba films, 134; of nationalist theater, 40
Census gathering, by Spanish rulers, 26
Census of 1903–5, 24, 25–39, 40, 46; aims of, 25–26; categories used in, 32–33; comparisons with nationalist plays,

Census of 1903–5 (*cont.*)
46, 51; data-gathering mechanisms of, 29–31; Filipino collaboration in, 26, 27–28, 32; photographs in, 37–38, *38, 39, 40, 41*; photographs of census workers, 37, *40, 41*; and race, 32, 35–39; resistance to, 28; wild/civilized distinction used in, 32–34, 35
Chinese: as characters in nationalist plays, 48; rumors about, during Japanese occupation, 120–21
Chinese mestizos, 6, 36
Christ: as heroic image, 211–12
Christianity: and census classification, 33; fundamentalism, 7, 180. *See also* Catholic Church/Catholicism
Christian salvation: as freedom metaphor, 13
Civilized/wild distinction in census of 1903–5, 32–34, 35, 37–38
Civil War (U.S.), photography and, 87, 89
Class conflict, 24, 139–40
Class hierarchy. *See* Social hierarchy
Class identity: and language use, 8, 9, 167–70, 197–200, 201
Climate: in colonial women's writings, 67–68
Collaboration, Filipino: in census of 1903–5, 26, 27–28, 32; portrayed in nationalist plays, 50; rhetoric of, under Japanese occupation, 109–14; with U.S. rule, 24, 26, 27–28, 32, 42, 100
Colonialism: collaboration's support of, 26, 42; reflected in Filipino nationalism, 13–14. *See also* Benevolent assimilation; Spanish colonization and rule; U.S. imperialism; U.S. rule
Colonial women's writings, 56–65; anxiety in, 59–60, 62, 63–64; climate in, 67–68; on domestic architecture, 67–68; domesticity in, 58–59; landscape descriptions in, 60–62; self-consciousness in, 63–65, 68; on servants, 59, 69, 70–72, 73–75; travel accounts, 57–59
Communism: and youth movement, 153–54
Communist Party of the Philippines, 4, 153, 154
Condict, Alice Byram, 64
Consumer identity, 180
Contemplacion, Efren, 226
Contemplacion, Flor: death of, 213–15; film industry interest in, 216, 217, 224; funeral of, 220, 221; responses to death of, 216–17, 219–23, 224; show biz gossip about, 223–27
Counterrevolution, 3, 7, 11–12. *See also* Revolution
Cruz, Juan Matapang (*Hindi Pa Aco Patay*), 44, 49

Daily Globe, 192
Damay (sympathy/mourning), 42, 43, 49
Dauncy, Campbell, 67, 68
Death: funeral rites and customs, 217–19, 226. *See also* Mourning
de Jesus, Gregoria, 195
de la Cruz, Nicolas, 6
De La Salle College, 153
del Pilar, Gregorio, 196
del Pilar, Marcelo, 195
del Rosario, Mila, 135–36
Demonstrations of 1970 (First Quarter Storm), 155–60
de Ocampo, Nick, 181
Dependency: idealization of, 12–13. *See also* Patronage
de Quiros, Conrado, 207–9, 220
de Tavera, Paz Pardo, 194
de Tavera, Trinidad Pardo, 195
Development: agricultural, 5; of capitalist economy, 139–40, 202, 204
Diaries of colonial women. *See* Colonial women's writings
Dogeaters (Hagedorn), 162–65

Domestic architecture: and privacy, 65–68
Domesticity, 52–56, 68–69. *See also* Colonial women's writings
Domestic workers. *See* Overseas contract workers; Servants
Drama. *See* Nationalist theater; Theater
Drinnon, Richard, 54

Economy: capitalist economic development, 139–40, 202, 204; deterioration after 1986, 180, 202; nineteenth-century influences on, 5; under U.S. rule, 12
EDSA (Epifanio de los Santos Avenue), 179
EDSA revolt (People Power revolt), 3, 12, 174, 179, 197–98
Education: language use in, 112, 170, 198
Elections, 140; 1969 Marcos reelection, 150
Elites. *See* Filipino elites
Embalming, 217–18
Embarrassment (hiya), 212–13
English: bakya use of, 172–73; dominance and spread of, 9, 112, 167–68, 170, 198–99; as language of collaborationist rhetoric, 111–14; Marcos' use of, 197; Ocampo's use of, 196, 199–202; post-EDSA use of, 198–202
Epifanio de los Santos Avenue (EDSA), 179
Esclamado, Alex, 205
Estrada, Joseph, 3, 198
Ethnic groups, 6; in census classifications, 32, 35. *See also* Race; *names of specific groups*
Ethnological photographs, 78–81, *78–80*, 83, 90, 96
Ethnological surveys, 27
Executive Council, 109

Face to Face (newspaper column), 223
The Fateful Years: Japan's Adventure in the Philippines, 1941–1945 (Agoncillo), 115–19, 121

Fee, Mary, 57, 60–61, 63, 67, 71, 72, 74
Felipe II, 4, 17
Feminist views of imperialism, 55
Filipino (language), 169, 170. *See also* Tagalog
Filipino: history and use of term, 6–8, 17, 213
Filipino-Americans, 2–3, 210. *See also* Balikbayans
Filipino-American War, 3, 19, 28; contemporary U.S. views of, 20–21; and photographs of war dead, 87, *87–88*, 89–91
Filipino elites: collaboration with Japanese, 109–14; language use by, 112; "official" nationalism of, 10–11, 107–9; and revolution of 1896, 9–12; threats to power of, 107–8, 139; under U.S. rule, 12, 107–8
Filipino identity. *See* National identity
Filipinos: homogenization of, as goal of colonial rule, 32; naming of, 6–8, 17; U.S. notions about, 20–23, 32, 33–35
Filipinos abroad, 2, 7, 14, 180, 205–6; balikbayans, 206–9, 214; movies and, 181; overseas contract workers, 206, 207, 209–14, 215, 216, 219 (*see also* Contemplacion, Flor)
Film: bakla figures in, 185–88; bomba movies, 133, 134–37, 150 (*see also* Bomba stars); Filipino audiences, 181–82, 189; Filipino film industry, 181; Filipino film stars, 187–89, 224–25; industry as purveyor of gossip, 223; industry interest in Flor Contemplacion story, 216, 217; languages of, 168, 170, 182; portrayals of the dead in, 224–25; portrayals of women in, 123, 134–36, 187; Taglish in Filipino movies and show biz talk, 182–88, 223; trivialization of issues by, 216–17; viewer's experience of, 133–34, 162, 163, 164, 185, 188
First Couple. *See* Marcos, Ferdinand and Imelda (First Couple)

The First Filipino (Anderson), 1
First Ladies, role of, 132. See also Marcos, Imelda Romualdez
First Quarter Storm (demonstrations of 1970), 155–60
Freedom, 11, 12–13
Freedom (Malaya) (Remigio), 49
Fundamentalism, Christian, 7, 180
Funeral rites and customs, 217–19, 226; departures from, in deaths of Flor Contemplacion and Ninoy Aquino, 221–22

Gancayco Commission, 216, 221–22, 226
Gender: in census of 1903–5, 47–48; vs. sex, 47, 48
Gender roles/identity: bakla figures in film, 185–88; in nationalist plays, 47, 48–51; OCWs as feminized, 214. See also Men; Women
Geography of the Philippines, 6
Ghosts, 218–19
The Golden Chain (Tanikalang Guinto) (Abad), 44
Gonzalez, Andrew, 112, 169
Gonzalez, Jacobo, 126
Gossip: and mourning, 204–5, 217–19, 223–27
Grieving. See Mourning
Guam, 5
Guerrilla resistance after Filipino-American War, 28
Guillermo, Alice G., 176
Gutierrez, Ruffa, 187–88

Hagedorn, Jessica (Dogeaters), 162–65
Harper's History of the War in the Philippines: photographs from, 80, 87, 88, 89
Heroism, 211–12, 214
Hindi Pa Aco Patay (I Am Not Yet Dead) (Cruz), 44, 49
Hinduism, 8

Historiography, 4, 202–3; Agoncillo on, 115, 118; area studies, 2, 3
Hiya (embarrassment), 212–13
Home: private nature of, 65. See also Domesticity
Hong Kong, 10
Hubble, Winnifred, 70
Huk (Hukbalahap) Rebellion, 12, 139, 140
Humor, 119; political cartoons, 174–79, 175, 178

I Am Not Yet Dead (Hindi Pa Aco Patay) (Cruz), 44, 49
Igorota (film), 134
Igorots, 37, 61–62, 78–79, 79, 84
Ikabod (comic strip), 174–79, 175, 178
Ileto, Reynaldo, 11, 12, 43, 211
Ilustrados, 165, 194, 199, 200
Imperialism. See Spanish colonization and rule; U.S. imperialism
Inangbayan (motherland), 42, 43
Independence: 1896 uprising, 1, 9–10, 194. See also Revolution
Independent Movement of New Women, 177
Indios, 6, 11
Institute of National Language, 169, 171
Intelligentsia: vs. bakya, 171–74
Irony, 4; in colonial women's writings, 57; in work of Ambeth Ocampo, 194
Islam, 8, 33, 36

Japan, 12, 13; pre-war Filipino attitudes toward, 103, 105–7
Japanese occupation, 109; circulation/function of rumors during, 117–21; elite collaboration under, 109–14
Jenks, Albert, 27; The Bontoc Igorot, 79
Jenks, Maude Huntley, 71, 74
Jesus Christ. See Christ
Joaquin, Nick, 6, 17, 18, 193
Jopson, Edgar, 153

Journalism, 192–93, 202; political humor, 174–79; show biz gossip, 223–26. See also News media; *names of specific journalists*

Kabataang Makabayan (KM), 153, 155
Kahapon, Ngayon, at Bukas (Yesterday, Today, and Tomorrow) (Tolentino), 44–45, 48, 49
Kalayaan, 12–13, 43
Katipunan, 41, 211
Keithley, June, 179
Kerkvliet, Benedict, 139
Kinship ties, 46–47
KM (Kabataang Makabayan), 153, 155
Komedya, 42–43
Kramer, Paul, 27

Labor, export of, 180, 205–6. See also Overseas contract workers
Lacaba, Jose, 156, 157, 158–59, 171–74
Lakasdiwa, 153
Landscape: in colonial women's writings, 60–62
Language: and collaborationist rhetoric, 111–14; and film, 168, 170, 182; and linguistic hierarchy in the Philippines, 8, 9, 167–70, 196–200, 201; national, efforts to establish, 8–9, 169, 170; and national identity, 106, 113; use in demonstrations of 1970, 156–57, 159. See also Rhetoric, forms and functions of; *specific languages*
Laurel, Jose P., 110, 114, 120
Laurel-Langley Agreement: protests against, 153
Laxa, Maricel, 183
Lee Kwan Yew, 213, 226
Letters by colonial women. *See* Colonial women's writings
Liberal party, 151, 157–58
Lingua franca: Tagalog as, 169, 170; Taglish as, 171, 198. *See also* National language

Liwayway, 111
Llamas, Antonio Garcia, portrait of Imelda Marcos, 148, 149–50
Looking. *See* Spectator experience/identity
Looking Back (newspaper column), 190, 192
Lopez de Legazpi, Miguel, 5
Lopez de Villalobos, Ruy, 4–5
Los Angeles Times, 205
Luhang Tagalog (Tagalog Tears) (Tolentino), 49, 51
Luna, Antonio, 194, 196
Luna, Juan, 194, 195
Lyceum, 153

Mabini, Apolinario, 194, 196
Macapagal, Evangelina, 132
MacArthur, Douglas, 110
Maga, Delia, 213, 216, 221
Magsaysay, Ramon, 139
Makati Avenue Office Girls (film), 182–85
MAKIBAKA (Malayang Kilusan Ng Bagong Kababaihan), 177
Malacañang palace, 122, 160
Malakas and Maganda legend, 122
Malaya (Freedom) (Remigio), 49
Malayang Kilusan Ng Bagong Kababaihan (MAKIBAKA), 177
Malays, 35, 36, 37, 82
Malls, 180
Malolos republic, 3, 10, 194
Manifest destiny, 54, 81. *See also* Benevolent assimilation
Marcelo, Nonoy, 174, 176; *Ikabod*, 174–79, 175, 178
Marcos, Ferdinand, 122, 136, 161; as bachelor, 125; biographical portrayals of, 127–28; and demonstrations of 1970, 155, 157, 160–61; language use by, 197; meets Imelda, 125–26, 130; portrait of, as Malakas, 122, 123; projects of, 137–38; rhetorical style of, 124; value of

Marcos, Ferdinand (cont.)
Imelda to, 124, 150, 161. See also
Marcos, Ferdinand and Imelda (First
Couple); Marcos regime
Marcos, Ferdinand and Imelda (First
Couple): continuing influence of,
202; image cultivated by, 122, 124, 131,
212; meeting and courtship of, 125–26;
as patrons, 141–43; portrayals of, in
commissioned biographies, 127–30,
136, 141–42; rehabilitation of, after
1986, 180; as royalty, 143; sources of
political success of, 141; as spectacle,
125, 126
Marcos, Imelda Romualdez, 122; ambition
of, 136; biographical portrayals of,
128–30, 136, 141–42; campaign style of,
124–25; criticism of, 150–52; cultural
projects of, 137–38; and demonstrations of 1970, 157; dress of, 124; media
portrayals of, 136–37, 143, 145, 151;
meets Ferdinand, 125–26, 130; parallels
with bomba stars, 136–37, 143, 145, 150;
as patroness, 141–43, 150; portraits of,
143–50, *144*, *146*, *148*; power and
charms of, 124, 128–31, 150; prominence of, 132, 137, 143, 150; rumored
presidential run of, 151; as singer, 124,
129–30. See also Marcos, Ferdinand
and Imelda (First Couple)
Marcos regime, 12; and balikbayans, 206,
207; criticism of, 150–52, 174 (see also
Political humor); encouragement of
Tagalog use by, 197; English use by, 197;
media monopoly of, 174–75, 179, 192;
opposition to (see Youth movement).
See also Marcos, Ferdinand; Marcos,
Ferdinand and Imelda (First Couple);
Marcos, Imelda Romualdez
Maricris Sioson: Japayuki (film), 182, 186–
88
Martial law babies, 191–92
Marx, Karl, 204

Mascardo, Tomas, 196
Masculinity: imperialism as validation of,
55
Mass media. See Media
McKinley, William, 19, 20
Media: Tagalog as lingua franca of, 170.
See also Film; News media
Media portrayals: of bomba stars, 133, 135–
36, 136–37, 143, 145; of Imelda Marcos,
136–37, 143, 145, 151
Melodramas. See Nationalist theater
Memoirs: by colonial women. See Colonial women's writings
Men: guilt over plight of Filipina workers
abroad, 222; imperialism as validation
of masculinity, 55. See also Gender
roles/identity
Mestizo/a identity, 165–67, 185–86; of film
stars, 188–89; link with Taglish, 167,
176–77
Mestizo/as, 6, 11, 36, 107, 108; historic
position of, 165, 166
Migration: wave theory of, 35–37
Migration of Filipinos, 2, 7, 206. See also
Filipinos abroad
Mimicry: in communication with servants, 72–73; in nationalist plays, 45–
46; as supposed character trait of Filipinos, 34–35
Mindanao chiefs, *80*
Money, 140–41, 143, 216, 226–27
Moses, Edith, 56, 57, 58, 64–65, 67; on servants, 69, 70–71, 72
Motherland (Inangbayan), 42, 43
Mourning (damay), 42, 43, 49
Mourning, 204–5, 216; commodification
of, 216, 226–27; and comparison of
deaths of Flor Contemplacion and
Ninoy Aquino, 220–23; and film, 216,
224–25; gossip and, 204–5, 217–19,
223–27; nationhood as imaged by, 214,
215, 219, 224
Movies. See Film

Movie stars, 187–89, 224–25. *See also* Bomba stars
Mr. & Ms., 192
Murillo Velarde, Pedro, 6
Muslim Malays, 36, 37
Muslims, 36; and census classification, 33

Naming: of Filipinos, 6–8; in nationalist plays and census report, 46; of the Philippines, 4–8
Nation, female personification of, 49–51
National Democratic Front (NDF), 191, 197
National identity, 17, 106–7, 116, 166; as imaged by mourning, 214, 215, 219, 224; as imaged by rumor, 116, 121; and language use, 106, 113; and overseas Filipinos, 204, 205, 206, 209
Nationalism, 3–4, 7–8, 13–14; and aestheticization of politics, 100, 150; conflictual nature of, 9; counterrevolutionary, 11–12, 27; Japan as model of, 105; "official," of Filipino elites, 10–11, 107–9; revolutionary, 11; in youth movement, 154
Nationalist Party, 157–58
Nationalist theater, 24–25, 39–51; antecedents of, 42–43; comparisons with census, 46, 51; gender roles in, 47, 48–51; mimicry in, 45–46; nation as family in, 47, 51; plot examples, 43–45; politicized character names in, 44–46; popularity of, 40–42; race in, 48
Nationalist Youth, 153
National language: efforts to establish, 8–9, 169, 170. *See also* Tagalog
National Union of Students of the Philippines (NUSP), 153, 155
Navarro-Pedrosa, Carmen, 124, 128
NDF (National Democratic Front), 191, 197
Negritos (Aetas), 36, 37, *38*, 78, *78*
News media: Marcos regime's control over, 174–75, 179, 192; opposition to Marcos in, 192–93; political humor in, 174–79; and show biz gossip, 223–26. *See also specific journalists and publications*
NGOs (nongovernmental organizations), 191
Noli me Tangere (Rizal), 18
Nongovernmental organizations, 191
NUSP (National Union of Students of the Philippines), 153, 155

Ocampo, Ambeth, 190–91; English use in work of, 196, 199–202; hallmarks of work of, 194–96; newspaper column of, 190, 192; popularity of work of, 193–94, 196, 202
OCWS. *See* Overseas contract workers
Osmeña, Esperanza, 132
Our Islands and Their People as Seen with Camera and Pencil: photographs from, *78*, *82*
Overseas contract workers (OCWS), 206, 207, 209–14, 215, 216, 219; Flor Contemplacion case, 213–17, 219–23; and guilt over plight of Filipina workers abroad, 222; as national heroes, 210–12, 215. *See also* Filipinos abroad

Palabrica, Raul J., 216–17
Pan-Asianism, 105
Partido Komunista ng Pilipinas (PKP). *See* Communist Party of the Philippines
Pasyon, 43, 211–12
Paternal imagery: in nationalist plays, 50, 51
Paternal metaphor for colonialism, 21, 22, 23, 54–55
Patronage, 138–43
Peasant revolts, 24; Huk Rebellion, 12, 139, 140
People Power Revolt (EDSA Revolt), 3, 12, 174, 179, 197–98
People's Court, 114
Philippine Assembly, 3, 26

283   *Index*

Philippine Commissions, 19, 27, 64; *Annual Reports of the Philippine Commission,* photos from, *80, 85*
Philippine Daily Inquirer, 192, 223
Philippine Free Press, 133, 143, 151
Philippines: naming and geography of, 4–8; peopling of, 35–37; Spanish colonization of, 5
The Philippines Past and Present (Worcester), *84*
Photographs and photography, 76–78, 83, 86–87, 101–2; in census of 1903–5, 37–38, *38, 39, 40, 41*; ethnological photography, 78–81, *78–80,* 83, 90, 96; images of natives transformed, 81, *82, 83, 84–86*; in other colonial documents, 38–39; portrait photography, 92–93, *94–98,* 96–101; viewer's identity/experience, 77, 83, 86–87, 91, 96, 101; war photography, 87, *87–89,* 89–92
Pilipino (language), 169, 170. *See also* Tagalog
PKP (Partido Komunista ng Pilipinas). *See* Communist Party of the Philippines
Plays. *See* Nationalist theater
Police: in demonstrations of 1970, 155–59
Political humor, 174–79
Ponce, Mariano, 103, *104,* 105
Pornography: in Marcos period, 133. *See also* Bomba films
Portrait photography, 92–93, *94–98,* 96–101
Portraits: of Imelda Marcos, 143–50, *144, 146, 148*; of Marcoses as Malakas and Maganda, 122, *123*
Privacy: and domestic space/architecture, 65–68
Promdi, 173. *See also* Bakya

Quezon, Aurora, 132
Quezon, Manuel, 110, 165, 197

Race: and census categories, 32, 35; colonial conception of racial hierarchy, 47, 48, 78–79, 81; in nationalist plays, 48; U.S. stereotypes of, 34; wave migration theory and racialization of Philippine history, 35–37. *See also* Ethnic groups
Radio Bandido, 179
Radio Veritas, 179
Ramos, Fidel, 215, 226; presidency of, 3, 180, 212, 214–15
Rape scenes: in bomba films, 134–35
Reciprocal obligation, tradition of, 47, 139, 141, 210
Recto, Claro M., 110, 113
Religion: Catholicism and Catholic Church, 12, 33–34, 191, 192; and census classifications, 33; Christian fundamentalism, 7, 180; Christian metaphors in Filipino politics, 12–13, 211–12; Islam, 8, 33, 36; Spanish missionary activity, 8–9, 168
Remigio, Tomas, 49
Resistance vs. collaboration: under Japanese occupation, 109–11
Revolution, 11; 1896 uprising, 1, 9–10, 194; elite attempts to contain, 11–12; Huk Rebellion, 12, 139, 140; peasant/worker revolts, 24. *See also* Counterrevolution
Revolutionary nationalism, 11
Reyes, Emmanuel, 185
Rhetoric, forms and functions of: collaborationist, 111–14; gossip, 204–5, 217–19, 223–27; irony, 4, 57, 194; rumor, 114, 116–21, 151, 155, 160, 217; slogans, 156–57. *See also* Mimicry
Riggs, Arthur Stanley, 41, 44, 45, 49, 50, 51
Rizal, Jose, 105–6, 165; as national hero, 211–12; in work of Ocampo, 191, 194, 195; writings of, 18
Roman Catholic Church. *See* Catholic Church/Catholicism
Romualdez, Vicente Orestes, 126, 128
Romualdez family, 128

284

Roosevelt, Theodore, 28
Root, Elihu, 20
Roxas, Manuel, 114
Rumor(s), 114, 116–17, 217; circulation/function of, during Japanese occupation, 117–21; of Imelda Marcos presidential run, 151; of imposition of martial law by Marcos, 160

Samahang Demokratiko ng kabataan (SDK), 155
Sanger, Joseph P., 25, 27, 32, 34
Sangley, 6
SCAUP (Student Cultural Association of the University of the Philippines), 153
Schurman Commission, 19. *See also* Philippine Commissions
SDK (Samahang Demokratiko ng kabataan), 155
Sedition Law, 40
Seditious dramas. *See* Nationalist theater
Seeing. *See* Spectator experience/identity
Self-government by Filipinos: U.S. notions about, 22–23, 54
Servants: colonial women's relationships with, 58–59, 69–75
Seven Years' War, 5
Sex: vs. gender, 47, 48
Sexual orientation/identity. *See* Gender roles/identity
Shamelessness (walang hiya), 208
Shunk, Caroline, 62–63, 64, 68, 71, 72, 73–75
Sin, Jaime, 80, 179
Singapore: diplomatic breach with, 223. *See also* Contemplacion, Flor
Sison, Jose Maria, 153
Slapping, 120
Slogans, 156–57
Social hierarchy: and class conflict, 24, 139–40; impulse to maintain, 12; and language use, 8, 9, 167–70, 196–200,

201; and patronage, 138–39; and revolution, 9, 11, 12. *See also* Filipino elites
Spanish-American War, 10
Spanish colonization and rule, 5, 33–34; 1896 uprising against, 1, 9–10, 194; influence on language, 8–9
Spanish language, 1, 8, 112, 168, 199
Spectacle: First Couple as, 125, 126; Imelda Marcos as, 150; white women as, 63–65
Spectator experience/identity, 158–59; anonymity of, 133–34, 162, 164, 185, 188; film and, 133–34, 162, 163, 164, 185, 188; photography and, 77, 83, 86–87, 91, 96, 101; and viewing of corpses, 217–18
Spirits, 218–19
Stoler, Ann, 55
Student Cultural Association of the University of the Philippines (SCAUP), 153
Student movement, 153, 177. *See also* Youth movement
Suarez, Francisco, 6
Sun Yat Sen, 103, *104*
Supreme Court: banning of nationalist plays by, 40
Swardspeak, 188

Taft, Helen, 52, 56, 64
Taft, William Howard, 20, 22, 26, 32, 34–35
Tagalog, 168–70; connotations of word for freedom in, 12–13; nationalist plays in (*see* Nationalist theater); as national language, 9, 169; post-EDSA use of, 197–98; use encouraged by Japanese, 111; use in demonstrations of 1970, 156–57
Tagalogs, 79, 81, 82
Tagalog Tears (Luhang Tagalog) (Tolentino), 49, 51
Taglish, 170–71, 176–77, 181; in film, 182–88; as language of dissent, 174, 177, 179, 198; and mestizo/a identity, 167, 176–77; in political humor, 174–79; politicization of, 179; post-EDSA use of, 198
Tahimik, Kidlat, 181

285   Index

Tanikalang Guinto (The Golden Chain) (Abad), 44
Tejeros Convention, 3
Theater: development and forms of, 42–43. *See also* Nationalist theater
Tisoy (comic strip), 174
Tolentino, Aurelio, 44–45, 48, 49, 51
Tourism: and Marcos regime's courting of balikbayan tourists, 207
Travel writings by women. *See* Colonial women's writings

U.S. aid: and Huk Rebellion, 139
U.S. imperialism: as aberrant, 53; aims of, 21; as validation of white masculinity, 55. *See also* Benevolent assimilation; U.S. intervention; U.S. rule
U.S. intervention: contemporary views/justifications of, 20–23. *See also* Filipino-American War; Spanish-American War
U.S. rule, 10–11; elite oligarchy under, 10–11, 12, 107–8; Filipino collaboration with, 24, 26, 27–28, 32, 42, 100
University of the Philippines, 153

Vargas, Jorge B., 111
Verano, Severa, 125
Violence: rumors about, during Japanese occupation, 120–21
Votes as commodities, 140–41

Wainwright, Jonathan, 117–18
Walang hiya (shamelessness), 208
War photography, 87, 89; images of Filipino dead, 87, 87–88, 89–91

Wave migration theory, 35–37
White love, 23. *See also* Benevolent assimilation
Wild/civilized distinction in census of 1903–5, 32–34, 35, 37–38
Wilson, Woodrow, 22–23
Women: bomba stars, 133, 135–37, 143, 145, 150; Filipina workers overseas, 222 (*see also* Contemplacion, Flor); journalists, 192; personification of nation and freedom as, in nationalist plays, 48–51; portrayal of, in bomba films, 133, 134–35, 150; portrayal of, in other films, 123, 187; roles of white women in colonial society, 48, 53–54, 55–56, 64; white women and their servants, 58–59, 69–75; white women as objects of attention, 63–65. *See also* Colonial women's writings; Gender roles/identity
Worcester, Dean C., 19, 20, 22, 27, 38; *The Philippines Past and Present*, 84
Worcester, Nona, 58, 59, 61–62, 74
World War II, 12, 108. *See also* Japanese occupation
Writing: introduction of Latin alphabet, 8. *See also* Language

Yesterday, Today, and Tomorrow (Kahapon, Ngayon, at Bukas) (Tolentino), 44–45, 48, 49
Youth: as social category, 152
Youth movement, 152, 153–61; demonstrations of 1970, 155–60; group origins and dynamics, 153–54

Earlier versions of most of the chapters in this book appeared in the publications listed below. I thank the respective publishers for permission to reprint portions of them here.

"White Love: Census and Melodrama in the U.S. Colonization of the Philippines" is a revised version of an essay in Amy Kaplan and Donald E. Pease, eds., *Cultures of United States Imperialism* (Durham, N.C.: Duke University Press, 1993), 185–210.

"Colonial Domesticity: Engendering Race at the Edge of Empire, 1899–1912," appeared in *American Literature* 67, no. 4 (December 1995): 639–66, and has been revised here.

"Anticipating Nationhood: Identification, Collaboration, and Rumor in Filipino Responses to Japan," is a revised version of an essay in *Diaspora* 1, no. 1 (spring 1991): 67–82.

A shorter version of "Patronage, Pornography, and Youth: Ideology and Spectatorship during the Early Marcos Years," appeared in *Comparative Studies in Society and History* 32, no. 2 (April 1990): 282–304.

"Taglish, or the Phantom Power of the Lingua Franca" was published in *Public Culture* 8, no.1 (fall 1995): 101–26, and appears here in revised form.

"Writing History after EDSA" served as the introduction to Ambeth Ocampo, *Luna's Moustache* (Pasig City, Philippines: Anvil Publishing, Inc., 1997), 1–14.

"'Your Grief is Our Gossip': Overseas Filipinos and Other Spectral Presences" was published in *Public Culture* 9, no. 2 (winter 1997): 267–91.

Vicente L. Rafael is Professor in the
Department of Communication at the University
of California, San Diego. He is the author of
*Contracting Colonialism: Translation and Christian
Conversion in Tagalog Society under Early Spanish
Rule* (Duke) and editor of *Discrepant Histories:
Translocal Essays on Filipino Cultures* (Temple) and
*Figures of Criminality in Indonesia, the Philippines,
and Colonial Vietnam* (Cornell).

Library of Congress Cataloging-in-Publication Data
Rafael, Vicente L.
White love and other events in Filipino history /
by Vicente L. Rafael.
p. cm.
Includes bibliographical references and index.
ISBN 0-8223-2505-5 (alk. paper)
ISBN 0-8223-2542-X (pbk. : alk. paper)
1. Philippines—History—20th century.
I. Title.
DS685 .R24 2000
959.904—dc21
99-050790

www.ingramcontent.com/pod-product-compliance
Lightning Source LLC
Chambersburg PA
CBHW030525230426
43665CB00010B/772